11 Essentials
of Effective
Writing

ANN MARIE RADASKIEWICZ McNEELY
Western Piedmont Community College

WADSWORTH
CENGAGE Learning

Australia • Brazil • Japan • Korea • Mexico • Singapore • Spain • United Kingdom • United States

WADSWORTH
CENGAGE Learning·

11 Essentials of Effective Writing
Ann Marie McNeely

Director of Developmental Studies:
  Annie Todd

Assistant Editor: Elizabeth Rice

Editorial Assistant: Luria Rittenberg

Media Editor: Christian Biagetti

Market Development Manager: Linda Yip

Content Project Manager: Dan Saabye

Art Director: Faith Brosnan

Manufacturing Planner: Betsy Donaghey

Rights Acquisition Specialist: Ann Hoffman

Production Service: Christian Holdener,
  S4Carlisle Publishing Services

Text Designer: Shawn Girsberger

Cover Designer: Roycroft Design |
  roycroftdesign.com

Cover Image: © Digital Vision/
  Getty Images

Compositor: S4Carlisle Publishing Services

Dedicated to
Marty, Mark, and Kayla.

For product information and technology assistance, contact us at
Cengage Learning Customer & Sales Support, 1-800-354-9706
For permission to use material from this text or product,
submit all requests online at **cengage.com/permissions**
Further permissions questions can be emailed to
permissionrequest@cengage.com

Library of Congress Control Number: 2012953885

Student Edition:

ISBN-13: 978-1-285-09275-1
ISBN-10: 1-285-09275-9

Wadsworth
20 Channel Center Street
Boston, MA 02210
USA

Cengage Learning is a leading provider of customized learning solutions with office locations around the globe, including Singapore, the United Kingdom, Australia, Mexico, Brazil, and Japan. Locate your local office at **international.cengage.com/region.**

Cengage Learning products are represented in Canada by Nelson Education, Ltd.

For your course and learning solutions, visit **www.cengage.com.**

Purchase any of our products at your local college store or at our preferred online store **www.cengagebrain.com.**

Instructors: Please visit **login.cengage.com** and log in to access instructor-specific resources.

Printed in the United States of America
1 2 3 4 5 6 7 16 15 14 13 12

Contents

PART I   ESSENTIAL CHARACTERISTICS OF ALL COMPOSITIONS   1

CHAPTER 1   Essential #1: Clear Subject, Audience, and Purpose   2

CHAPTER 6   Essential #6: Coherent Paragraphs   104

CHAPTER 9   Essential #9: Interesting Openings   172

APPENDIX 2   Eleven Common Errors in English   243

Index to Essays by Method of Development

Preface

11 Essentials of Effective Writing transcends the various expository genres and defines the key characteristics that are always present in effective expository writing of any type. By organizing good writing into 11 easy-to-remember qualities, this book helps students understand how to compose clear, interesting prose that establishes their college-readiness. Rather than organizing the book by steps in the writing process or by types of compositions (rhetorical modes), *11 Essentials of Effective Writing* accelerates the teaching of writing by defining and illustrating the necessary qualities of the finished product. It shows students exactly what they need to shoot for, and then gives them specific strategies for getting there.

11 Essentials of Effective Writing covers the fundamental competencies that students need to be able to write *anything* in their academic, personal, and professional lives. It includes coverage of the academic essay, but also demonstrates how all other types of successful expository writing—including letters, reports, and e-mail messages—possess the same key traits. Examples from real student and professional writing illustrate how each essential trait is present in any type of effective composition.

11 Characteristics of Good Writing

Different from most writing texts, *11 Essentials* provides students with a student-friendly framework for understanding all of the qualities and features of effective writing. Information about a variety of different skills and concepts is boiled down into 11 main qualities that are easy to remember during planning, composition, and revision:

Clear subject, audience, and purpose
Conventional form and features
Clear sentences
Vivid language
Complete paragraphs
Coherent paragraphs
Cohesive paragraphs
Clear organization
Interesting openings
Effective closings
Sensitivity and tact

"I am simply in love with the simplicity of this text."
—Shelley Palmer, Rowan-Cabarrus Community College

"The organization and approach of the book is clear and consistent, using lots of good examples and providing writing ideas throughout."
—Laurie Watson, Le Cordon Bleu College of Culinary Arts

"I really appreciate its general focus on writing across disciplines and for different purposes. There's so few texts out there that do this well, and I would think it would help students considerably to see that writing matters outside of the walls of our classroom, too."
—Emily Berg, Reedley College

This concise framework arranges topics with natural connections in a way that eliminates unnecessary divisions and redundancies, streamlines instruction, and offers the potential to accelerate students' progress through their developmental writing coursework. For example, Chapter 2, "Essential #2: Conventional Form and Features," connects an explanation of essay form to the explanation of paragraph form because once students understand the form and features of a paragraph, they can quickly and easily grasp the concept of essay structure. Verbal and visual analogies in conjunction with diagrams and ample activities give students the opportunity to connect new information to what they already know.

Powerful Application of the Writing Process

Students learning to be better writers must feel comfortable following the steps of the writing process. Each chapter addresses prewriting, writing, and revising to make a clear connection between each essential characteristic and how to achieve it with specific strategies for each stage of the writing process. Whether in the classroom or in the workplace, students will find that the steps of the writing process are applicable. Additionally, each chapter covers the writing process through these features:

- **Tips** about writing and the writing process appear throughout each chapter to serve as reminders of how the topics covered relate to the writing process.
- **Checklists** at the end of each chapter provide students with a tool for self-evaluation or peer-evaluation during the writing process. A comprehensive checklist of the essentials, which can be found on the book's inside front cover, is also included to holistically evaluate longer pieces of writing.

Real-World Practice Opportunities

Exercises throughout the chapters have applications in the classroom and in the workplace, so students have the opportunity to practice writing for a variety of situations and develop skills that are transferable to their other college courses and beyond. All models and exercises are based on high-interest topics that are relevant to students' lives right now, including college success skills, career planning, and practical life skills.

- **Exercises.** The 11 chapters and Appendix 2, Eleven Common Errors in English, include exercises that give students immediate practice with a particular concept or technique.
- **Suggested Writing Activities.** These lists of possible composition topics found at the end of each chapter reinforce the idea that the essential characteristics apply to *all* writing—not just the essay. Each list contains suggested topics for personal, academic, and professional compositions.

- **Model Compositions.** These examples found in Appendix 1 offer a variety of academic, personal, and professional writings that illustrate the 11 essentials and demonstrate the quality expected from students' practice opportunities.

Additional Resources

Instructor's Manual and Test Bank

The Instructor's Resource Manual includes sample syllabi and lesson plans, an answer key for exercises in the book, chapter quizzes, midterm and final exams, and a map to applicable Aplia tutorials and exercises.

Aplia for Basic Writing Levels 1 and 2

Founded in 2000 by economist and Stanford professor Paul Romer, Aplia is dedicated to improving learning by increasing student effort and engagement. Aplia is an online, auto-graded homework solution that keeps your students engaged and prepared for class, and has been used by more than 850,000 students at over 850 institutions. Aplia's online solutions provide developmental writing students with clear, succinct, and engaging writing instruction and practice to help them build the confidence they need to master basic writing and grammar skills. Aplia for Basic Writing: Level 1 (sentence to paragraph) and Aplia for Basic Writing: Level 2 (paragraph to essay) feature ongoing individualized practice, immediate feedback, and grades that can be automatically uploaded, so instructors can see where students are having difficulty (allowing for personalized assistance). Visit www.aplia .com/cengage for more details.

Acknowledgments

My thanks go first of all to the instructors who provided excellent feedback and advice for this edition of *11 Essentials of Effective Writing*:

Melissa Adams, Red Rocks Community College
Matthew Allen, Wright College
Eugenia Antonio, Lonestar College
Tina Arduini, Penn State Dubois
Jackie Atkins, Penn State Dubois
Kathleen Barlow, Martin University
Emily Berg, Reedley College
Mary Anne Bernal, San Antonio College
Randy Boone, Northampton Community College
Annie Burns, Meridian Community College
Judy Covington, Trident Technical College
Marcia Cree, Long Beach City College
Michelle Cristiani, Portland Community College
Cindy Dupre, Shasta College

"The integration of the writing process into the chapters is a very effective strategy, for it keeps the writing process in perspective and allows students to focus on writing more consistently."
—Judy Covington, Trident Technical College

"[The exercises] effectively focus on issues that are important to students."
—Mary Ann Bernal, San Antonio College

"The biggest advantage is the up-to-date, relevant topics for today's students."
—Dianne Krob, Rose State College

Julie Engstrom, Brigham Young University
Sonja Evans, Central Georgia Technical College
Tamara Ferguson, Bluefield State College
Tim Florschuetz, Mesa Community College
Shauna Gobble, Northampton Community College
Aileen Gum, City College
Curtis Harrel, North West Arkansas Community College
Dianne Krob, Rose State College
Zeba Mehdi, Central Piedmont Community College
Christopher Morelock, Walters State Community College
Shelley Palmer, Rowan-Cabarrus Community College
David Pendery, National Taipei College of Business
Alan Reid, Brunswick Community College
Jennifer Schaefer, Lord Fairfax Community College
Debra Slaton, Cisco College
James Sodon, St. Louis Community College
Karen Taylor, Belmont Technical College
Laurie Watson, Le Cordon Bleu College of Culinary Arts
Jodeen Wink, Riverland Community College
Michelle Zollars, Patrick Henry College

In addition, I would like to thank the team at Cengage Learning—including Annie Todd, Acquisitions Editor; Elizabeth Kendall, Senior Product Manager; Elizabeth Rice, Assistant Editor; Dan Saabye, Content Project Manager; Christian Holdener, Project Manager at S4Carlisle Publishing Services; and Kirsten Balayti, Copyeditor— for the outstanding expertise and guidance they provided throughout the writing and production process.

Finally, I am grateful to my husband Marty McNeely and my children, Mark and Kayla, for their love, support, and patience as I worked. This book is dedicated to them.

Ann Marie Radaskiewicz McNeely
Western Piedmont Community College

INTRODUCTION

The Writing Process

In a recent survey, 302 employers were asked what knowledge and skills they wanted in college graduates seeking to work for them. Eighty-nine percent of these employers selected "the ability to effectively communicate orally and in writing" as one of the most important qualifications of applicants to their organizations.[1] Good writing skills are critical not only for workplace success, but also for academic and personal success. But what is the best way to go about acquiring these skills so that you can achieve your goals?

First, commit to strengthening your skills in four specific ways. Second, always approach every one of your writing tasks as a process with separate and distinct steps. These strategies are explained in the following sections.

Improving Your Writing Skills

You can become a better writer by strengthening your skills in four specific ways:

1. **Improve your knowledge of specific concepts and your skill in using specific techniques that produce effective writing.** For example, expand your vocabulary, learn the rules of grammar and punctuation, and familiarize yourself with patterns and structures that result in clear sentences, strong paragraphs, and well-developed longer documents, such as essays.

   To help you develop this knowledge, this book is organized according to the 11 essential characteristics that any composition must possess to achieve its purpose:

   Clear subject, audience, and purpose
   Conventional form and features

---

[1] Hart Research Associates. *Raising the Bar: Employers' Views on College Learning in the Wake of the Economic Downturn: A Survey Conducted on Behalf of the Association of American Colleges and Universities by Hart Research Associates.* January 10, 2010. http://www.aacu.org/leap/documents/2009_EmployerSurvey.pdf.

Clear sentences
Vivid language
Complete paragraphs
Coherent paragraphs
Cohesive paragraphs
Clear organization
Interesting openings
Effective closings
Sensitivity and tact

Every chapter of this book includes explanations of each of these characteristics as well as numerous opportunities to practice each one so that you can incorporate them into your own compositions.

2. **Read examples of good writing.** As you learn specific concepts and skills of writing, read models of effective writing and study why they are effective. When you increase your awareness of the techniques being used in the models you read, you gain ideas about how you can achieve similar effects in your own compositions. You will see how the specific concepts and skills of writing that you've learned about are being put to use successfully. This book includes many paragraphs and essays that serve as good examples to imitate.

3. **Practice writing.** As you are improving your knowledge and skills, you must practice incorporating them into your own compositions. This book includes many topic suggestions, and your writing course will provide you with many valuable opportunities to practice your writing skills.

4. **Get feedback about your writing's strengths and weaknesses.** You need to take advantage of opportunities to have people who write well (such as writing instructors, writing tutors, and writing course classmates) read your writing and help you identify areas for improvement. Your writing course and your college's writing lab will provide you with chances to get this valuable feedback, and this book includes some tools, such as checklists, that will help you or the reviewers of your writing know what to evaluate.

As you begin studying and practicing effective writing, the first important concept to understand and apply to your own compositions is the three-step writing process.

The Three Steps of the Writing Process

Writing requires a number of different kinds of mental tasks. You must generate ideas. You must organize your thoughts. You must find the right words to express those thoughts. You must make sure that what you've written makes sense and is grammatically correct. You might be tempted to do several of these tasks at the same time. However, these are all distinct activities that should be performed separately. Doing them simultaneously slows you down. Combining them also makes composition more difficult.

Writing is most effective when it occurs as a process with three main steps. During the **prewriting step**, you decide on the kind of document you're going to write, you generate ideas about your topic, you determine the main idea of your composition, and you organize the ideas and information you plan to include.

During the **writing step** of the process, you put your thoughts into sentences and paragraphs as you compose a draft of your paper.

During the final **revising and editing step**, you check over what you've written to make sure that your ideas are clearly explained and progress logically from one to the next. You also verify that your sentences adhere to the rules for grammar, punctuation, and spelling. You share one or more drafts with peers, instructors, or writing tutors to get helpful feedback and suggestions for improvement.

Think of the writing process as a cycle, as shown in Figure 1. Writers start with prewriting, move on to writing, and then rewrite last. Notice, however, that the arrows in Figure 1 point in both directions, indicating that writers sometimes must go back to previous steps during the composition process. For example, you might be writing a draft and realize that you need to return to prewriting to generate more details for a particular section of your paper. You may be rewriting and decide that you want to go back to the writing stage to compose a new paragraph that will strengthen your essay. You can always move forward and backward in the process as needed to create your finished product.

By deliberately completing each of these steps as separate tasks, you will improve the quality of your writing. The remainder of this Introduction presents some specific strategies you can use to accomplish each step.

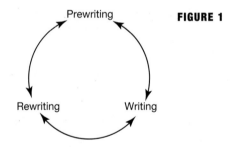

Prewriting

Rewriting   Writing

FIGURE 1

TIP

To better understand the writing process, compare it to the steps involved in cooking a meal. When you're going to prepare dinner, for example, you first decide what you're going to make. You assemble all of the necessary ingredients and equipment. Also, you determine the order in which you need to make the entrée and side dishes so that they will all be finished and ready to eat at about the same time. This same kind of preparation and planning is required when you set out to create a composition. Next, as you are actually cooking, you are mixing, heating, or chilling ingredients to create each dish, just as you are forming sentences and paragraphs to express your ideas during the writing step. Finally, you sample each dish to make sure that it is properly prepared, and you make changes to improve the taste. For example, you might add more salt or remove excess liquid from your potatoes. If you made a mistake and burned something, you might throw out that part. When you write, you improve your creation during the rewriting step by adding, removing, or rearranging information and by correcting mistakes.

Step #1: Prewriting

The prewriting step of the writing process includes the following three tasks:

1. Generate ideas about your topic.
2. Determine your composition's main idea.
3. Organize your ideas and information.

Generating Ideas: Seven Useful Strategies

For some of the subjects you write about, the ideas will flow easily, and you won't have any trouble thinking of what you want to say. For other subjects, however, coming up with the right ideas will be more challenging. When that happens, the worst thing you can do is sit in front of a blank piece of paper or a blank computer screen, hoping that the ideas will suddenly appear. Instead, you need to use a more *active* approach to discover what you need to include in your paper. Seven effective strategies for producing ideas are described in the next sections of this Introduction and summarized in Figure 2.

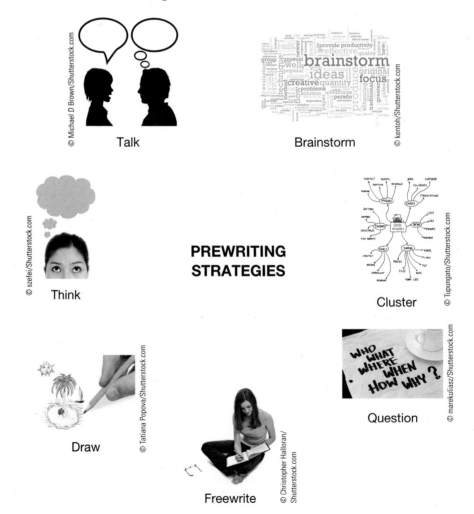

PREWRITING STRATEGIES

Talk

Brainstorm

Think

Cluster

Draw

Freewrite

Question

FIGURE 2

Always use at least one of these strategies to gather ideas *before* you write. The actual composition of any type of paper is a challenging mental activity that requires you to consider the best arrangement of smaller units (your words, your sentences, and your paragraphs) while keeping the big picture (your overall structure and goal) in mind. Writing is like flying by helicopter into a forest. As you approach in the air from far away, you can see the whole forest, its overall size, its shape, its edges, and its general features. As you fly closer, you lose sight of the boundaries, but then you can begin to distinguish individual trees. As you descend among those trees, you begin to notice the leaves, bark, and roots of the ones closest to you. When the helicopter deposits you in the middle of the forest, you'll easily lose your way if you can't remember the overall size and shape of the forest that you saw on your way in. Writing, too, requires you to pay attention to the details while also remembering the overall size and shape of the whole composition. You will make the composition process harder for yourself if you try to think up ideas while you compose, so get in the habit of using techniques for generating and understanding your thoughts before you begin to write.

Think

One useful technique for generating ideas is simply to clear your mind of all other thoughts and focus your full attention for an extended period of time on the topic you need to write about. This activity requires you to concentrate on that one subject and ignore everything else, so you will need to take steps to eliminate or reduce distractions and interruptions. Turn off your cell phone. Go someplace where you can be alone with your thoughts. Then, consider what you already know about your subject. Identify the beliefs and opinions you hold. Determine what you still need to find out.

This technique also works when you engage in activities that you do automatically, without having to give them much thought. When you're doing the dishes, walking your dog, taking a shower, jogging, or even driving your car, try turning off the radio, the television, the iPod, or any other source of stimulation and turning your thoughts to the topic you need to write about. This technique will probably work best if you follow it by capturing ideas on paper using one of the other techniques described in this Introduction.

If this method is difficult for you, don't give up on it after just one try. Remember that we are bombarded all day long with sensations and information that compete for our attention. You may have to practice with ways that you can create periods of time just for thinking.

▌ Exercise A

Find a 20-minute period of your day when you can eliminate or reduce distractions. Spend that time thinking about a topic you need to write about.

Talk

The talk strategy simply involves discussing your topic informally with someone. It requires no pen or paper, just an interested or supportive person who will listen to you and perhaps ask questions as you explain aloud what you need to write about.

This method relies on the power of language as a tool for helping us understand our thoughts. Many of the topics we must write about are ones we've never written about or even discussed with someone before. Therefore, even though we may have some ideas or opinions about the subject, as long as they remain unexpressed in our minds, they tend to be fuzzy, shadowy, and incomplete. Only when someone asks us to express those ideas, either in speech or in writing, do they form more clearly. Can you remember the last time someone asked you what you thought about a particular topic, perhaps a current event or issue? In the act of searching for the words you needed to communicate your ideas, you probably clarified in your own mind what you knew or believed about that subject. When we must find the right words to express what we're thinking, our thoughts become clearer, and we know better what we think simply by having found the language to share those thoughts with others. As W. H. Auden put it, "How do I know what I think, until I see what I say?"

TIP

Increasing the size of your vocabulary is an important component of developing good writing skills. The more words you know, the more accurately you can express your ideas and opinions. Excellent tools for building your vocabulary include:

- books on vocabulary development
- websites such as Vocabulary.com
- vocabulary-builder apps for smart phones and tablet computers

Talking about your ideas with others before you compose can be a valuable step in the process of writing. You will, of course, have to find the right words when you finally sit down to write, but you will find this challenging mental task to be a lot easier if you've already experimented in an informal conversation. Oral discussion will also produce the additional benefit of helping you identify gaps in your information or aspects of the topic you're still not sure about. Then you can gather the missing data or spend more time thinking before you begin to write. If you begin writing when you're still fuzzy about what you think, your writing, too, will be unclear.

Exercise B

1. With a partner, talk about a current news topic that you've never discussed or written about before. Notice how your thinking about this topic becomes clearer as you discuss it.
2. With a group of your classmates, discuss your next writing assignment. Talk about ideas you are considering for the paper you will write. Ask your group members questions about the topics they are considering.
3. Form a study group with other classmates enrolled in a course you're taking. Notice how oral discussion of the facts and concepts you're learning helps you understand them better.
4. For your next writing task, use the talk strategy to find and clarify ideas before composing.

Draw

For some topics, you may want to draw pictures of your mental images. This method involves generating ideas by tapping into your visual memory and sketching pictorial details. You do not have to possess artistic talent to use this technique. Don't worry about creating a masterpiece. The point is to tap into the part of your brain that stores pictures and then use those pictures to jump-start your writing process.

The drawing technique is especially well suited for writing tasks that ask you to describe a person, place, or object or to explore your memories. For example, your supervisor might ask you to propose a new layout of furniture and equipment to improve the efficiency and productivity in your workplace. One of your relatives might like more information about the hotel where you stayed in the Bahamas. Or you might need to describe storm damage to your house for an insurance company. For topics like these, the drawing strategy can help you get ideas before writing.

Because you will eventually have to find words to convey your thoughts to the reader, this method works best when you follow it by using one of the other idea-generation strategies that relies on language.

Exercise C

As you complete one or more of the following activities, notice how these techniques help you remember key details that would be important in a written description.

1. Visualize in your mind a place (such as a neglected public playground, the intersection of two roads, an abandoned building, or an area in your workplace) that is dangerous or unsafe. Sketch it on paper.
2. Sketch a toy you played with when you were a child.
3. Draw the perfect outfit to wear to a job interview.
4. Draw a map that shows the shortest route from your college's campus to your home.

Freewrite

Freewriting involves recording the flow of thoughts through your mind. When you freewrite, you literally take dictation from your brain, letting your thoughts arise freely without controlling them in any way. You can begin with a particular topic to focus on, or you can just record the random thoughts that arise one after the other. Figure 3 provides an example of a student's freewriting in response to the topic *A Needed Change*.

This method is not only an excellent tool for generating ideas about a wide variety of writing tasks, but it will also help you understand what you already know about a topic you need to write about.

In order to freewrite most effectively, follow these guidelines:

Write for a prescribed length of time, perhaps 10 or 15 minutes. During that time, do not stop writing. If your mind goes blank, write

A Needed Change

The closing time of my daughters day care center, Wee Care,upsets me—parents just can't get there sometimes by 5:30 I can't get off work til 5:00 and then I have to drive 15 miles across town to the day care so when theres traffic I can't make it by 5:30, three times I had to pay the $10 penalty fee even though I was just 5-10 minutes late and I can't afford these extra charges–the day care bill is already high but I don't want to change day care centers cause Hannah likes going to this one her best friend Brittany is there and she and Hannah have played together since they were two years old. But the staff members are very carring and really love the kids. Why can't they take turns staying an extra half hour, parents like me would be less stressed out and greatful.

FIGURE 3

"my mind is blank my mind is blank" over and over until another thought occurs to you.

Don't censor your thoughts. Write down everything you're thinking, even if it seems silly or irrelevant. Don't judge or evaluate your thoughts; just get them down onto the page. If your train of thought moves away from your original topic to another subject, let it.

Forget about grammar and spelling. Don't worry about punctuation, capital letters, or the spelling of words. When you freewrite, you will be more productive if you abandon all of the rules. Don't slow yourself down by wondering whether you should insert a comma or a semicolon. Write as fast as you can, and don't worry about organizing your thoughts or even creating complete sentences. The brain thinks in fragments and phrases, so your freewriting should be a collection of partial and half-formed thoughts. As a result, you'll probably end up with sloppy, seemingly incomprehensible scribblings. If others were to read your freewriting, it probably wouldn't make much sense to them. However, it's not meant for others to read. No one but you will see these pages. This activity is a tool for you to use to explore your ideas. Later on, you'll shape them into a document suitable for your readers' eyes.

TIP

Beyond generating ideas, freewriting can be helpful in other ways. First, it can be an effective tool for problem solving. Exploring your thoughts with freewriting can be a good way to identify the source of the problem and then generate some possible solutions. Also, freewriting is a useful way to clear your mind of clutter before you begin an important task, such as taking a test, that will demand your full attention. If you give your thoughts your full attention during a 10- to 15-minute freewriting session, they'll be less likely to intrude when you need to focus on something else.

When you finish freewriting, look back over what you have written, and highlight, circle, or underline ideas that seem useful or relevant to your writing task.

Exercise D

1. Freewrite for 10 minutes on one of the following topics: *A Challenge I Face, My Goals,* or *Things About Myself I'd Like to Improve.*
2. Choose one particular topic from your field of study that you're interested in knowing more about. Freewrite on this topic for 10 minutes to discover what you already know about it.
3. Freewrite without beginning with a specific topic. Simply record the random thoughts flowing through your mind.

Brainstorm (or List)

Brainstorming involves quickly writing down words and phrases that occur to you as you consider your topic. You can record these words and phrases in the form of a list or spread them out over the page, as Figure 4 illustrates. This technique is based on free association, the concept that one thought triggers another thought. For example, when you hear the word *orange*, another word or image immediately pops into your mind. When you brainstorm, you record that word or phrase, and then the next one that occurs to you, and then the next, and so on. For example, if you began with the word *airplane*, you might generate something like the brainstorm shown in Figure 4.

To most effectively use the brainstorming technique, follow these guidelines:

Don't try to organize your thoughts in any way. Just let them arise randomly. Don't record them in any certain order, either, even if your paper gets messy. Fill up a sheet of paper by writing down each word or phrase anywhere on the page, as the example in Figure 4 illustrates.

Don't censor any of your ideas. Write down every word or phrase that pops into your mind, even if one seems silly or irrelevant. You can weed out the useless or unrelated ideas later. During brainstorming, don't evaluate or judge, just record.

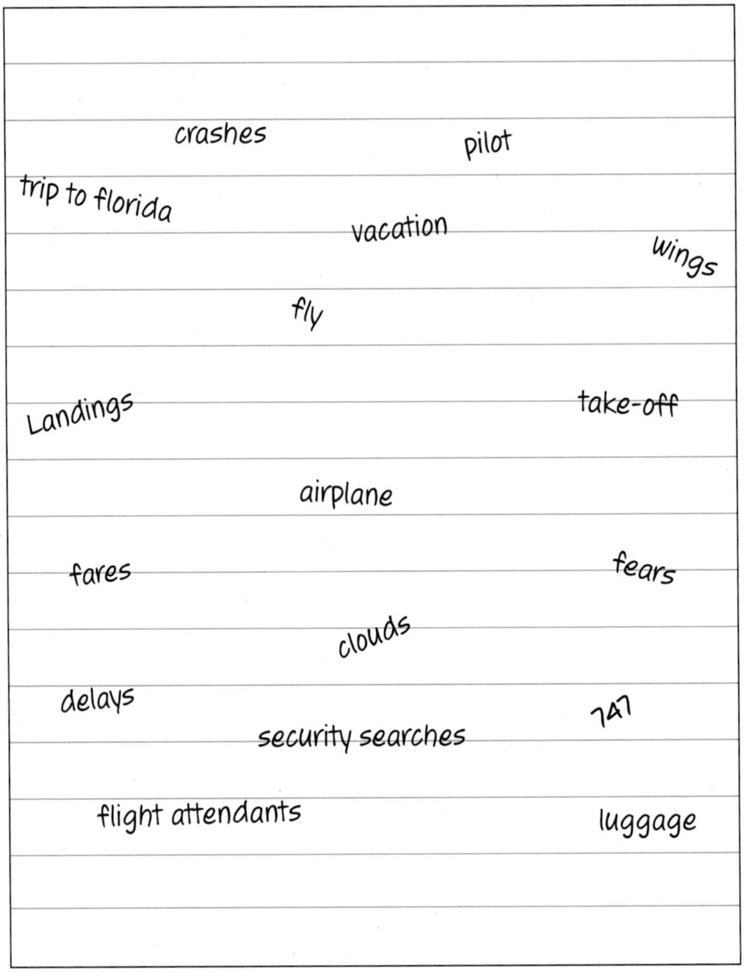

crashes   pilot

trip to florida

               vacation

                                        wings

           fly

Landings   take-off

           airplane

fares   fears

              clouds

delays   747

          security searches

flight attendants   luggage

FIGURE 4

Write as fast as you can and continue to record ideas until they stop coming to you. Then, go back over what you wrote and highlight, circle, or underline ideas that seem useful or relevant to your writing task.

Brainstorming is an effective, informal way to generate ideas. It's also a good technique for narrowing ideas. For example, if your history professor requires you to write a term paper on the Vietnam War, you might brainstorm on the topic to help you zero in on some specific aspect to focus on. Then, you could brainstorm again about your new, limited topic, such as one specific battle or one particular military commander.

TIP

Like freewriting, brainstorming can be a useful tool for problem solving.

Exercise E

1. Brainstorm ideas about a memorable holiday or birthday celebration.
2. With a group of your classmates, brainstorm together on this topic: What inventions does the world need?
3. Write about study techniques that have worked for you, using the brainstorming technique to generate ideas.
4. Think of a personal problem you need to solve. Brainstorm some possible solutions.

Cluster

Like brainstorming, clustering is based on free association, the mind's tendency to link one thought to another. Clustering, though, groups words and phrases loosely into strings of related ideas or "clusters." This method is a little more organized than brainstorming because you link ideas together in a chain in the order in which they occur to you, exhausting one set of associations before beginning another set. For example, you begin, as in brainstorming, with a topic. You write down the first word or phrase you think of when you consider that topic. Then, you write down what that word or phrase makes you think of, and so on. So, for example, if you began with the word *security*, your clustering might look something like the one in Figure 5.

FIGURE 5

When clustering, you follow a train of thought as far as you can, then return to your original topic to begin another train of thought. Like brainstorming, this technique is most effective when you don't censor yourself; instead, write down words and phrases quickly to capture every idea and image. When you finish, you'll have several sets of associations, or clusters. Then, you can evaluate which ones include relevant details for the composition you're planning to write. You can ignore the clusters that you won't need. Another way to use the clusters you generate is to select one group to focus on. For example, the writer who produced the cluster about the word *security* may want to tell a story about a memorable encounter with security personnel in an airport. Or, that writer might decide to describe how to improve home security, or describe effective strategies for achieving financial security. The cluster in Figure 5 helps to identify a specific direction, and then additional prewriting can be used to generate more details.

Exercise F

1. Create a cluster of ideas for one of the following words: *summer, pets, grandmother, college.*
2. Think of an idea or a concept you recently studied in one of your classes. Cluster it.
3. With a group of your classmates, create a cluster for the topic *stress.*

Question

When reporters go out to collect information about an event or situation, they get answers to all of the following questions: *Who? What? When? Where? Why? How?* Asking these questions and finding the answers to them can be an effective way to generate ideas about a topic you need to write about. For example, if one of your instructors wants you to write a report about a disease or disorder that has affected you or a family member, you could explore your topic by asking questions about it. Figure 6 provides a sample of the questions generated for the topic *Attention Deficit Disorder.*

Investigating the answers to these questions should provide you with a lot of good ideas for the report you need to write.

Exercise G

Create a list of questions for one of the following topics:

1. A historic person, place, object, or event
2. An unsolved mystery
3. Your career goal

There is no one best way to go about generating ideas. Different techniques work for different writers. You may prefer brainstorming, for example, whereas a

Attention Deficit Disorder (ADD)
WHO *is affected by ADD?*
WHO *are famous people with ADD?*
WHAT *are the symptoms of this disorder?*
WHAT *are the causes?*
WHEN *was the disorder first identified?*
WHERE *is the disorder most common?*
WHY *is there controversy about this disorder?*
HOW *is it diagnosed?*
HOW *is it treated or managed?*
HOW *does it affect patients' lives?*

FIGURE 6

classmate finds that freewriting works best for him. Find the methods that work best for you. Keep in mind, though, that certain techniques are suited for certain kinds of writing tasks, and be willing to try several different techniques. If you need to describe a place or an object, for instance, you might want to use the clustering method, which is a good technique for exploring memories and images. If you need to write an explanation of a new policy for your co-workers, you might want to use the question method, which is a good way to generate information about all of the different aspects of a topic.

Determining the Main Idea

The next task in the prewriting stage takes place after you have finished generating ideas. Before you write any document, you need to determine the overall point you want to make about your topic. What one idea or opinion do you want your readers to believe or to accept upon reading your composition? The answer to that question becomes your **main idea**. It's important for you, the writer, to understand your main idea. If you're not sure what that idea is, you won't communicate it successfully to your readers.

A main idea statement has two parts:

1. A **topic** (the subject of the paragraph or the longer composition)
2. A **point** about that topic

For example, the main idea of the Introduction you are reading now is

TOPIC	POINT
Your writing	will improve if you complete all three steps of the writing process.

The main idea of a paragraph is called the **topic sentence**, and the main idea of an essay or longer composition is called the **thesis statement**. Because both of these main idea sentences are important necessary features of paragraphs, essays, and longer documents, they are covered more thoroughly in Chapter 2 of this book as one of the essentials of effective writing.

To determine your main idea, review the thoughts you came up with when you used one or more of the strategies for generating ideas. Some of these details will lead you to form a certain conclusion about your topic. Details that don't fit can simply be ignored. For example, take a look back at Figure 3, the student's freewriting on *A Needed Change*. The student's topic is *the closing time of the Wee Care Day Care Center*. The writer believes that this closing time causes problems for parents; therefore, it should be changed. The main idea could be stated like this:

TOPIC	POINT
The closing time of the Wee Care Day Care Center	should change to 6:00 p.m.

Exercise H

Look over the ideas you generated when you completed Exercises A–G of this Introduction. Select one set of ideas, and write a main idea statement that arises from those details. Begin your main idea statement with your topic, and add the point you want to make about that topic.

Organizing and Outlining

After you have generated ideas and determined your composition's main idea, the next prewriting task involves organizing your thoughts and figuring out the best order in which to present them in your composition.

Many inexperienced writers are tempted to skip this important task. They assume that they will be able to combine it with the writing step, thus saving themselves some time. However, trying to organize ideas and write the draft at the same time often leads to serious problems that undermine the quality of the entire composition. It's actually more efficient and effective to work out an organization plan prior to writing. Making the effort to sketch out a plan for the composition ahead of time usually improves the quality of the first draft and decreases the amount of rewriting necessary in the final stage of the process.

Clear organization is one of the 11 essentials of effective writing; therefore, it is covered completely in Chapter 8 of this book. There, you will find a discussion of several concepts and techniques that will help you improve this step of your writing process. Briefly, though, organization involves:

1. Reviewing the ideas you generated and identifying the ones that relate to your main idea
2. Determining the reasons, examples, facts, or other details that will best support or prove your main idea
3. Deciding on the best order to use for presenting those details
4. Creating an outline that reflects this order

Consider, for example, the student's freewriting about *A Needed Change* (see page xxvi). Her main idea is *The closing time of the Wee Care Day Care Center should change to 6:00 p.m.* The writer should first review her freewriting, identify her reasons for the needed change, and continue freewriting if she has not yet produced enough information. Once she feels as though she has enough reasons, she should create an outline that lists her reasons in the order she will discuss them, and then sort the additional relevant details into the appropriate sections. Details that are not relevant are not included. An informal outline for this composition might look like this:

Main Idea: *The closing time of the Wee Care Day Care Center should change to 6:00 p.m.*

Reason #1: Parents work until 5:00 p.m. and can't always get there by 5:30 p.m.

Example: I work until 5:00 p.m. and sometimes cannot complete the 15-mile drive across town in just 30 minutes.

Reason #2: Parents cannot afford the penalty fee.

Example: I can't afford the $10 late fee, which I've had to pay three times.

This detailed plan provides an excellent guide to follow while writing.

▋ Exercise I

Create an outline for the main idea statement you wrote for Exercise H. List the reasons, examples, facts, or other details that you would include in the order in which you would present them.

Step #2: Writing a Draft

Once you have completed all three prewriting tasks—generating ideas, determining the main idea, and organizing and outlining—you're ready to move on to the second main step of the writing process: writing a draft. In this step, you follow the outline you created and express your ideas and information in the form of sentences and paragraphs.

This book discusses several essential characteristics of effective sentences and paragraphs that writers must be aware of as they compose. You'll learn more about these qualities in the following parts of this book:

- **Part II (Chapters 3 and 4) explores the features of effective sentences.** Chapter 3 covers the rules for writing clear sentences, and Chapter 4 demonstrates how to write sentences containing vivid language.
- **Part III (Chapters 5, 6, and 7) explains the three C's of effective paragraphs:** complete, coherent, and cohesive.
- **Part IV (Chapters 8, 9, 10, and 11) covers the components of effective essays and longer compositions.** Chapter 8 shows how to organize ideas, Chapters 9 and 10 provide techniques for interesting opening and closing paragraphs, and Chapter 11 covers some important do's and don'ts when trying to persuade readers to agree with you.

Exercise J

Using the outline you generated in Exercise I, write a composition to support or prove your main idea.

Step #3: Rewriting and Editing

The final step of the writing process, the rewriting step, includes the following three tasks:

1. Get feedback about your draft.
2. Revise your draft (make larger-scale changes as needed).
3. Proofread and edit errors in your sentences.

Getting Feedback

After completing a draft, it's often useful to get feedback about your paper's strengths and weaknesses. Ask your writing instructors, you college's writing tutors, or your fellow writing course classmates to read your paper and help you identify needed improvements. You could ask your readers some general questions about your draft, such as:

Is my main idea clear?
Have I included enough supporting information?
Does my paper convince you to accept my main idea?
Does the organization of my paper make sense?
Is anything confusing, unclear, or difficult to understand?
Do you see any errors that need to be corrected?

You could also provide your reviewers with a copy of the comprehensive checklist on the inside cover of this book, which can serve as a helpful guide. In addition, you could have your readers evaluate only certain qualities of your paper, especially those that have been identified in the past as areas you need to improve. You could give them a copy of a checklist focused on a specific writing quality—each chapter of this book includes a checklist that can be used as a guide (such as Chapter 9's "Checklist for Interesting Openings," p. 169).[2]

Exercise K

Ask an instructor, a tutor, or a classmate to read the draft you produced for Exercise J and offer you some suggestions for improvement.

Revising

Revising involves carefully reading and evaluating your draft to decide what you need to improve. When you revise, you consider major aspects of your composition, such as main-idea sentences, organization, support, unity, the opening, and the closing. You may move, change, expand, or delete whole sections of your paper during this step. The goal of revision is to produce the final draft that you will submit to your instructor or your intended audience.

The checklist on the inside cover of this book, as well as the checklists focused on specific qualities in each chapter, can provide you with helpful guides for conducting your evaluation.

Proofreading and Editing

Proofreading involves carefully going over every sentence of your revised draft to find errors in grammar, punctuation, capitalization, spelling, and word choice. Correcting these errors is called **editing**.

The proofreading and editing task is a very important part of the writing process. Errors can confuse your readers, lead to misunderstandings, and/or cause your readers to form a negative opinion about you, the writer. Therefore, you should always leave time to correct these mistakes. You may also want to get into the habit of asking people with good writing skills to help you find and eliminate the errors in your documents.

Chapter 3 and Appendix 2 of this book will give you practice with proofreading and editing common errors.

Exercise L

Revise, proofread, and edit the draft you produced for Exercise J.

Each of the chapters that follows covers one essential characteristic of all effective writing and explains what you can do to incorporate that quality into your own writing as you prewrite, write, and rewrite your drafts.

---

[2] See the checklists on pages 11, 33, 61, 81, 102, 129, 142, 170, 185, 194 and 208.

PART I

Essential Characteristics of All Compositions

CHAPTER 1

Essential #1: Clear Subject, Audience, and Purpose

In both your personal life and your professional life, you will often have to communicate with people in writing. For example, you will compose e-mail messages to send to friends and family members. You will write memos and reports for your co-workers and supervisors. You will compose letters to send to potential employers. You may even write journal entries that no one but yourself will read. Figure 1.1 summarizes some of the different people and groups to whom you may need to write.

Any written document, regardless of its type, covers a topic for a reader or group of readers for the purpose of achieving some goal. Therefore, every writing task should begin with a clear understanding of the composition's subject, audience, and purpose. Together, they make up the first essential of all effective writing. Because these three components affect all of the choices you make about *what* you include in your composition and *how* you say what you need to say, all three should be clear in your own mind so that they can guide your writing during every step of the writing process—prewriting, writing, and rewriting.

Subject

The **subject** of a paper is the person, place, thing, or idea you are writing about. In the college courses you take, you may have some choice in your selection of subjects. In your English class, for instance, your instructor may ask you to write an essay about a topic that interests you. In your history class, a research paper assignment may permit you to choose from a list of various topics covered in the course.

More often, however, life "assigns" us topics that arise from a need. We write mostly to achieve some goal (for example, to convince a potential employer to schedule a job interview or to get a refund for an unsatisfactory product) or to fulfill one of our reader's needs (for example, to update the boss about a project or to give a friend advice about a problem). Most of the time, then, we don't have to think up topics to write about; they are supplied by the situations and people in our lives.

Whether the subject is your choice or not, you will need to give some thought to its scope, or size. The scope of the topic needs to be appropriate for the type of

Teachers, mentors, or role models

Yourself

Friends

Fellow students

Relatives

People who disagree with you

Supervisors

Companies or businesses

Potential employers

Co-workers

FIGURE 1.1

document you are writing. Although no type of document has any one set length, some are by nature shorter than others. The majority of the documents you will probably be writing, such as letters, summaries, reviews, editorials, and essays, tend to be relatively brief (one to five pages). Other kinds of documents, such as formal reports and research papers, may be longer. You will need to be able to cover the topic completely, so you must make sure that your subject is not too big to fully explain in the type of document you are expected to write. If your instructor asks you to write an essay, for example, he or she is probably expecting a shorter document of four to eight paragraphs in length that is focused on one particular aspect of a topic, not everything there is to know about that topic.

> **TIP**
>
> In college, grades are always based solely on the quality of the *finished product* (your paper, your test, your project, your presentation), not on the effort you put into preparing that product. By focusing on the qualities of effective compositions, this book will help you understand and incorporate those qualities.

Audience

The **audience** of a paper is the person or people who will read it or who need to read it. For everything you write, you will need to consider three specific qualities of your intended readers:

- their characteristics
- their prior knowledge about the topic
- their needs

When considering the characteristics of your audience, you will need to answer questions such as: *How old are my readers? Are they male, female, or a combination of both? To what ethnic, racial, and socioeconomic groups do they belong? Are they married? Do they have children? How do they earn a living? What challenges are they facing? What are their interests? What beliefs do they hold? What are their objections to my ideas or suggestions?* By answering these questions, you will consider characteristics of your readers that could affect how they respond to your thoughts about your topic. Anticipating and addressing these responses will be important to achieving your purpose. For example, if you write an e-mail to try to convince one of your instructors that you were unexpectedly absent from class on a test day for a good reason, your instructor's interests, beliefs, and possible objections should affect the way you present your argument. Also, your readers' characteristics will affect the words you choose. Language that could potentially insult or offend your audience will undermine your purpose and should always be avoided. In Chapter 11 of this book, you will learn more about how to avoid this kind of language.

It's also important to think about your audience's level of prior knowledge about the subject. If you believe that readers have some knowledge about the topic, you will not have to provide as many explanations and definitions of terminology as you might if the audience knows relatively little about the subject. For example, if you are writing a set of instructions for a co-worker, you would need to explain the topic in much more detail for a new employee who is in training than you would for an experienced co-worker.

Finally, consider your audience's needs. What are your readers' goals? What do they need to achieve? Are they interested in saving time, money, or labor? Your job as the writer is to make it clear how your ideas and information will help fulfill their needs. For example, if you are writing to convince a manager of a business to grant you a job interview, you need to explain how you would be able to use your knowledge and skills to help that manager maintain a smoothly running workplace.

Purpose

Your **purpose** for writing is the goal you are trying to achieve. There are just three purposes for writing anything:

- to entertain
- to inform
- to persuade

If your purpose is to entertain, your goal is to provide your readers with a pleasurable experience, perhaps by telling them an interesting story or by making them laugh. This is usually the primary goal of fictional writing such as novels and short stories. If your purpose is to inform, your goal is to increase your readers' understanding of the topic or to teach them how to do something. Textbooks, summaries, assembly instructions, and many newspaper and magazine articles are types of writing with a mainly informative purpose. If your purpose is to persuade, your goal is to convince your readers to change a belief or a behavior. Editorials, proposals, and many essays have a persuasive purpose.

One of these three purposes will be your main reason for writing, but some of the documents you compose could have a second purpose, too. For example, a letter of application sent to a prospective employer will inform the reader about your qualifications *and* attempt to persuade that reader to call you to schedule a job interview.

Prewriting for a Clear Subject, Audience, and Purpose

In the Introduction to this book, you learned that the prewriting step of the writing process includes three tasks: generating ideas about the topic, determining the composition's main idea, and organizing thoughts in preparation for writing. As you complete each of these tasks, you should maintain a constant awareness of your intended subject, audience, and purpose and adjust any or all of these components as needed so that they match.

In a well-written document, the subject, the audience, and the purpose always fit together, or match. It's helpful to think of these three components in a triangle shape of interlocking puzzle pieces, as shown in Figure 1.2.

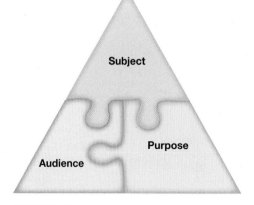

FIGURE 1.2

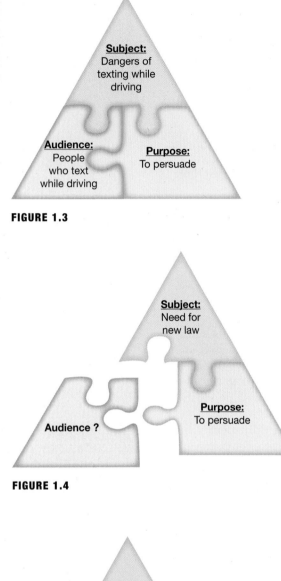

FIGURE 1.3

FIGURE 1.4

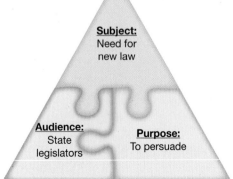

FIGURE 1.5

The three essential components—subject, audience, and purpose—should fit together just as puzzle pieces fit together. For example, let's say you want to persuade people who try to drive and text at the same time that they should stop doing this. Your topic would be the dangers of simultaneous driving and texting. Your audience would be cell phone users who drive and text at the same time. Your purpose would be persuasive because you want to convince them to stop. This subject, audience, and purpose fit together, as Figure 1.3 shows.

If one of these components changes, however, changes may need to be made to one or both of the other components. Now let's say that you feel so strongly about the dangers of texting while driving that you believe it should be outlawed. Is your purpose and your audience still the same? Although you may still include information about the dangers of texting while driving, your topic changed to the need for a new law that makes this activity illegal. If you envision a triangle puzzle diagram, your "puzzle piece" for the topic has changed shape (see Figure 1.4).

Your purpose is still persuasive because you want to argue in favor of passing that new law. Your new topic, though, does not fit the audience and will need to change. Instead of writing to the people who engage in the dangerous behavior, you will want to write to the people who can do something about it, so your audience needs to change to your state's legislators. You must change the "puzzle piece" for the audience so that it will fit the altered topic (Figure 1.5).

> **TIP**
>
> Chapter 11 explains how to select information and ideas that match your readers' needs and goals.

▌ Exercise 1.1

On your own paper, create three different triangle diagrams by matching one of the subjects from the first list with one of the audiences and one of the purposes from the second and third lists. For

each diagram, draw a triangle divided into three parts like the one below, and write one subject in the top section, one audience in the bottom left section, and one purpose in the bottom right section.

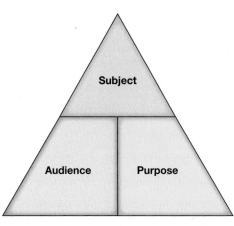

SUBJECT	AUDIENCE	PURPOSE
how to write an effective résumé	college students	to entertain
a funny story about talking rabbits	senior citizens	to inform
features of a good child's car seat	children	to persuade
reasons why you should not "friend" your students on Facebook	job seekers	
	parents	
effective test-taking techniques	teachers	
new treatments for arthritis		

Exercise 1.2

For each set of subject, audience, and purpose, use the information given to determine what the missing component should be. Write the missing information on your own paper.

1. Subject: The features of a good day care center
Audience: Working parents of young children
Purpose: ?

2. Subject: The benefits of working as a volunteer
Audience: ?
Purpose: To persuade

3. Subject: ?
   Audience: A person who doesn't know how to operate his new iPod
   Purpose: To inform

4. Subject: Reasons for violating a course's attendance policy
   Audience: The instructor for the course
   Purpose: ?

5. Subject: Available scholarships
   Audience: ?
   Purpose: To inform

6. Subject: ?
   Audience: People who never exercise
   Purpose: To persuade

Exercise 1.3

Select two of the writing assignments listed on page 14. On your own paper, create triangle diagrams that identify the subject, audience, and purpose for each composition.

Writing for a Clear Subject, Audience, and Purpose

The intended subject, audience, and purpose of a composition affect all aspects of that composition, including its content, its organization, and its wording. Therefore, the prewriting step of the process is the best time to carefully consider and select these important elements. Once you've determined your topic, your readers, and your purpose, you will make decisions throughout the writing stage, as you compose, to ensure that all three continue to fit together.

You chose a specific subject to fit a specific audience and purpose; therefore, as you write, you will need to be careful not to stray from that subject by including related but irrelevant ideas or information. For example, if you are writing to persuade a teenage relative of yours that dropping out of high school is a bad idea, don't include a story about a friend who quit a job. That particular example may be about quitting, but it's not about quitting *school*, so it would not be meaningful. As you write, make sure that every sentence you include directly relates to your composition's specific topic.

Also, select the reasons or other details that best fit your reader's situation, needs, or goals. If you are trying to prevent a 16-year-old from dropping out of high school, for instance, you will want to focus on the negative financial or social consequences. You would leave out any argument that this particular reader would not find very persuasive. Chapter 11 of this book explains how to select ideas and information that match readers' needs and goals.

As you write your sentences, use words that clearly reflect your purpose. For example, it's usually appropriate to directly address readers as "you" when teaching them how to do something (as in "Next, *you* press the enter button on *your* keyboard") or when persuading them to change a behavior or a belief (as in " *You* should begin exercising at least three times a week"). However, "you" is usually inappropriate and unnecessary when your goal is to provide readers with information about a topic. Informative compositions should also avoid certain other words and phrases—such as *should, must,* and *ought to*—that communicate a persuasive purpose.

Your choice of words and the types and lengths of sentences you write also need to fit your audience's characteristics in the following ways:

- Use language that fits your readers' age and educational background. For example, if you are trying to persuade middle school students to join a club or participate in a project, don't use college-level vocabulary or long, complex sentences.
- Define all specialized or unfamiliar terms if your readers are not experts on the topic. For example, if you are explaining to the average computer user how to solve a computer problem, include definitions for terms such as *router, modem, encryption,* and *reboot.*
- Choose language that communicates respect, especially when you are asking for something from the reader. Don't "talk down" to the reader or insult him or her in any way. Chapter 11 of this book explains how to avoid offensive and insulting language.
- Use a level of formality appropriate to the situation. For example, when writing an e-mail to one of your college professors, don't write what looks like a text message filled with abbreviations, misspellings, punctuation mistakes, and other errors.

Exercise 1.4

Consider each statement along with the writer's intended subject, audience, and purpose. Explain why the statement does not match one or more of those elements. Write your answers on your own paper.

1. yo - cud u give me more time to rite my paper cuz it aint done yet

Subject:	Extension of an assignment deadline
Audience:	A college instructor
Purpose:	To persuade

2. Replacement of the disposable power devices contained within a hydrocarbon particulate detection system should occur biannually.

Subject:	Maintenance of smoke detectors
Audience:	Homeowners
Purpose:	To inform

3. Learning how to speak a foreign language can expand your career opportunities.

 Subject: Reasons to learn a foreign language
 Audience: Retired senior citizens
 Purpose: To persuade

4. In a restaurant, we diners should not be forced to listen to a screaming child at another table.

 Subject: Four ways to respond effectively to a toddler's temper tantrum
 Audience: Parents of toddlers
 Purpose: To inform

5. Because you have no idea what you're doing, you gave me a bad haircut, and you need to give me my money back.

 Subject: Request for a refund
 Audience: Hairstylist
 Purpose: To persuade

6. A motor vehicle operator is required to maintain a reduced rate of speed and expand the distance between his or her vehicle and the preceding vehicle during periods of inclement weather.

 Subject: Driving safely in rain, snow, and fog
 Audience: Teenagers who are learning how to drive
 Purpose: To persuade

7. I hope you'll agree to switch shifts with me at work. If you start working nights and I can switch to the day shift, I'll be able to see my girlfriend more often.

 Subject: Reasons to trade work schedules
 Audience: A co-worker
 Purpose: To persuade

8. Hey, Rob! Whassup? I'm not gonna make your algebra class tonight. Holla!

 Subject: Absence from class
 Audience: A college instructor
 Purpose: To inform

9. You should start volunteering because you can include the experience in the work history section of your résumé.

 Subject: My experience as a volunteer tutor
 Audience: Readers of a newsletter for volunteer tutors
 Purpose: To inform

10. I am married with two children, two dogs, and one cat.

 Subject: My work history
 Audience: A manager who needs to hire a new employee
 Purpose: To inform

Rewriting for a Clear Subject, Audience, and Purpose

After you have written a draft, you will want to evaluate it carefully to make sure that its subject, audience, and purpose are clear and fit together. Consider using the following checklist to guide you in looking at specific features. If you find details, language, or other elements that do not match your subject, your audience, or your purpose, be willing to rewrite to change or remove them.

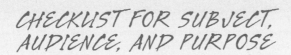

CHECKLIST FOR SUBJECT, AUDIENCE, AND PURPOSE

Use this checklist during the rewriting step of the process to make sure that you are considering important aspects of your subject, your audience, and your purpose and generating ideas that match.

☐ The scope (size) of the subject is appropriate for the document's typical length.

☐ The composition is appropriate to the audience's key characteristics.

☐ The composition is appropriate to the audience's level of prior knowledge about the subject.

☐ The composition is appropriate to the audience's needs and goals.

☐ The writer's purpose for writing the composition is clear.

☐ The composition's subject, audience, and purpose fit together.

In the following paragraph, the student writer intended to explain to people who want to quit smoking how she herself successfully kicked the habit. If you were helping this writer identify problems related to subject, audience, and purpose, what revisions would you recommend?

> I was finally able to quit smoking by following a three-step plan that worked for me. First, you have to go to your doctor and tell him or her to give you a prescription for a drug called Chantix®. Then, as you begin taking this drug, you should slowly decrease the number of cigarettes you smoke every day. At the same time, whenever you get a craving for nicotine, just substitute something else for that cigarette you want. For example, get a soda or a piece of chewing gum or try going for a walk. That's all there is to it! You'll soon be a non-smoker like me if you do what I did.

This writer set out to write an informative composition about the steps that she followed to quit smoking, and her topic sentence (the first sentence) does indicate her original intentions. However, although she does go on to explain each of the steps she followed, she presents them in the form of instructions for the reader to follow. Notice, too, that she uses persuasive language such as *you need to, you have to,* and *you should.* For this topic, that's a problem. The writer is not a doctor, and she cannot assume that her readers can (or should) do exactly what she did. They may not be healthy enough to take a drug, for instance. She also does not address her readers' characteristics and needs. They are probably struggling with their addiction and find it very difficult to deal with a craving. This writer, though, makes it sound as though substituting something else for a cigarette is easy.

Exercise 1.5

Using the checklist on page 11, evaluate each of the following paragraphs and explain to the writer what needs to be revised to better match the subject, the audience, and/or the purpose. The underlined sentence states the writer's main idea.

1. My work experience and skills make me an excellent candidate for your available work-study position in Madison College's Financial Aid Office. Getting this job would really help me cover my expenses. I've been struggling to pay for my tuition, books, and transportation to and from the campus, and I've concluded that I have to have an additional source of income. If I don't start earning some money, I might have to drop out of school, and I really don't want to do that. So I hope that you'll hire me.

2. College students, you should give Fred's Famous Pizza & More a try. Not only do we have the best pizza in town and unlimited soda refills, but we also offer a complete kids' menu. Even the pickiest of eaters will find something they like at Fred's. While they're waiting for their food, children can have fun climbing, sliding, and tumbling in our huge, padded play area. Every hour, our mascot, Freddie the Turtle, comes out to greet the kids and dance with them.

3. Next time you buy a car, you should seriously consider purchasing an electric vehicle. The Chevrolet Volt, for example, has a lithium-ion battery that stores energy. This battery powers the car electrically for about 35 miles, until its charge has been used up. At that point, a gas engine takes over to keep the car running, allowing it to go another 375 miles. When you return home, you plug the car into an electrical outlet, and the battery fully recharges in about 10 hours.

Exercise 1.6

Working with one or two of your classmates, rewrite the paragraph about quitting smoking on page 11 to correct its mismatched subject, audience, and purpose.

Exercise 1.7

A. Use the checklist on page 11 to evaluate a paragraph or essay you have recently written. If you revised this composition, what would you change to create a better match among the composition's subject, audience, and purpose?

B. Use the checklist to evaluate a paragraph or essay written by one of your classmates. What changes would you recommend to create a better match among the composition's subject, audience, and purpose?

SUGGESTED WRITING ACTIVITIES

Complete all of the steps of the writing process as you write one or more of the following compositions. As you prewrite, think carefully about your subject, your audience, and your purpose. Create a triangle diagram to match these three components. Then, keep your purpose and your audience in mind as you write.

ACADEMIC WRITING

1. Write an e-mail to one of your instructors to make a request. For example, request extra time for completing an assignment, or ask the instructor to excuse one of your absences.
2. Explain a concept, a term, or an event that you learned about in one of your classes.
3. Write to introduce yourself to your fellow students in an online course you're taking.

PROFESSIONAL WRITING

4. Write an e-mail to a co-worker to describe the procedure to follow to complete a task in your workplace.
5. Write to your supervisor to propose a change to a policy or procedure that causes problems in your workplace.
6. Convince customers or clients that your workplace's product or service is superior to that of your competitors.

PERSONAL WRITING

7. Describe a place (such as neglected public playground, the intersection of two roads, an abandoned building, or an area at your children's school) that is dangerous or unsafe. What individual, group, or organization could improve this place? Write to persuade this audience to make those improvements.
8. Write a letter to thank someone who gave you a gift or did a good deed for you. Explain the benefits you gained from this gift or deed, or acknowledge the reader's specific sacrifices in giving you this gift or performing this deed.
9. Write an e-mail to a manufacturer to complain about a product that you recently purchased.

CHAPTER 2

Essential #2: Conventional Form and Features

All effective writing is presented using conventional form (one that readers expect) and includes certain components that assist readers in following and comprehending the ideas or information. In all compositions, whether they are one paragraph long or several paragraphs or pages long, the reader will usually expect you to do four things:

1. Introduce the subject.
2. State your main idea.
3. Provide evidence or explanations to support that idea.
4. Tie your thoughts together with a satisfying closing.

Paragraph Form

A **paragraph** is a group of sentences that state and then support one main idea. As Figure 2.1 shows, the first line of a paragraph is indented. The left side of the paragraph lines up along the left margin of the paper.

To accomplish the four things readers expect from you, your paragraph will include up to four parts: an opening sentence or two, a topic sentence, a body, and a concluding sentence. These parts are discussed in the sections that follow. Figure 2.1 includes a paragraph with these four parts labeled.

Opening Sentence(s)

The purpose of including an **opening sentence** or two is to introduce the paragraph's topic. Sometimes, opening sentences also prepare the reader for the main idea by providing some background information or by establishing the situation. Opening sentences are optional. However, with each paragraph you write, ask yourself if your reader would better understand your main idea if you provided a little introductory information. If the answer is yes, begin your paragraph with one or two opening sentences.

INDENT ———— You've set the goal of earning your college degree, and you're
FIRST LINE ready to get started on your journey. The path won't always be
easy, so how can you keep yourself going even when you get tired,
frustrated, or discouraged? By doing three things, you will keep
yourself moving toward your goal even when you're tempted to quit.
First of all, eliminate the word *can't* from your vocabulary. Instead of
saying, "I just can't do math," for example, say "I'm going to have
to put in more time and effort to understand my math homework."
Remain determined, and tell yourself constantly that NOT doing
something is just not an option. Second, write down your ultimate
goal, "I will earn my college degree," and post it in plain view—on a
note stuck to your computer, on the first page of your notebook, or
on a whiteboard beside your desk. Read your goal often and even
more frequently when the going seems especially tough. Finally, do
something every day that moves you even one tiny step closer to your
goal. Remember that every assignment you complete, every paper
you write, every test you take, and every class you complete gets you
further down the path. By doing these three things, you will be more
likely to accomplish what you set out to do.

OPENING
SENTENCES

TOPIC SENTENCE
(MAIN IDEA)

BODY
(SUPPORT)

CLOSING
SENTENCE

FIGURE 2.1

T!P

An opening sentence is most appropriate when the entire composition is only one
paragraph long. Paragraphs that form the body of longer compositions will often lack
opening sentences.

Topic Sentence

The **main idea** of a paragraph is the one point or opinion that you want your readers to believe or to understand when they are finished reading your paragraph. The
sentence in the paragraph that states this main idea is called the **topic sentence**.
This sentence must contain two components: the *topic* of the paragraph and the
overall point the writer wants to make about that topic.

TOPIC	OVERALL POINT
Walking just two miles a day	will result in a number of health benefits.
The recycling process	includes six main steps.
My grandfather	is the most generous person I've ever known.

Include a clear topic sentence in every paragraph you write. The topic sentence does not have to appear at the beginning of the paragraph; it may be appropriate to present it in the middle or at the end of the paragraph. At first, however, get in the habit of stating your main idea early in the paragraph. Later, as you continue to develop your skills, you can experiment with placing it elsewhere.

Exercise 2.1

Rewrite the following topic sentences on your own paper. Then, for each sentence, circle the topic and underline the point the author wants to make about that topic.

1. My brother and I are similar in some ways but very different in other ways.
2. Expanding your vocabulary is one of the best things you can do for yourself.
3. The Wee Care Preschool should extend its closing time from 5:30 p.m. to 6:00 p.m.
4. Safe lifting of heavy objects requires the use of three specific techniques.
5. The installation of a traffic light at the intersection of Mull Road and Town Center Drive would improve safety for both motorists and pedestrians.

Exercise 2.2

On your own paper, list the topic sentences in the following paragraphs: distance learners on page 73, attending community college on page 87, and errors in logic on page 101. Do each of these sentences clearly state the paragraph's topic and the author's point about that topic?

Exercise 2.3

Write a topic sentence for each of the following topics. Begin each statement with the topic, and then add a point you want to make about that topic.

1. Taking public transportation (such as the bus or subway)
2. One technique for saving money
3. One thing students should *not* do in class
4. Fast food
5. Reality shows on television

Exercise 2.4

Highlight the topic sentence in a paragraph you wrote recently. Does this sentence include the paragraph's topic and a clear point about that topic? How would you revise it to improve it?

Selecting a Point of View

Your topic sentence should reveal to the reader the point of view you have selected for your composition. **Point of view** relates to your decision to refer to *yourself* (first-person point of view), to refer to the *reader* (second-person point of view), or to refer to *neither* (third-person point of view). The chart on page 25 summarizes the three points of view.

When using **first-person point of view**, the writer refers to himself or herself by using the pronouns *I, me, my, we, us,* or *our*, as in the following example:

> I formed a study group to improve **my** learning and **my** grades.

This point of view is appropriate when telling a story about a personal experience. Whenever your goal is to focus on yourself and your own thoughts and feelings, you may use first-person point of view.

> *TIP*
>
> First-person point of view is usually not appropriate for academic assignments and some workplace documents.

In **second-person point of view**, the writer directly addresses the reader using the pronouns *you* and *your*. Here is an example:

> You should form a study group to improve **your** learning and **your** grades.

This point of view is most appropriate when giving the reader instructions for how to do something or for persuading the reader to change a belief or a behavior.

When using the **third-person point of view**, the writer refers to neither herself nor himself nor the reader. This point of view is expected in most academic and professional writing, especially when the focus is on the *subject*, not on the writer or the reader. Here is an example:

> **Students** who form study groups often improve **their** learning and **their** grades.

> *TIP*
>
> In general, the three different points of view fit one of the particular purposes for writing described in Chapter 1:
>
> · When writing to *entertain*, perhaps by telling a funny story about a personal experience, the writer may choose first-person point of view.
> · If the purpose of the writing is *informative*, third-person point of view will often be the best choice unless the composition is explaining how to perform a task; in that case, second-person point of view is usually acceptable.
> · When writing to *persuade*, either second-person or third-person point of view is usually most effective.

Once you have established your point of view, stick to that point of view throughout your composition, and don't shift from one to another as you write.

Exercise 2.5

On your own paper, write the point of view (first-person, second-person, or third-person) that is used in each of the following topic sentences.

1. You should cast your vote for Leslie Johnson, candidate for governor.
2. The ABC Daycare Center uses three different discipline strategies in response to unacceptable behavior.
3. I was able to heal my broken heart through a combination of willpower, self-discipline, and time.
4. The Basics of Self-Defense course will teach you valuable crime-prevention techniques.
5. The Seafood Shack has good food, reasonable prices, and excellent service.

Exercise 2.6

On your own paper, rewrite the sentences in Exercise 2.5 to change them to a different point of view.

Exercise 2.7

On your own paper, identify the point of view in the following paragraphs: apps for college students on pages 110-111, body language on page 110, and credit cards on page 126.

Like a lawyer in a courtroom trial, the writer must present enough information to support an idea or opinion and convince readers it's correct.

Body

The **body** of your paragraph consists of all of the sentences that support (explain or prove) the idea or opinion you presented in your topic sentence. Common types of support include examples, facts, data, statistics, explanations, and reasons. Chapters 5, 6, and 7 of this book present a complete explanation of how to support a paragraph.

To understand how support works in the body of a paragraph, think about a lawyer involved in a courtroom trial. The lawyer's main idea is either "The defendant is guilty" (if the lawyer is a prosecutor) or "The defendant is not guilty" (if the lawyer is a defense attorney). All of the evidence and information presented during the trial to convince the jury is the lawyer's support. In your paragraph, you will state your idea or opinion, and then you—like a lawyer—will present enough information to support your idea or opinion and convince your readers that it is correct.

Closing Sentence

The **closing sentence** of a paragraph ties all of your thoughts together and ends the paragraph in a satisfying way. This sentence should not simply repeat what you've already said, nor should it introduce a new idea. Closing sentences often present some consequence or implication of the information or ideas you presented in your paragraph.

Like opening sentences, closing sentences are optional, especially in the body paragraphs of multiparagraph documents such as essays. However, documents that are only one paragraph long will often be strengthened by a sentence that provides a satisfactory closing.

> ### TIP
>
> How long does a paragraph have to be? The answer is: *As long as it needs to be to prove or explain the idea in the topic sentence.* In some paragraphs, five or six sentences will be enough. Other paragraphs will require 10 or more sentences to get the job done.

Exercise 2.8

Read the following paragraph and answer the questions that follow. Write your answers on your own paper.

¹ Writing is viewed by many college students as a tough skill that's too much trouble to master; consequently, they view their writing courses as classes that simply must be endured in order to complete the requirements for their degree. ² In reality, though, thoroughly learning the skills taught in writing courses is absolutely critical to one's future success. ³ First of all, writing is one very important way an individual communicates an image of himself or herself as a clear, logical thinker who is dedicated to producing high-quality work. ⁴ Instructors, colleagues, professionals, and other members of the community judge others—their work, their knowledge, their abilities, and their overall intelligence—by how well they write. ⁵ Because writing is always a direct reflection of the writer's ability to think, anyone who wants others to believe that he or she is a smart and capable person must become a competent writer. ⁶ Second, good writing skills help prevent sometimes costly mistakes. ⁷ When people do not express themselves clearly in writing, misinterpretations and misunderstandings frequently occur. ⁸ For example, a badly written memo can lead to errors that cost a company money. ⁹ A poorly written contract can create serious legal difficulties. ¹⁰ On the other hand, because writing is still an extremely important form of communication in college and in the workplace, good writing skills help people acquire the things in life they most desire: good grades, a great job, promotions, respect, authority, and financial success. ¹¹ For all of these reasons, college students are investing in themselves and their own futures when they put in the time and effort necessary to hone their writing skills.

1. Which sentence is the opening sentence?
2. Which sentence is the topic sentence?
3. What point of view is used in this paragraph?

4. Which sentences make up the paragraph's body?
5. Which sentence is the closing sentence?

Exercise 2.9

Select one of the following paragraphs in Chapter 6 of this book: drugs on page 114, concentrating on pages 112–113, or apps for college students on pages 110–111. Highlight the paragraph's different parts (opening sentence, topic sentence, body, and closing sentence) using different-colored highlighter markers. Or, list the following on your own paper: (1) the paragraph's opening sentence, (2) the paragraph's topic sentence, (3) the sentences that begin and end the body of the paragraph, and (4) the paragraph's closing sentence. Finally, identify the point of view used in the paragraph.

> ### TIP
>
> As you compose your first drafts of the paragraphs you write for this class, consider highlighting the different parts using different colors so that you don't forget to include any of them.

Form for Essays and Multiparagraph Documents

As Figure 2.2 shows, an essay—like a paragraph—includes four parts. Each part accomplishes one of the four things readers expect from you. These parts are an

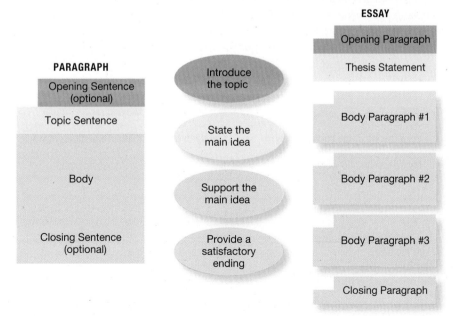

FIGURE 2.2

opening paragraph, a thesis statement, two or more body paragraphs, and a concluding paragraph. Figure 2.3 includes an essay with these four parts labeled.

How will you know if you should write a paragraph or an essay or other type of longer document? The length of your paper will depend upon your topic and main idea. Some topics and ideas can be fully supported in just one paragraph. Others are broader subjects that will require more support than you can achieve in just one paragraph.

Title

A **title** is a phrase that identifies the composition's topic. Therefore, it should always be clear and brief. It should not mislead readers by suggesting that the composition will be about something that it's not. A title can also be used to pique the reader's interest, so it might include some clever wordplay, humor, a surprising or unexpected statement, or some other wording that readers find interesting. However, its most important characteristic is clear identification of the paper's topic.

Here are some additional guidelines for effective titles:

- Limit the words in the title to about five or six.
- Capitalize the first word and all of the major words in the title. Don't capitalize very short words such as *a, an, and, the,* and *of* unless that word is the title's first or last word.
- Center the title above the opening paragraph of your essay.

Opening Paragraph

The purpose of the **opening paragraph** is to introduce the topic, get the reader interested, provide background information, and state the main idea. Techniques for writing effective opening paragraphs are covered in detail in Chapter 9 of this book.

Thesis Statement

Your **thesis statement** is your composition's main idea. It's the one point or idea you want your readers to understand or believe after reading your entire document. Like a topic sentence, a thesis statement includes two components: the *topic* of the composition and the *overall point* the writer wants to make about that topic.

TOPIC	OVERALL POINT
Burke County	is a great place to live and raise a family.
Volunteering at the soup kitchen	has been rewarding in several different ways.
My education and work experience	will make me a valuable asset to your company.

TIP

Both the thesis statement and the topic sentences indicate main ideas. The thesis statement expresses the main idea of the entire composition. Topic sentences express the main ideas of body paragraphs.

The AAS Degree: Another Path to a Great Career

OPENING PARAGRAPH

Before enrolling in college, you may have set the goal of completing a bachelor's degree program to prepare for a specific career. Many career fields, such as teaching, engineering, and computer systems analysis, will definitely require you to earn a bachelor's degree for entry into the profession. However, other occupations that may be of interest to you do not necessarily require that level of education. In fact, many stable jobs with very good wages require only a two-year associate's degree from a community college.

THESIS STATEMENT

If you are still unsure about your career choice, you should seriously consider the many associate in applied science degree programs that are pathways to great careers.

BODY PARAGRAPH #1

Most associate in applied science (AAS) degree programs will prepare you for an interesting, rewarding career in a stable or growing field. Nursing, computer science, horticulture, machining, accounting, and video game design are just a few of the many career fields that may provide you with opportunities to spend your workdays engaged in tasks you truly enjoy. Many of these jobs also tend to be more plentiful than jobs that require a bachelor's degree. Consider that about 10% of our country's workforce hold jobs that require at least a bachelor's degree, whereas twice that number, or 20%, use specialized or technical skills that can often be obtained with just two years of college education. Gaining these skills by completing an AAS program can result in better job security for you now and in the future.

BODY PARAGRAPH #2

Another reason to consider enrolling in an associate level program is the high wages being earned by AAS graduates. In fact, 83% of all workers holding associate degrees have the same or higher annual earnings as those with a 4-year degree. For example, students who earn health care AAS degrees and go to work as nurses, dental hygienists, and radiation technicians usually have annual starting salaries at $45,000 or more. As of 2011, the salaries for engineering technician positions ranged from $50,000 to $75,000. Compare the average starting salary of an inexperienced graduate with a bachelor's degree in marketing, which is about $40,000 per year. The average starting salary of a person who earns a bachelor's degree in psychology is $31,000 per year, and the average first-year teacher's salary is $32,722.

BODY PARAGRAPH #3

One final reason to look into an AAS program is something you usually DON'T get—two additional years without income and a large amount of educational debt. Associate's degree graduates can enter the professional workforce two years before bachelor's degree candidates do, so they begin earning a professional level of income much earlier. Plus, the cost of a community college education is usually significantly lower than the cost of an education at a university or four-year college. Many AAS graduates are able to cover their expenses with grants and scholarships that do not have to be paid back, so they graduate with little or no student loan debt. Students in bachelor's degree programs, on the other hand, often have to take out loans to help pay for their tuition, books, and living expenses. In fact, the average student loan debt of bachelor's degree recipients is now over $22,000. Many also owe thousands more in credit card debt, which takes years to pay back.

CLOSING PARAGRAPH

To find out more about the wide range of associate in applied science degree options, you can browse your local community college's catalog or website, or you can visit your college's career center. If you find an AAS program that interests you, you may be just two years away from the beginning of a high-paying and satisfying career.

FIGURE 2.3

▌ Exercise 2.10

Rewrite the following thesis statements on your own paper. Then, for each statement, circle the topic and underline the point the author wants to make about that topic.

1. A successful job interview requires preparation and practice.
2. Four different types of financial aid will help you pay for your college expenses.
3. High school and college differ in several important respects.
4. Extreme, sustained stress has negative mental, psychological, and physical effects.
5. All successful leaders usually have five specific traits in common.

▌ Exercise 2.11

On your own paper, list the thesis statements in the essays on pages 227, 239, and 241. Do each of these statements clearly identify the essay's topic and the author's point about that topic?

▌ Exercise 2.12

Write a thesis statement for each of the following topics. Begin each statement with the topic, and then add a point you want to make about that topic.

1. Effective parenting
2. High school
3. Repairing a damaged relationship
4. Social media websites such as Facebook
5. Preventing crime

▌ Exercise 2.13

Highlight the thesis statement in an essay you wrote recently. Does this sentence include the essay's topic and a clear point about that topic? How would you revise it to improve it?

Selecting a Point of View

Earlier in this chapter, on page 18, you learned that **point of view** relates to your decision to refer to *yourself* (first-person point of view), to refer to the *reader* (second-person point of view), or to refer to *neither* (third-person point of view). You must make this decision when writing essays as well as paragraphs.

The chart below summarizes each type of point of view and lists examples and appropriate uses.

POINT OF VIEW	PRONOUNS	EXAMPLE	APPROPRIATE USES
First-person point of view	I we me us my our	I didn't get married until I was 31 years old.	👍 Telling stories about personal experiences 👍 Sharing personal thoughts and feelings
Second-person point of view	you your	You should postpone marriage until you are in your 30's.	👍 Giving instructions 👍 Persuading the reader to change a belief or behavior
Third-person point of view	he/she his/her they/their	The median age of first marriage has risen to 28 for men and 26 for women, indicating that many Americans are waiting until they're older to get married.	👍 Writing academic or professional documents that focus on the subject, not the writer or reader

Exercise 2.14

On your own paper, write the point of view (first-person, second-person, or third-person) that is used in each of the following thesis statements.

1. Your selection of a pet should depend upon factors such as your activity level, your financial resources, and your available time.
2. Today's humans are taller than humans who lived a century ago for two main reasons.
3. I found out the hard way that honesty is always the best policy.
4. Hiking in the wilderness provides both physical and mental benefits.
5. My family's New Year's Eve celebration includes several fun traditions.

Exercise 2.15

On your own paper, rewrite the thesis statements in Exercise 2.14 to change them to a different point of view.

Exercise 2.16

On your own paper, identify the point of view in the essays on pages 212, 214, and 227.

Body

The **body** of your essay or longer composition consists of two or more paragraphs that provide information to support your main idea. Chapters 5, 6, 7 cover the qualities of effective body paragraphs, and Chapter 8 explains how to organize the body.

Closing Paragraph

The **closing paragraph**, or **conclusion**, of an essay or longer composition should provide readers with a sense of closure by tying your thoughts together in a satisfying way. This paragraph, which is often only three or four sentences long, should not simply repeat what you've already said, nor should it introduce a new idea. Techniques for writing effective closing paragraphs are discussed in detail in Chapter 10 of this book.

TIP

How long does an essay have to be? The answer is: *As long as it needs to be to prove or explain the idea in the thesis statement.* Essays always include at least four paragraphs: an opening paragraph, at least two body paragraphs, and a closing paragraph.

Exercise 2.17

Read the following essay and answer the questions that follow. Write your answers on your own paper.

Emotional Intelligence: Five Traits to Develop for Success in Life

[1] True or false: In a group of people, the smartest and most educated will always get the best jobs, make the most money, and live the most satisfying lives. According to American psychologist Daniel Goleman, the answer is false. Intelligence and education certainly do contribute to a person's success in life. However, an individual's level of "emotional intelligence" is an even better predictor of how well he or she will probably do personally and professionally. Goleman's concept of emotional intelligence includes five characteristics.

[2] The first characteristic is self-awareness. People who are self-aware understand their own strengths and weaknesses, and they regularly conduct honest assessments of themselves to identify areas that need improvement. Self-aware people can also name the specific feelings they experience. Rather than saying they are feeling "good" or "bad," they can describe their emotions more precisely as "loved," "proud," "angry," "confused," "frustrated," and so on. They know how each of these different emotions affects them. This ability to recognize and understand feelings is crucial to controlling them and to using them to make good choices and relate positively to others.

[3] A person with a high level of emotional intelligence is not only in touch with his or her emotions but is also able to manage them effectively, so the second characteristic of emotional intelligence is mood management. People who can manage their moods don't let emotions such as worry, fear, jealousy, and anger overwhelm them and cause them to make bad decisions. Instead, they refuse to let their feelings hijack their ability to think calmly and clearly. They acknowledge their feelings, but they maintain the ability to determine a rational, productive response to every situation.

[4] The third characteristic of emotional intelligence is motivation. Emotionally intelligent people know that it's rewarding to work hard to get something or understand something, and they're willing to put in the time and effort it takes to achieve a goal. They understand that this process often involves choosing to work instead of play. For example, emotionally intelligent students always choose to do their homework or study for a test instead of watch television or chat with friends on the phone. They are willing to defer their immediate satisfaction for the later satisfaction of accomplishing a worthy goal.

[5] The fourth characteristic of emotional intelligence is empathy, the ability to understand others' thoughts, feelings, needs, and desires. People who possess empathy can put themselves in other people's shoes and understand their perspective. This characteristic allows them to account for differing opinions, compromise, and find better solutions to problems. Being empathetic helps people build and maintain positive relationships and work with others more effectively to achieve goals.

[6] The fifth and final characteristic of emotional intelligence is good social skills. People who interact effectively with others know how to listen, share, cooperate, collaborate as part of a team, resolve conflict, and treat others with kindness and compassion. As a result, they are able to build and maintain good relationships that help them achieve results.

[7] Emotional intelligence can be the deciding factor in whether or not a person achieves what he or she is after. After setting any goal, an individual should perform an honest evaluation of his or her level of emotional intelligence and work on strengthening any weak areas that could hinder success.

1. Which paragraph is the opening paragraph?
2. Write the sentence that expresses the essay's thesis.
3. What point of view is used in this essay?
4. Which paragraphs form the essay's body?
5. Which paragraph is the closing paragraph?

Exercise 2.18

Select one of the essays on pages 212, 227, 239 of this book. Highlight the essay's different parts (opening paragraph, thesis statement, body, and closing paragraph) using different-colored highlighter markers. Or, identify the paragraph number(s) of each of these parts. Finally, identify the point of view used in the essay.

TIP

As you compose your first drafts of the essays you write for this class, consider highlighting the different parts using different colors so that you don't forget to include any of them.

Guidelines for Document Format

Any document that you write to send or give to someone—including class assignments, e-mail messages, letters, and written documents at your workplace—should always have the following characteristics:

Printed Documents

- Typed in black ink on white, straight-edged paper
- Neat, clean, and professional looking (free of smudges, wrinkles, tears, and messy corrections)
- Attractive and easy to read, with uniform margins and a balance of text and white space
- Adheres to conventions for capital and lowercase letters (don't use all capital letters)
- Free of grammar, punctuation, and spelling errors

Electronic Compositions

- Words in black font with a size and style that is easy to read
- Attractive and easy to read, with uniform margins and a balance of text and white space
- Adheres to conventions for capital and lowercase letters (don't use all capital letters)
- Free of grammar, punctuation, and spelling errors

Keep in mind that people will tend to see your written documents as an indicator of your overall quality of work. Therefore, you should always put time and effort into making your compositions reflect that you are a person who adheres to standards and produces high-quality work.

The following sections illustrate additional formatting guidelines you should follow when writing specific types of documents for your college courses, on the job, or for personal reasons.

Academic Assignments

Each instructor you have will usually provide you with specific instructions for the required components of written assignments you must produce. Figure 2.4 illustrates the first page of an assignment with some typical elements (the student's name, course information, date, and assignment information) requested by instructors.

FIGURE 2.4

Sherry Wilkinson   1

POL 101

Professor Huggins

12 September 2013

Chapter 3 Discussion Questions

Letters

Letters are a common form for academic, professional, and personal writing, so you will need to know their parts and their conventional format. Letters written for academic or professional purposes should be typed, and they should also follow standard business-letter format. Figure 2.5 illustrates one common type of format (block format), with the required parts labeled.

WRITER'S ADDRESS	123 Winner's Road New Employee Town, PA 12345
DATE	March 16, 2001
RECIPIENT'S NAME AND ADDRESS	Ernie English 1234 Writing Lab Lane Write City, IN 12345
GREETING	Dear Mr. English:
TEXT OF LETTER	The first paragraph of a typical business letter is used to state the main point of the letter. Begin with a friendly opening; then quickly transition into the purpose of your letter. Use a couple of sentences to explain the purpose, but do not go in to detail until the next paragraph. Beginning with the second paragraph, state the supporting details to justify your purpose. These may take the form of background information, statistics or first-hand accounts. A few short paragraphs within the body of the letter should be enough to support your reasoning. Finally, in the closing paragraph, briefly restate your purpose and why it is important. If the purpose of your letter is employment related, consider ending your letter with your contact information. However, if the purpose is informational, think about closing with gratitude for the reader's time.
CLOSING	Sincerely,
WRITER'S SIGNATURE	*Lucy Letter* Lucy Letter

FIGURE 2.5

TIP

For additional illustrations of different business-letter formats, type the words "Purdue Online Writing Lab" into an Internet search engine. Then, in the search box labeled "Search the OWL," type in "business letters."

E-mail Messages

An e-mail message is often a very informal form of communication when sent to friends or relatives. However, when e-mailing people such as college instructors or officials, supervisors, or co-workers, you will need to carefully consider your audience because they affect *what* you include in your message and *how* you say it. In Chapter 1, you learned that it's important to think about three qualities of your readers: their characteristics, their prior knowledge about the topic, and their needs. People such as college officials and workplace supervisors are busy professionals who probably deal with many people and receive many e-mails. Therefore, following a polite greeting, such as "Dear Professor Huggins" or "Dear Mr. Smith," your e-mail needs to identify right away who you are, what the situation is, and what you need. For example, if you are writing to an instructor who teaches hundreds of students every semester to ask a question, you need to state the specific class in which you are enrolled (for example: "I am a student in your POL 101 class, and I have a question about our research paper topic."). If you are writing to a manager in your workplace, you need to briefly remind the reader about the situation that is prompting you to write (for example: "At our staff meeting last week, you asked me to compile a list of our old computers that need to be replaced.").

In addition, you will need to adhere to all of the guidelines for creating professional-looking documents. E-mail messages should be treated as formal types of communication when sent to people who are not close friends or relatives. Follow this list of do's and don'ts when composing e-mail messages:

- DO carefully type the reader's e-mail address so that it's accurate.
- DO include the e-mail message's subject in the subject box.
- DON'T write e-mail messages using the writing style commonly used for text messages. Instead, write e-mail messages in complete sentences that are properly punctuated, and spell out words; don't abbreviate.
- DO create paragraphs just as you would if you were writing any other kind of document. Don't type your message as one long paragraph with no breaks.
- DON'T type your message in all capital letters.
- DO politely thank the reader, especially if you have made a request.
- DO sign your message with your first and last name.
- DO follow all of the rules for correct grammar, punctuation, and spelling.

Figure 2.6 provides a sample e-mail message from a student to an instructor.

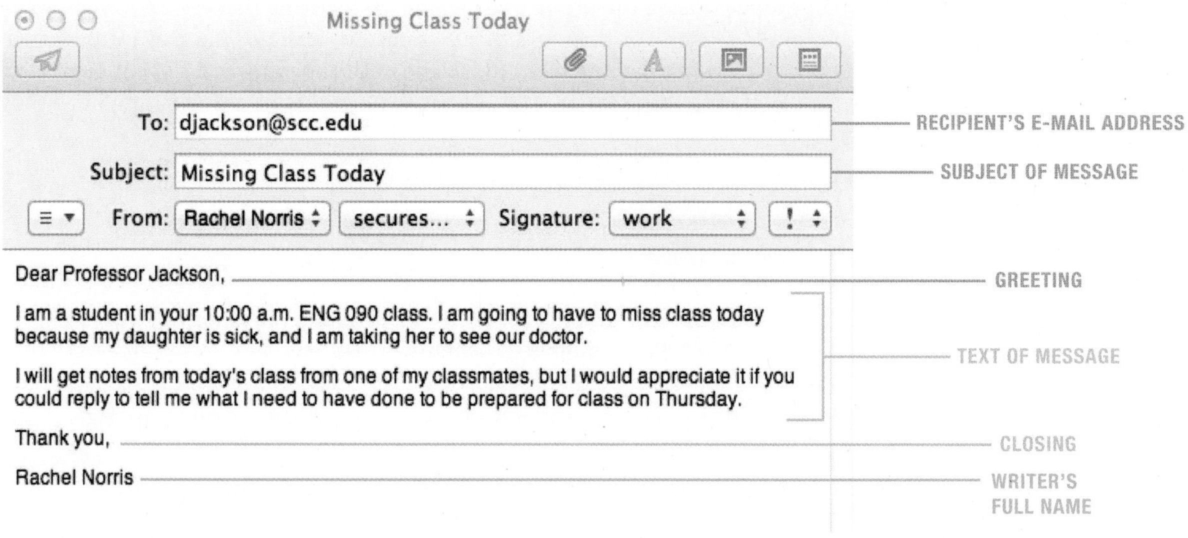

○ ○ ○   Missing Class Today

To: djackson@scc.edu ————————————————— RECIPIENT'S E-MAIL ADDRESS

Subject: Missing Class Today ————————————————— SUBJECT OF MESSAGE

≡ ▼   From: Rachel Norris ⇕   secures... ⇕   Signature: work ⇕   ! ⇕

Dear Professor Jackson, ——————————————————————————— GREETING

I am a student in your 10:00 a.m. ENG 090 class. I am going to have to miss class today
because my daughter is sick, and I am taking her to see our doctor.

I will get notes from today's class from one of my classmates, but I would appreciate it if you ——— TEXT OF MESSAGE
could reply to tell me what I need to have done to be prepared for class on Thursday.

Thank you, ———————————————————————————————————— CLOSING

Rachel Norris ——————————————————————————————————— WRITER'S
                                                                                        FULL NAME

FIGURE 2.6

Exercise 2.19

**Read the following e-mail from a student to a college's Director of Financial
Aid. On your own paper, list the improvements you would recommend to
this writer.**

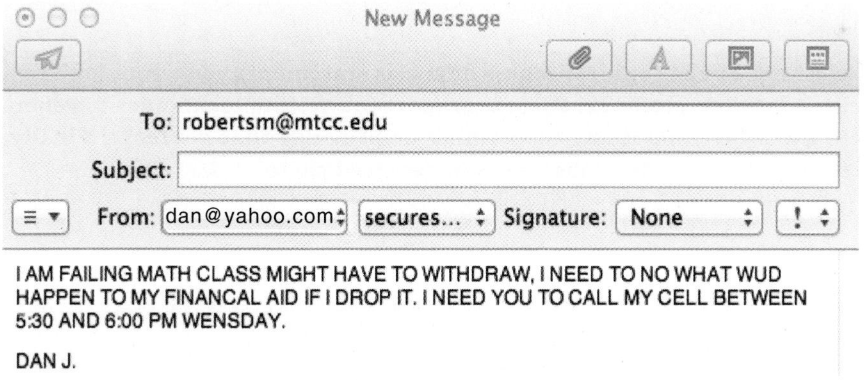

○ ○ ○   New Message

To: robertsm@mtcc.edu

Subject:

≡ ▼   From: dan@yahoo.com ⇕   secures... ⇕   Signature: None ⇕   ! ⇕

I AM FAILING MATH CLASS MIGHT HAVE TO WITHDRAW, I NEED TO NO WHAT WUD
HAPPEN TO MY FINANCIAL AID IF I DROP IT. I NEED YOU TO CALL MY CELL BETWEEN
5:30 AND 6:00 PM WENSDAY.

DAN J.

Prewriting for Conventional
Form and Features

One of the best ways to ensure that you include all of the required features and
parts of your composition is to remind yourself by adding labels to the outline

TIP

Chapter 8 discusses outlines in more detail.

you generate during the prewriting step of your writing process. When you write your outline, list all of the parts that you need to include. You may even want to jot down a few notes about what to include in the opening and closing. Here is an example of an outline for an essay about the benefits of participating in a study group:

OPENING PARAGRAPH:	Explain what a study group is.
THESIS STATEMENT:	Participation in a study group can bring students a number of benefits.
BODY:	Benefit #1: Deeper, richer, longer-lasting learning experiences Benefit #2: Improved performance on tests, better grades Benefit #3: Meet new people, form new friendships
CLOSING PARAGRAPH:	Recommend trying it

As you write, follow this outline to make sure that you don't leave out any of the important elements.

Exercise 2.20

Select one of the topic sentences or thesis statements you wrote for Exercise 2.3 or Exercise 2.12. Use one or more prewriting techniques to generate ideas for supporting (explaining or proving) that sentence. Finally, create an outline that labels all four required parts.

Writing for Conventional Form and Features

During the writing step of the process, you can make sure that you're including all required parts of your composition by color coding them. As you write or type, use one color ink or font for the opening, switch to another color ink or font for the main idea statement, and so on. Doing so will help you to remember to include all necessary features. Later, when you generate your final draft of the composition, you can change the entire composition to black ink.

If you are composing a specific type of document, such as a letter, you might want to use a template when you create your draft. A **template** is a model that shows the page layout and parts of a particular document. It will show you the specific features you need to include and tell you where to place each one. You can find specific templates by typing in the one you need (for example, "business letter template") in an Internet search engine.

TIP

For longer assignments, divide the writing task into stages that you complete over several days instead of trying to complete the whole project all at once. Set deadlines for each step of the process—prewriting, writing, and rewriting—with breaks built in between each one. Use a calendar to record the date the final product is due. A few days prior to that, schedule a date to complete the rough draft. A few days prior to that date, set a deadline for creating an organization plan. Spread the entire procedure over a longer period of time, and achieve each of your smaller goals according to schedule.

Exercise 2.21

Using different-colored highlighter markers, highlight the four different parts of a paragraph or essay you are working on now. Are any of the required parts missing? If so, add them.

Rewriting for Conventional Form and Features

After you have composed a draft, you can verify that you've included all of the necessary parts and features by using a checklist like the following as a guide.

CHECKLIST FOR CONVENTIONAL FORM AND FEATURES

Use this checklist during the rewriting step of the process to make sure that you are including all conventional components of your paragraphs, essays, and other compositions.

☐ The composition begins by introducing the subject.

☐ The composition's main idea is clearly stated in a topic sentence (for paragraphs) or thesis statement (for essays and longer compositions).

☐ The topic sentence (paragraphs) or thesis statement (essays) indicates the composition's point of view.

☐ Each topic sentence includes the paragraph's topic and the writer's point about that topic.

☐ The body of the paragraph or essay offers evidence or explanations to support the composition's main idea.

☐ The essay ends with a satisfying closing.

☐ The layout of the document follows the guidelines for this type of document.

Exercise 2.22

A. Use the checklist on page 33 to evaluate a paragraph or essay you have recently written. If you revised this composition, what would you change to ensure that it adheres to conventional form and includes conventional features?

B. Use the checklist to evaluate a classmate's paragraph or essay. What changes would you recommend?

SUGGESTED WRITING ACTIVITIES

Complete all of the steps of the writing process as you write one or more of the following compositions. As you plan, write, and revise, check your composition for conventional form and features.

ACADEMIC WRITING

1. Explain the essential qualities of effective parents or teachers.
2. List and explain the factors that should affect a student's selection of a major or career goal.
3. Find an editorial that you disagree with. Write a letter of rebuttal; in other words, argue *against* the editorial writer's opinions.

PROFESSIONAL WRITING

4. Argue to your supervisor that you deserve a raise in pay.
5. Write an account of an accident or dispute that occurred in your workplace.
6. Write to your supervisor to nominate one of your co-workers for an "Employee of the Month" award.

PERSONAL WRITING

7. Write an e-mail to a distant friend or relative to persuade him or her to visit you.
8. Write a letter to your local school board to argue against a recent proposal or decision.
9. Write a letter to a scholarship committee to explain why you deserve to receive the scholarship.

PART II

Essential Characteristics of Effective Sentences

CHAPTER 3

Essential #3: Four Rules for Clear Sentences

In 2011, the National Association of Colleges and Employers surveyed companies and asked, "What do employers want in new hires?" The top five skills and personal characteristics identified as desirable in candidates included a strong work ethic, teamwork skills, analytical skills, and initiative. Topping that list, however, was verbal communication skills; employers said that the ability to communicate clearly and concisely is *the* most important skill in the workplace.[1]

In another nationwide survey conducted by NFI Research, 85 percent of the senior executives and managers in large companies said that the writing they receive from their employees is too long. One survey participant wrote, "Being clear and concise is probably the most important key to effective business writing. I've seen brilliant ideas from brilliant coworkers go unnoticed for no other reason than they were buried in way too much text."[2]

Clear and concise writing begins with your sentences. They must be written so that they do not have to be read twice. They should not get in your reader's way as he or she attempts to understand the ideas on the screen or the page. To construct sentences that accurately convey your meaning and are easy to understand, you will need to follow the four simple rules explained in this chapter:

Rule #1: Use strong verbs.

Rule #2: Avoid wordiness.

Rule #3: Vary sentence types and lengths.

Rule #4: Adhere to rules for grammar, punctuation, and spelling.

Prewriting for Clear Sentences

In the Introduction to this book, you learned that the thoughts you have never expressed in either conversation or writing tend to be fuzzy and incomplete. When we find the language to express what we're thinking, the words we choose actually help us understand more clearly what we know or believe.

---

[1] Huhman, Heather. "5 Job Skills in Demand in 2011." Careerealism.com, 18 Feb. 2011. Web. 18 Feb. 2012.
[2] Martin, Chuck. "The Key to Better Communication: Shorter Memos." CIO.com, 28 Jan. 2008. Web. 18 Feb. 2012.

You can make this process a little easier on yourself by spending an adequate amount of time generating as many ideas and details as possible during the prewriting stage. The more you have thought about and jotted down ideas, the more raw material you'll have when it's time to compose the sentences and paragraphs of your document. Writing that is confusing, rambling, or monotonous is often a direct result of insufficient thinking at the beginning of the writing process. Therefore, it's a good idea to get in the habit of using at least one (or, better yet, a combination) of the seven strategies for generating ideas that were explained in the Introduction of this book.

Writing Clear Sentences

Writers often get frustrated during the composition process because they think that sentences just flow naturally from the pens and computer keyboards of everyone else except theirs. They don't. Words and sentences often come out the first time messy and inaccurate. Quite often, the wording that first comes to mind is not the one that is exactly right. Even experienced writers must try out many different wordings until they find the ones that best convey their meaning. The rules covered in this chapter will give you some ways to avoid dull, excess words and boring or flabby sentence constructions. By practicing these rules until they are second nature, you should be able to reduce the amount of revision and editing you'll have to do later.

However, the most important thing when composing is to complete a draft. During the rewriting stage, which will be discussed later in this chapter, you can go back to evaluate your sentences again according to these rules and make the necessary corrections.

Rule #1: Use Strong Verbs

When you write, pay special attention to the verbs in your sentences. These are the words that convey actions, so they should be precise and lively. The first way to

© Pixsooz/Shutterstock.com

All writers—even professional writers—have to try out many different wordings until they find the ones that are exactly right.

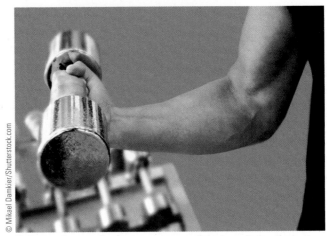

Verbs are the muscle of your sentences. Select precise, action-oriented verbs for clear, interesting sentences.

ensure interesting, action-oriented verbs is to avoid two common sentence patterns—*There is* sentences and *It is* sentences—that will always force you to settle for dull, weak verbs.

Avoid *There Is* Sentences

Any time you begin to write a sentence that starts with *There is, There are, There was,* or *There were,* stop! These sentences allow the writer to rely heavily on a weak *to be* verb, often burying the strongest verb choice somewhere else in the sentence. Notice how the following revised sentences are more interesting because they begin with a subject that performs an action:

WEAK VERB:	There was a cold wind blowing from the North. [The strongest verb is hiding as an adjective, *blowing*.]
BETTER:	A cold wind blew from the North.

WEAK VERB:	There will be new and better restaurants opening in our town. [The best verb is hiding as an adjective, *opening*.]
BETTER:	New and better restaurants will open in our town.

In addition to relying on a weak *to be* verb, *there is* phrases also tend to weigh the sentence down with unnecessary words. We can often dramatically improve a sentence by deleting *there is* and rewriting to begin the sentence with the subject that is performing the action. In the following examples from student writing, the *there is* phrases are unnecessary. Note how each revision substitutes a more action-oriented verb.

WORDY:	There is no doubt that drugs are a main factor in the crime rate. [14 words]
BETTER:	Undoubtedly, drugs contribute to the crime rate. [7 words]

WORDY:	Today, there are many misfortunes that result in one-parent families. [10 words]

BETTER: Today, many misfortunes create one-parent families. [6 words]

WORDY: There are others like me who have rescued abused animals and found it very rewarding. [15 words]

BETTER: Others like me have discovered rewards in rescuing abused animals. [10 words]

WORDY: There are a river, pond, and lake nearby that will provide campers with many opportunities for canoeing and fishing. [19 words]

BETTER: Campers can canoe and fish on a nearby river, pond, and lake. [12 words]

Avoid *It Is* Sentences

Sentences that begin with *It is* often suffer from the same problems—dull verbs and wordiness—that plague *there is* sentences.

WORDY: It is a constant battle between people who support gun control and people who oppose it. [16 words]

BETTER: Advocates for gun control endlessly battle those who oppose it. [10 words]

WORDY: It's up to the parents of a child to monitor the child's homework. [13 words]

BETTER: A child's parents should monitor that child's homework. [8 words]

WORDY: It is good for your vehicle's fuel efficiency when you limit your speed. [13 words]

BETTER: Limiting your speed improves your vehicle's fuel efficiency. [8 words]

> *TIP*
>
> For more practice with writing sentences that contain strong verbs, see pages 71–74 of Chapter 4.

Exercise 3.1

On your own paper, rewrite each of the following sentences to eliminate *There is* or *It is*.

1. It is buying products made in America that helps create and maintain U.S. jobs.
2. There are two different solutions to our problem.
3. There is usually a gradual onset of high blood pressure.
4. It was helpful information for all of us.
5. There is a lot of variation in your time sheet hours from week to week.
6. It was lack of organization that contributed to my low grade in my Art Appreciation class.
7. There are three local businesses sponsoring this year's fundraiser.

Avoid Passive-Voice Sentences

Sentences can be written in active voice or passive voice. In **active voice**, the subject of the sentence is the performer of the action, and the thing that receives the action is the object:

subject verb object
Phil mowed the **lawn**.

The active voice is clear and direct. The **passive voice**, on the other hand, reorganizes the sentence so that the subject of the sentence is the thing that is *receiving* the action:

subject verb
The **lawn was mowed** by Phil.

In a passive-voice sentence, what should be the object (the thing being acted on) becomes the subject—and therefore the focus—of the sentence.

PASSIVE:	Your investment **will be managed** by financial experts.
ACTIVE:	Financial experts will manage your investment.
PASSIVE:	A memo **is written by** an employee to other employees within the organization, whereas a letter **is written by** an employee to others outside the organization.
ACTIVE:	An employee writes a memo to other employees within the organization and a letter to others outside the organization.
PASSIVE:	Each year, funds **are requested** for these programs, but these requests **are turned** down by the county commissioners.
ACTIVE:	Each year, we request funds for these programs, but the county commissioners turn down those requests.

Most of the time, passive-voice sentences are less effective than active-voice sentences, and they should be avoided for the following reasons:

- Passive voice does not emphasize the performer of the action. Readers usually have to wait until the end of the sentence to find out who the performer is.
- Passive voice allows the writer to omit the performer altogether, leaving the reader with unanswered questions.

> Jim Clark **was given** [By whom?] a watch as token of gratitude for his many years of faithful service.

> The military's promises about jobs or training **are written** [By whom?] in a contract so that the recruit **can be assured** [By whom?] that the promise **will be kept** [By whom?].

- Passive-voice sentences are usually wordier than active-voice sentences. Using the indirect, passive construction often requires the writer to pile on unnecessary words to get the sentence to make sense. The next section of this chapter will further discuss this problem.

TIP

For more practice with active-voice and passive-voice sentences, see pages 46–47 of this chapter.

Contrary to popular belief, passive voice does not make writing sound more authoritative, more scholarly, or more professional; instead, overuse of the passive voice results in writing that is plodding or pretentious. When you occasionally write in the passive voice, do so intentionally to achieve a specific purpose. Do not use this sentence pattern when the active voice would produce a clearer, more interesting sentence.

TIP

Use passive voice for one of the following three situations: (1) when you don't know the subject who performed the action (*example:* The computer *was damaged* sometime between 8:00 p.m. and 6:00 a.m.), (2) when you need to hide the subject who performed the action for diplomatic reasons (*example:* Another candidate *has been selected* for the position), and (3) when the receiver of the action actually *is* more important than the performer of the action (example: Mr. Lee was presented the award by Senator Byrd).

Exercise 3.2

On your own paper, rewrite the following passive-voice sentences to change them to active-voice sentences.

1. Insomnia can be caused by stress.
2. A good salary, paid vacations, medical insurance, and retirement benefits are provided to our employees.
3. To help detect breast cancer, yearly mammograms are recommended for women over age 50.
4. Video cameras could be used by the security guards to monitor the entire building.
5. Release of information regarding a patient's condition is governed by hospital policy.
6. Last year, over 60,000 people were served by United Way agencies.
7. The final budget draft is presented by the president to the board of directors.

Select Verbs with the Correct Meaning

When you're experimenting with strong verbs in your sentences, make sure that you choose verbs with the correct meaning. The subjects in your sentences should actually be able to perform the actions conveyed by the verbs. In the following examples, all drawn from student writing, note the mismatch between the subject (in blue) and the verb (in green), which results in a confusing or meaningless sentence:

Reckless drivers make any road hazardous, but a heavily traveled **road** already **obtains** that potential. [How can a road obtain a potential? This sentence doesn't make any sense.]

One negative **effect** of required courses stems from the view that students must become well-rounded thinkers. [This sentence includes a number of imprecise word choices. How can an effect stem from a view?]

Though many popular television programs have included profanity for many years, the **degree** of this profanity is becoming more tasteless. [How can a degree become tasteless?]

Succeeding in math contains several key factors. [How can succeeding contain factors?]

The **vote** was lost by 27 votes. [The vote was lost by votes?]

▊ Exercise 3.3

On your own paper, write a more accurate verb to replace each of the bold-faced verbs in the following sentences.

1. Joe blundered into the room, gasping for air and clutching his chest.
2. Messages gushed into his e-mail inbox.
3. By eating low-calorie foods and walking every day, Rosita surrendered 50 pounds.
4. A student who hands in a paper found on the Internet has executed an act of plagiarism.
5. After Victoria posted her vacation plans on Facebook, thieves read the information and gutted her house while she was away.
6. The catcher launched the ball to the second baseman, who tagged the runner as he lurched headfirst for the base.
7. The elderly couple perched on the park bench and inspected the ducks swimming in the pond.

Rule #2: Avoid Wordiness

Blaise Pascal, a 17th-century French scientist and philosopher, once penned to a friend, "I have made this letter longer than usual, only because I have not had the time to make it shorter." His statement reminds us of an interesting paradox about writing: It actually takes *more* time and effort to write concisely, with fewer words. When we're trying to find the words to communicate our thoughts, we usually use too many words in our first attempt. That's fine, of course, when we're engaged in the difficult process of finding language for thoughts that we've never before expressed. We should go ahead and write down the sentences as we think of them so that we can record our ideas quickly. However, clear, effective writing always expresses an idea in as few words as possible. We never want to make our reader wade through a lot of unnecessary words to get to our meaning. Therefore, we have to be willing to reexamine our first version and experiment with different wordings to get rid of any debris that is clogging up our sentences.

iStockphoto.com/uros ravbar

Reading wordy documents is like trying to wade through thick mud.

| **WORDY:** | Skepticism is an attitude that is very healthy for a student to possess. [13 words] |
| **BETTER:** | Skepticism is a healthy attitude for students. [7 words] |

| **WORDY:** | The teacher of a stop-smoking course I took (and failed) said he was told by people who were once addicted to cocaine that quitting smoking was even more difficult than giving up their drug habits. [35 words] |
| **BETTER:** | Former cocaine addicts told my stop-smoking course teacher that quitting smoking was more difficult than giving up cocaine. [18 words: This revision changes passive to active voice and changes some wording; for example, *people who were once addicted to cocaine* becomes *former cocaine addicts.*] |

| **WORDY:** | One difference I found between the two teachers was their opinion about the students they were teaching. [17 words] |
| **BETTER:** | The two teachers differed in their opinions about their students. [10 words] |

| **WORDY:** | As for hunters, wolves have been subject to a tremendous amount of animosity from them. [15 words] |
| **BETTER:** | Hunters hate wolves. [3 words] |

As you examine your writing to look for places where you can trim unnecessary words, watch for the common wordy expressions in the chart on page 46.

SOME COMMON WORDY EXPRESSIONS	
WORDY EXPRESSION	**ONE-WORD SUBSTITUTION**
due to the fact that	because
at this point in time	now
in the event that	if
until such time as	until
despite the fact that	although
at all times	always
in view of the fact that	since
in the near future	soon
in most cases	usually
a large number of	many

As you compose your first draft, expect to have to reevaluate every sentence for possible wordiness. Many of them will have to be rearranged or pruned to better convey your ideas.

> ## TIP
>
> "The most valuable of all talents is that of never using two words when one will do."
>
> —*Thomas Jefferson, author of the Declaration of Independence*

Avoid Redundant Words

As you search for wordiness in your writing, look for words and phrases that simply repeat information already stated. These words and phrases are *redundant* and can be eliminated. The bold parts of the following sentences are redundant:

> After implementing the procedure and putting it to use, our firm saved $100,000 per year.
>
> Volunteers who are donating their time and energy to our cause will be asking for your pledge soon.
>
> Because I am overworked and have more projects than I have time to do them, I am going to need additional help and assistance.

If you expressed a thought clearly the first time, you should not need to repeat it.

Avoid Passive Voice

In an earlier section of this chapter, you learned that passive-voice sentences tend to be longer and wordier than they need to be. Writing in active voice instead will help to keep your sentences free of unnecessary words.

| **WORDY:** | These walls **will have to be removed** by the contractor in order to make improvements to the actual design. [19 words] |
| **BETTER:** | The contractor will have to remove these walls to improve the design. [12 words] |

| **WORDY:** | A survey **was distributed by** the Council to everyone in June, and the answers it received **were used** to determine the agenda for the next meeting. [26 words] |
| **BETTER:** | The Council distributed a survey to everyone in June and used the results to determine the next meeting's agenda. [19 words] |

| **WORDY:** | There are two main points that **are argued** by people who support gun control and want to keep many from having guns. [22 words: This sentence has three problems. In addition to being passive, it begins with *There are,* and it includes redundant wording.] |
| **BETTER:** | Gun control advocates argue two main points. [7 words] |

Avoid Hedging and Disclaimers

Two types of phrases add unnecessary words to sentences. The first group of phrases can be described as **hedging**, or suggesting that the statements being made *might* be true, but they are presented as merely the writer's beliefs or opinions, and he or she is being too cautious to come right out and state them assertively as truth. Some common hedging phrases include:

It seems to me that

It's possible that

I think that

I believe that

I feel that

In my opinion

These phrases not only call into question your confidence in what you are saying, but they also add useless words. Because you are writing the statement, you obviously believe it, think it, or feel it; therefore, it's unnecessary to say so.

Note how the revisions of the following examples result in statements that are more confident and less wordy:

| **HEDGING:** | **I really feel that** our training program is one of the best in the industry. |
| **BETTER:** | Our training program is one of the best in the industry. |

| **HEDGING:** | **I think that** careful attention to financial details will allow us to meet our objectives. |
| **BETTER:** | Careful attention to financial details will allow us to meet our objectives. |

HEDGING:	In my opinion, the legal drinking age should be lowered from 21 to 18.
BETTER:	The legal drinking age should be lowered from 21 to 18.

Disclaimers are another type of wordy phrase that will also reduce the reader's confidence in you as a trustworthy source of information about the topic. *To disclaim* means "to disown," which involves rejecting responsibility for a statement. These phrases are not only wordy, but they also make you seem uncertain about what you are saying; therefore, they encourage your readers to reject your ideas. Common disclaimers include phrases such as:

I don't really know that much about this, but . . .

I'm not really sure, but . . .

I'm no expert, but . . .

I don't have a degree in this, but . . .

I haven't done enough research on this yet, but . . .

I'm not sure if this is accurate, but . . .

This may or may not be true, but . . .

I could be wrong, but. . .

Including such phrases weighs down the sentence with extra words and also weakens your credibility for your readers, who will probably dismiss your statements as unreliable. If you really don't know what you need to know to write about a topic, then don't write about it until you gather more information. On the other hand, if you do understand the topic and can offer appropriate evidence to support your ideas, state those ideas confidently, without hedging phrases and disclaimers.

█ Exercise 3.4

On your own paper, rewrite each of the following sentences to eliminate hedging phrases and disclaimers.

1. In my opinion, our public school teachers deserve a raise.
2. I really believe that I could have made a B in algebra if I had studied more.
3. I could be wrong, but I think that using a tanning bed increases your risk of skin cancer.
4. You may be having an allergic reaction, but I'm not an expert, so I'm not 100 percent sure.
5. If we want to finish this project on time, it seems to me that we'll have to find a way to compromise.
6. Some people oppose same-sex unions, but I feel that same-sex couples should have the right to marry.
7. It's possible that the defendant is not guilty.

Rule #3: Vary Sentence Types and Lengths

Writing that is interesting to read includes sentences of different lengths and types. This combination provides variety and rhythm that readers find pleasing and therefore more enjoyable to read. To understand this concept, think about a popular song you like to hear or sing. That song undoubtedly includes a series of verses (sections with identical music but different lyrics) with a chorus (a repeated section that follows each verse). Songs can also include other elements, such as an introduction, a bridge, an instrumental solo, and a coda, which add variety. All of these parts include melodies, which are sequences of notes that make up musical phrases. This combination of repetition and variation is pleasing to our ears.

Likewise, the paragraphs and essays you write have different parts, which you learned about in Chapter 2 of this book. Each of those parts includes sentences that can be compared to the musical phrases in songs. Those phrases include different notes of different lengths to create different sounds. The sentences you write, too, need to be of different types and lengths to give your writing a pleasing and varied rhythm.

Write Sentences of Different Types (Simple, Compound, Complex)

Writers can use three basic patterns to construct their sentences. **Simple sentences** are sentences that contain just one independent clause (a group of words with a subject-verb relationship that can stand alone as a complete sentence).

subject   verb
College causes a great deal of new stress for students.

© Ghenadie/Shutterstock.com

Just as combinations of different notes make a musical composition interesting and pleasing to our ears, different lengths and types of sentences make written compositions more pleasing to read.

3 subjects   one verb
Deadlines, the pressure to succeed, and financial strains can be stressful.

subject   verb #1   verb #2
Stress damages health and **reduces** quality of life.

Compound sentences, the second type, contain two or more independent clauses. They include two different sets of subject-verb relationships.

subject/verb #1   subject/verb #2
Severe, prolonged **stress can be** harmful, **so students must use** some coping strategies.

subject/verb #1   subject/verb #2
You should not **commit** to more than you can handle, **and you should keep** up with all of your academic work.

subject/verb #1
Warning signs can signal out-of-control stress; for example,

subject/verb #2
stomach problems, lack of sleep, and **frequent headaches are** often symptoms.

Compound sentences are created by joining two independent clauses with a conjunction (*for, and, nor, but, or, yet, so*). You can use the acronym FANBOYS to remember these seven words. In the first two example sentences above, the conjunctions are green. Compound sentences can also be created by joining two independent clauses with a conjunctive adverb. In the third example sentence above, the conjunctive adverb is green. Here is a list of some common conjunctive adverbs organized by the type of relationship they convey:

SOME COMMON CONJUNCTIVE ADVERBS	
Addition	also
	in addition
	furthermore
	moreover
Cause and effect	therefore
	because
	as a result
	consequently
	thus
Contrast	however
	on the other hand
	instead
	nevertheless

Comparison	likewise
	similarly
Example	for example
	for instance
Time	then
	now
	meanwhile
	next
Choice	otherwise

The third type of sentence is the **complex sentence**, which contains one independent clause and one or more dependent clauses (clauses that provide more information about an independent clause and cannot stand alone as complete sentences).

independent clause   dependent clause
Deal with a stressful situation whenever it arises.

dependent clause   independent clause
If you can't change a stressful situation, you can change your reaction to that situation.

dependent clause   independent clause
A person who manages stress effectively is more likely to reach his or her goals.

Complex sentences are created with subordinating conjunctions and relative pronouns. In the first two example sentences above, the words *whenever* and *if* are subordinating conjunctions. In the third example, the relative pronoun *who* begins the dependent clause. Here are lists of common subordinating conjunctions and relative pronouns:

COMMON SUBORDINATING CONJUNCTIONS

after	as though	even though	since
although	because	if	so that
as	before	once	than
as if	even if	rather than	though
unless	until	when	whenever
where	whereas	wherever	while

COMMON RELATIVE PRONOUNS

who/whom	that
whoever/whomever	which
whose	

TIP

Pages 258–260 of Appendix 2: Eleven Common Errors in English explain and provide practice with common relative pronoun errors.

Mature, sophisticated writing includes a mixture of all three of these types of sentences. As you read the following example, notice the effect that lack of sentence variety has:

> Most newborn babies need a full bath only three or four times a week. Every day, wash your baby's face, chin, neck, and bottom. Wash your baby's head and face first while the water and washcloth are cleanest. You do not need to use soap on the baby's face. Mild soap and water can be used on areas that need frequent washing, like the baby's bottom. Rinse your baby well with the washcloth. When you are through bathing your baby, wrap her in a towel and pat dry. Rubbing irritates your baby's skin and may cause peeling.

Buie, Mary, et al. *Your Baby's First Year*. Raleigh, NC: Department of Environment, Health, and Natural Resources, 1996. Print.

This paragraph consists of eight sentences, five of which are simple. This lack of variety creates a boring, monotonous style. The style becomes more interesting, however, and the information becomes clearer, when the writer combines and reorganizes several of the sentences:

> Although you should wash your baby's face, chin, neck, and bottom every day, most newborn babies need a full bath only three or four times a week. Wash your baby's head and face first while the water and washcloth are cleanest. Don't use soap on the baby's face, but do use mild soap and water on areas that need frequent washing, like the baby's bottom. When you are through bathing your baby, wrap her in a towel and pat her dry because rubbing irritates your baby's skin and may cause peeling.

This revision contains three complex sentences and one compound sentence.

If your writing contains a lot of simple sentences, experiment with different ways to combine some of them into compound and complex sentences for increased variety. Use coordinating conjunctions or conjunctive adverbs to join two sentences and create one compound sentence. Use subordinating conjunctions or relative pronouns to combine two sentences and create one complex sentence.

TIP

To learn how to use commas to properly punctuate compound and complex sentences, see pages 270–271 of Appendix 2: Eleven Common Errors in English.

Exercise 3.5

On your own paper, identify each of the sentences in the following paragraph as simple, compound, or complex.

[1] Having a criminal record makes an already stressful job search even more difficult. [2] Most job applications include a question about prior convictions, and companies often use that information to reject applicants. [3] If an applicant has been convicted of a crime, he or she might be tempted to omit that information on job applications. [4] Some states do prevent employers from asking about certain offenses, so job seekers should research the specific requirements. [5] When they are required to report a criminal past, they should always resist the temptation to lie. [6] The majority of companies now conduct some kind of background check for potential employees. [7] They will uncover any lies and fire the dishonest employee. [8] An applicant with a criminal record should always provide information about the offense on the job application, but he or she should also include an explanation of the circumstances.

Handwritten notes:
1. Simple
2. Compound
3. Complex
4. Compound
5. Complex
6. Simple
7. Simple
8. Compound

Exercise 3.6

Write three simple sentences, three compound sentences, and three complex sentences.

Exercise 3.7

Identify each of the sentences in a paragraph you have written recently as simple, compound, or complex.

Avoid a Lot of Short Sentences

If your writing contains a lot of short sentences, one after another, your reader will judge your composition to be monotonous and unsophisticated. Consider the following example from a letter of application:

> I would like to apply for a job at ABC Day Care. I think I am very qualified. I found out about your opening in the newspaper.
> I am majoring in education at Clark Community College. I am on the Dean's List. I like working with children. I worked at another day care center for a year. I helped with infants and toddlers.
> I would like to meet with you. My resume is enclosed. Perhaps we could schedule an interview. I look forward to talking to you.

Adapted from *Writing for the Real World*
by Ann Marie Radaskiewicz.

Although an adult wrote this letter, it sounds as though a child composed it. The short, choppy sentences are childlike and dull. Notice how much more mature the letter sounds when it is rewritten to combine some of the short sentences:

> I would like to apply for a job at ABC Day Care. I read about the opening in the newspaper, and I am very qualified for this position.
>
> I am majoring in education at Clark Community College, where I am on the Dean's List. I like working with children; I worked with infants and toddlers at another day care center for a year.
>
> I would like to meet with you for an interview after you have reviewed my enclosed résumé. I look forward to talking to you.

If your writing contains a lot of short sentences, experiment with ways to combine some of them to vary their lengths.

Avoid a Lot of Long Sentences

At the other extreme is the overuse of long sentences. Whereas short sentences are monotonous and immature, too many long sentences can be rambling, confusing, or pretentious. Overly long sentences try to pack too much information into one sentence, and readers can become frustrated with writing that asks them to absorb too much at one time.

The following sentence from a student's summary of a magazine article about gymnast Kerri Strug forces the reader to take in too much information:

> She had to do one more vault for her team even though she was in pain because she thought the United States would lose if she didn't do the vault, but she did do it and did very well, earning 9.712, but should found out later that the United States would have won even if she hadn't done the vault.

Although this sentence is long, it sounds as unsophisticated as a series of short sentences because the writer is not in control of the information.

Another example is from a student's descriptive essay:

> His tie was green and covered with colorful cartoon characters and spread about four inches wide at the bottom and was clipped about halfway down between the knot and the end, which hung about two inches below his western style belt, and he claimed that he made the tie clip himself from a hood ornament and no one knew cars like he did.

This writer tried to pack too much information into one overly long compound sentence. Readers need a break long before they get one.

TIP

Overly long sentences are often in danger of becoming run-on sentences or comma splices. These two major sentence errors are explained on pages 247–250 of Appendix 2: Eleven Common Errors in English.

Exercise 3.8

On your own paper, rewrite passage A to combine some of the short sentences. Rewrite passage B to break up overly long sentences into shorter ones.

A.   Successful people achieve the goals they set for themselves. These people have a habit. They all use their time wisely. They do not waste time. They know that time is limited and fast-moving. They choose to devote their hours to completing tasks. These tasks will move them closer to where they want to be. Successful people also control their time. They stay focused and refuse to allow interruptions and digressions. Others cannot easily pull them away from a task.

B.   An effective computerized slide show, such as a PowerPoint presentation, should enhance the audience's interest, understanding, and memory, so you should make it easy to read by using contrasting colors and large font size with upper- and lowercase letters, not all capital letters, but without too much text because then the audience is reading the slides rather than listening to what you're saying, so the slides should list just key terms to complement the verbal message you're delivering, not replace it. Also, the slides should be visually pleasing, not cluttered with too much clip art, animations, photos, graphs, or charts, and spacing and indenting should be used to show the relationships between the key terms and short phrases on each of the slides because that will reinforce the audience's understanding of the information you're presenting.

TIP

The type of sentences you write, along with the words you choose, creates your writing *style*. Style is the "flavor" of your writing, which might be described as conversational, academic, or journalistic, to name just a few of the many different styles. No matter what style you adopt or develop, strive to write sentences that are clear and interesting.

Rewriting and Editing for Clear Sentences

After you write a draft of a paragraph or essay, you should reevaluate all of the sentences you've written to make sure that they adhere to the first three rules for clear sentences explained in this chapter. In addition, you will need to make your document adhere to the fourth rule for clear sentences by carefully proofreading and editing it. In the Introduction to this book, you learned that **proofreading** involves carefully examining every sentence of your revised draft to find errors in grammar, punctuation, capitalization, spelling, and word choice. Correcting these errors is called **editing**.

Rule #4: Adhere to Rules for Grammar, Spelling, and Punctuation

Readers expect the writing they encounter in academic settings, the workplace, and the media to use Standard English. Unlike conversational English, Standard English demands that we follow a strict set of rules for grammar, punctuation, and spelling. The readers of your compositions will expect you to follow all of these rules, and, if your writing contains grammatical or spelling errors, they are likely to make one or more of the following conclusions about you:

1. You did not care enough about your document to make it conform to the rules for Standard English.
2. You were too lazy to take the time to make your composition correct.
3. You do not know Standard English, so you must be unintelligent or uneducated.

All are harsh, perhaps unfair, pronouncements about you and your work. Nonetheless, readers will indeed make these judgments if errors plague your writing. Even if your thoughts are brilliantly creative, your readers may fail to understand them or give them the attention they deserve if you do not express them using Standard English.

Use Proper Grammar and Punctuation

The rules for Standard English are logical and necessary. Adhering to these rules will prevent misunderstandings between you and your readers. When just one comma can change the whole meaning of a sentence, for example, it's important to know the rules for commas so that your readers don't misinterpret.

Following the rules will also help you write sentences that don't get in readers' way as they try to comprehend your ideas. If they are constantly being tripped up and slowed down by errors that require them to stop, figure out the problem, and mentally correct it, they will be distracted from the thoughts you are trying to express.

> ### TIP
> For practice eliminating common grammatical errors from your writing, see Appendix 2 of this book, Eleven Common Errors in English.

The following sentences, for example, all contain errors that force readers to stop and figure out what the writer really meant:

Children come into the clinic with tooth decay. [A misplaced modifier suggests that the clinic has tooth decay, but the writer meant that the children have it.]

This year's election campaign disappointed all the candidates attacked each other repeatedly. [This run-on sentence forces the reader to stop, sort out where one thought ends and the next begins, and then make mental corrections before proceeding.]

Fred eats pork as much as chickens. [A parallelism error makes it sound as though the chickens eat pork.]

Grammar, punctuation, and spelling errors are like litter strewn across a landscape. No matter how lovely or interesting the scene, it will be marred by these mistakes.

© rj lerich/Shutterstock.com

Grammar, punctuation, and spelling errors will mar your document like trash strewn over a scenic beach.

Exercise 3.9

On your own paper, rewrite each of the following sentences to correct the errors and correctly express the writer's meaning.

1. Let's eat Grandma.
2. Lying in the road, the jogger found a $20 bill.
3. Tom likes Brussel sprouts more than her.
4. If the customers don't buy all the hotdogs, throw them in the trash.
5. I didn't answer the phone, which was rude.
6. Today, I read newspaper articles about my friend Joe, a serial killer and our town's "Citizen of the Year."
7. I enjoy listening to music jogging on the treadmill.

Write Complete Sentences

A grammatically correct sentence is always *complete*, which means it contains a subject and a verb and expresses a complete thought. A sentence **fragment** results when the writer punctuates a part of a sentence as though it were a whole sentence (with a capital letter and a period).

FRAGMENT WITH NO VERB:	The chickens running around the front yard.
FRAGMENT WITH NO SUBJECT:	Laughed, joked, and talked all the way to the museum.
DEPENDENT CLAUSE FRAGMENT:	Because she did not get enough sleep.

Correct a sentence fragment in one of two ways. If the subject or the verb is missing, add it and continue to let the sentence stand by itself.

The chickens running around the front yard **clucked and squawked.**

The students laughed, joked, and talked all the way to the museum.

If the fragment is a dependent clause, delete the word that makes it a dependent clause, or attach it to the sentence that precedes or follows it:

She did not get enough sleep.

Because she did not get enough sleep, **she did not perform well on the test.**

Pages 243–246 of Appendix 2: Eleven Common Errors in English include more practice with locating and correcting sentence fragments.

TIP

Have someone read your writing aloud to you so that you can actually hear the sentences that need to be reworded.

▌ Exercise 3.10

On your own paper, rewrite each fragment to add the missing information or complete the thought.

1. Injured while jumping on a trampoline with no safety net.
2. Because I had done the reading assignment.
3. Left the front door standing wide open.
4. People who watch the news every day.
5. When I complete my college degree.
6. Sweeping, mopping, and then waxing the floor.
7. The document, found in the attic in a stack of old papers.

Check Your Spelling

Correct spelling is a requirement in every piece of writing you compose. Always check and double-check your spelling before sending your documents on to your readers. You can spell-check three ways:

1. Look up the spellings of words you're not sure of in a print or online dictionary.
2. Use your word processor's spell-checker to identify misspellings and suggest corrections.
3. Ask someone who is a good speller to proofread your work and point out misspellings.

Exercise 3.11

On your own paper, write the word in each group that is misspelled.

1. receive, probly, recognize, lightning
2. dependant, February, definitely, mathematics
3. salary, government, incredible, alright
4. seperate, calendar, writing, finally
5. knowledge, succede, library, happened
6. believe, judgment, untill, grammar
7. basically, similar, nessesary, really

Exercise 3.12

On your own paper, write the rules for clear sentences that are violated in each of the following sentences. (Sentences 1–4 violate only one rule. Sentences 5–8 violate two rules.) Then, rewrite each sentence to correct the errors.

RULES FOR CLEAR SENTENCES
RULE #1: USE STRONG VERBS.
Avoid *there is* sentences.
Avoid *it is* sentences.
Avoid passive-voice sentences.
Match subjects and verbs.
RULE #2: AVOID WORDINESS.
Check for redundant words.
Avoid passive-voice sentences.
Avoid hedging and disclaimers.
RULE #3: VARY SENTENCE TYPES AND LENGTHS.
RULE #4: ADHERE TO RULES FOR GRAMMAR, PUNCTUATION, AND SPELLING.

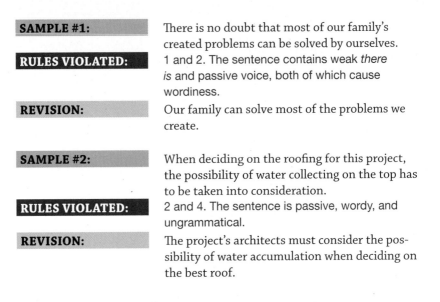

SAMPLE #1: There is no doubt that most of our family's created problems can be solved by ourselves.

RULES VIOLATED: 1 and 2. The sentence contains weak *there is* and passive voice, both of which cause wordiness.

REVISION: Our family can solve most of the problems we create.

SAMPLE #2: When deciding on the roofing for this project, the possibility of water collecting on the top has to be taken into consideration.

RULES VIOLATED: 2 and 4. The sentence is passive, wordy, and ungrammatical.

REVISION: The project's architects must consider the possibility of water accumulation when deciding on the best roof.

1. There are many mistakes that occur during the training of a dog.
2. Study for one hour. Then take a short break. Rest your mind for 10 minutes. Then go back to studying. You will concentrate better.
3. To speed up your note-taking during lectures, use abbreviations and write in cursive rather than print, and consider using a laptop if your professor allows, but make sure you sit near an electrical outlet in the classroom, and also use a pen that writes smoothly.
4. According to scientists, dark chocolate asparagus honey and coconut are foods that can improve you're mood and energy.
5. I suppose it's possible that we miscalculated and added the numbers incorrectly.
6. It is an individual's choice to drink alcohol or to say no. When offered an alcoholic beverage.
7. Two hikers who were lost in the woods and didn't know the way out were found by a search and rescue team that looked for them.
8. In my opinion, there are too many commercials aired during this television program.

▌ Exercise 3.13

Correct the grammar and spelling errors in a composition you've written recently. Use a colored pen to cross out each error and then write in the correction.

When you evaluate your sentences to make sure that they adhere to the four rules for clear sentences, consider using a checklist like the following as a guide.

CHECKLIST FOR CLEAR SENTENCES

Use this checklist to make sure that you are adhering to the four rules for clear sentences.

☐ Sentences do not begin with *there is*.

☐ Sentences do not begin with *it is*.

☐ Sentences are written in active voice rather than passive voice.

☐ Verbs convey accurate meanings.

☐ Sentences do not include redundant or wordy expressions.

☐ Sentences do not include hedging phrases or disclaimers.

☐ Sentences are a mixture of simple, compound, and complex.

☐ Sentences are a mixture of different lengths.

☐ Sentences adhere to the rules for grammar, spelling, and punctuation.

Exercise 3.14

1. Use the checklist above to evaluate a composition you have recently written. If you revised this composition, what would you change to improve its sentences?
2. Use the checklist to evaluate a classmate's paragraph or essay. What improvements would you recommend?

SUGGESTED WRITING ACTIVITIES

Complete all of the steps of the writing process as you write one or more of the following compositions. Check your draft to make sure that your sentences adhere to the four rules for clear sentences.

ACADEMIC WRITING

1. Write a summary of a book, a chapter, or an article that you were assigned to read in one of your classes.
2. Argue against a specific idea or opinion that you learned about in one of your classes.
3. What specific course or educational program should your college add to its academic offerings? Explain why this course or program would be a good addition.

PROFESSIONAL WRITING

4. Write a letter to your supervisor or your company's president to praise one of your co-workers for going above and beyond the call of duty.
5. Explain a procedure or a concept for the customers at your workplace.
6. What are three essential qualities of a good boss? Illustrate your ideas with specific examples of bosses you've known.

PERSONAL WRITING

7. Write an e-mail to a friend to persuade him or her that taking a specific class would be beneficial in some way or useful in achieving a specific goal.
8. Write to a 16-year-old to explain the difference between a "good driver" and a "bad driver."
9. Describe to your fellow students some specific stress-relief techniques that have worked for you.

CHAPTER 4

Essential #4: Vivid Language

The following passage is from a book that describes, based on survivors' eyewitness accounts, the tragic sinking of the great ship *Titanic*. Most of us would agree that this passage is an example of effective writing:

> In the distance, the *Titanic* looked an enormous length, her great bulk outlined in black against the starry sky, every port-hole and saloon blazing with light. It was impossible to think anything could be wrong with such a leviathan, were it not for that ominous tilt downwards in the bow, where the water was now up to the lowest row of port-holes. Presently, about 2 A.M., as near as can be determined, those in the life-boats observed her settling very rapidly with the bow and the bridge completely under water, and concluded that it was now only a question of minutes before she went. So it proved. She slowly tilted straight on end with the stern vertically upwards, and as she did, the lights in the cabins and saloons, which until then had not flickered for a moment, died out, came on again for a single flash, and finally went altogether. At the same time, the machinery roared down through the vessel with a rattle and a groaning that could be heard for miles, the weirdest sound surely that could be heard in the middle of the ocean, a thousand miles away from land. But this was not yet quite the end.
>
> To the amazement of the awed watchers in the life-boats, the doomed vessel remained in that upright position for a time estimated at five minutes; some in the boat say less, but it was certainly some minutes that at least 150 feet of the *Titanic* towered up above the level of the sea and loomed black against the sky.
>
> Then, with a quiet, slanting dive, she disappeared beneath the waters, and the eyes of the helpless spectators had looked for the last time upon the gigantic vessel on which that had set out from Southampton. And there was left to the survivors only the gently heaving sea, the life-boats filled with men and women in every conceivable condition of dress and undress, above the perfect sky of brilliant stars with no a cloud, all tempered with a bitter cold . . . a bitter cold unlike anything they had felt before.

> Adapted from Marshall, Logan, ed.
> *Sinking of the Titanic*. www.gutenberg.org

This passage tells a tragic story and evokes feelings of sadness, horror, and sympathy. These emotions are stirred in readers because this passage is well written using vivid language. **Vivid language** helps readers create mental images to understand the writer's meaning. This brief passage is effective because it contains all four aspects of vivid language: (1) factual and sensory details (times, positions of the ship, colors, sounds); (2) strong verbs (*tilted, roared, towered, loomed, disappeared*); (3) descriptive adjectives (*outlined in black, doomed, slanting, helpless, heaving, brilliant, bitter*); and (4) figures of speech (the *Titanic* is referred to as a female and a leviathan). These types of language will help you better communicate with your readers by creating pictures in their minds.

Prewriting for Vivid Language

Vivid language begins during the prewriting stage of the writing process. If you spend plenty of time using one or more of the strategies to generate ideas, you will have more details to work with when you begin to write your composition. Certain strategies—such as drawing, brainstorming, freewriting, and clustering—may be especially useful for producing details that will encourage you to write using vivid language.

Writing Sentences with Vivid Language

As you are composing, you will be searching for words to express the thoughts you need to share with your reader. Some of these words will be exactly the right ones when you first think of them, and some of them won't. Writing is a process of trying out different ways of saying something until you have found the most precise and interesting wording.

However, don't get bogged down in trying to make a sentence perfect before going on to the next sentence. Be aware of the various types of vivid language, and try to incorporate them as you compose, but remember that your most important goal is to complete a draft. During the rewriting stage, which will be discussed later in this chapter, you can go back to evaluate your sentences again and add vivid language to improve them.

Details

Words can be either general or specific. **General** words are those that refer to a broad range of things. More **specific** words are those that refer to fewer things or just one thing in particular. For example, examine the list in Figure 4.1.

The items in this list move from very general (*transportation*, a word that includes many different modes of travel, including bicycles, canoes, and camels) to very specific (one particular car). The more general the word you use, the greater the risk of the reader misinterpreting you. For example, when you use a word such as *vehicle*, readers will, at best, conjure up in their minds a shadowy image of something with four tires and, at worst, attach a meaning (truck or motorcycle, for example) that you did not intend at all. The more specific you are, the sharper and clearer the image you generate in readers' minds, and the less likely it is that they will misunderstand you.

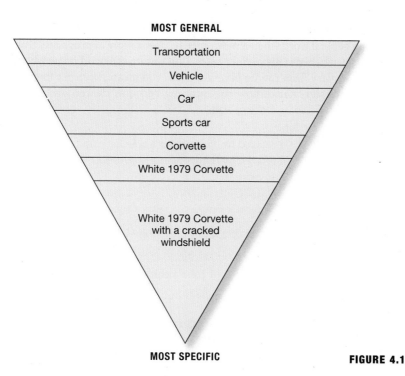

MOST GENERAL

| Transportation |
| Vehicle |
| Car |
| Sports car |
| Corvette |
| White 1979 Corvette |
| White 1979 Corvette with a cracked windshield |

MOST SPECIFIC

FIGURE 4.1

Ineffective writing is often filled with general language, words that are too vague or too broad to create a specific mental image for readers. If you're writing a memo to a co-worker asking her to send flowers to a client, she might send a bunch of carnations when you meant for her to send roses. If you're writing a letter to your local newspaper's editor to advocate for technology upgrades in a local school, the paper's readers will misunderstand your point if you don't describe the current state of computer labs and identify the specific equipment that needs to be replaced. In both instances, the writing will not fulfill its purpose because one or two general words led readers to decide on meanings the writer did not intend (see Figure 4.2).

FIGURE 4.2
The more general the word you use, the greater the risk of the reader misinterpreting you.

vehicle

© Tom Wang/Shutterstock.com

© Michel Borges/Shutterstock.com; © Michael Shake/Shutterstock.m

© BananaStock/Jupiterimages; © Rob Wilson/Shutterstock.com

© Yuri Arcurs/Shutterstock.com; © Margo Harrison/Shutterstock.com

As you compose, evaluate each word choice to determine whether you're choosing a general word when a more specific one is more appropriate. Don't write the word *dog* when you mean *Rottweiler*. Don't write the word *crime* when you really mean *burglary*. Don't write *beverage* when you mean *sweetened iced tea*. In the following examples, notice how the meaning becomes clearer when the general language is revised to be more specific:

GENERAL:	I relaxed by lying under a **tree** listening to **music**.
MORE SPECIFIC:	I relaxed by lying under a shady oak listening to an Aerosmith CD.

GENERAL:	The **man's operation** was a success.
MORE SPECIFIC:	Fred Davis's appendectomy was a success.

GENERAL:	**Menial labor jobs** await those without a high school diploma.
MORE SPECIFIC:	Frying hamburgers, sweeping floors, and stocking shelves are common jobs for those who lack a high school diploma.

GENERAL:	Prosthetics have advanced beyond **mere substitutions** to the **ability to restore function**.
MORE SPECIFIC:	Prosthetics have advanced beyond wooden legs and glass eyes to new devices, such as cochlear implants for the ears, that restore the patient's use of the missing or defective body part.

As a final example, read the following two versions of the same passage. The first relies heavily on general language. The second substitutes more specific words that make the meaning clearer.

According to the law, institutions are required to prevent discrimination against individuals with disabilities. They must ensure that everything is accessible to disabled individuals. Providing this access requires the addition of architecture, aids, services, policies, and procedures that allow the disabled to attend and participate in institutional activities.

This passage is difficult to comprehend even after two or three readings. Substituting more specific language makes the meaning much clearer:

According to the Americans with Disabilities Act, colleges and universities are required to prevent discrimination against students with disabilities. They must ensure that all of their programs, services, activities, and facilities are accessible to students in wheelchairs, blind or deaf students, and students who have learning disabilities. Providing this access requires the addition of handicapped ramps, elevators, interpreters, notetakers, closed captioning, and extra time on tests, for example, which allow students with disabilities to attend and participate in classes, presentations, performances, and other events.

▌ Exercise 4.1

On your own paper, rewrite each of these sentences to replace the general words or phrases in green with more specific choices.

1. When you come over, I'll make us **some good food**.
2. She was wearing too much **makeup**.
3. The kitchen staff must **practice good hygiene**.
4. The playground includes **playground equipment** along with an open area for children to play **games**.
5. **Elected officials** in the United States should legalize **drugs**.
6. I enjoy the **things** I learn in **my class**.
7. One of the candidates has **a strong education**, and the other has **experience**.
8. Thank you for **what you did for me**. I know you **sacrificed a lot**.
9. The **more you give**, the **more you get**.
10. He **has issues**.

Factual and Sensory Details

Clear and interesting writing includes not only specific word choices but also factual and sensory details. **Factual details** include information such as names, quantities, dates, and dimensions. For instance, in the list on page 65, the reader's mental image is sharpened with information such as "Corvette" (the type of car) and "1979" (the year of the car). Describing a person as 80 years old and five feet five inches tall provides factual details that help the reader form a clearer picture of the subject. In the following passage from a student's essay on the effects of clearcutting, the writer has not included many factual details. The questions indicate opportunities to provide more specific information:

> South American rain forests are vanishing [How fast?]. Plants in rain forests [Which ones?] supply a large percentage [How much?] of the earth's oxygen. As the trees are cut down [By whom?], plants [Like what?] used in medical cures [Like what?] are being destroyed [By whom?]. Also, animals [Which ones?] are left homeless when their habitat vanishes.

Adding the facts would bring the subject into crisper, clearer focus:

> South American rain forests are vanishing at the rate of 17 million acres per year, according to the United Nations. Because the trees, shrubs, vines, and other plants in rain forests supply the earth with 20 percent of our planet's oxygen, the rapid depletion of these forests is alarming. As timber companies cut down trees, they also destroy plants, such as the rosy periwinkle, that have become important to medical researchers searching for cures for cancer and other diseases. Also, the destruction of rain forests hastens the extinction of birds, insects, reptiles, and other animals, which are left homeless when their habitat vanishes.

Sensory details sharpen the reader's mental image by providing information about what something looks like, smells like, tastes like, sounds like, or

TIP

When you include facts and other details that you find through research, you will need to give the source of your information. See pages 97–98 of Chapter 5 for more explanation about including information from research.

feels like. For example, that five-foot-five-inch tall 80-year-old you're describing might have wispy gray hair (a sight detail); a raspy, cough-racked voice (a sound detail); and dry, papery skin (a touch detail). Each detail you add makes the subject come more alive on the page. In the image of the lemon below, note the difference between the factual details and the sensory details.

Factual Details

Weight: 6 ounces

Size of a fist

18.6 mg of vitamin C

4 tablespoons of juice

Sensory Details

Color: yellow

Smell: citrus scent

Shape: oblong

Taste: tart

© topseller/Shutterstock.com

In the following example from a student's essay about a motorcycle race, adding a few sensory details can bring the experience to life on the page.

First version:

I sat on the starting line, ready to go. I wasn't as nervous as I'd been earlier that day, but I still had a few butterflies in my stomach. A man held up a sign with a big number two, which meant two minutes until the gate dropped. All of the racers revved their motors and watched the sign. The man flipped it suddenly to reveal a number one: one minute to go. I was instantly nervous again.

This writer includes some effective sight details but could add more information about what his other senses—sound, smell, and touch—were experiencing to make his description more vivid.

Revised to add sensory detail:

I sat on the starting line, ready to go. The buzz of 20 idling motorcycle engines roared in my ears. My bike vibrated beneath me, eager to spring to life. The sharp smell of gasoline filled my head. I wasn't as nervous as I'd been earlier that day, but I still had a few butterflies in my stomach. The race official held up a sign with a big number two, which meant two minutes until the starting gate dropped. All of the other racers revved their motors, drowning out the cheers of the crowd, and watched the sign. The official flipped it suddenly to reveal a number one: one minute to go. I was instantly nervous again. My hands felt slippery inside my gloves, and my heart was pounding.

In the next passage from a student's essay on the benefits of walking, the writer has included few sensory details:

Walking improves your appearance. It helps firm, shape, and tone your body. Walking also improves posture.

Note how adding sensory information, in addition to a few factual details, helps the reader visualize the subject for improved understanding:

Walking improves your appearance by firming and shaping your body. You will lose excess flab from your legs and buttocks, so your thighs won't rub together anymore. Your calf muscles will become more taut and defined. Your buttock muscles will tighten and no longer sag. You'll lose fat around your torso, resulting in a more slender waistline. Finally, your posture will improve as your spine straightens from regular exercise, allowing you to breathe more efficiently.

█ Exercise 4.2

On your own paper, rewrite the sentences in the following paragraph to insert facts that would answer the questions in brackets.

During high school [Name of school? What grade?], I thought I could handle work and make good grades the same time. So I got a job [Where?] working [Doing what?] during the week [When?] and on weekends [When?], sometimes until late at night [How late?]. As a result, I never completed my assignments [For what classes?], and I never got enough sleep [How much did you get?]. Not surprisingly, my grades dropped [How much? To what?].

█ Exercise 4.3

On your own paper, fill in the blank in the following paragraph with the name of a specific area, and then rewrite the rest of the paragraph, adding factual details and sensory details.

_____ is one of the most attractive parts of this town [or campus]. The buildings and other structures look nice. The open areas are pleasing to look at. There are interesting things to see.

TIP
Try to write during the time of day when you're most alert. If you're at your mental peak in the morning, write in the morning. If you're a night owl, write at night.

Descriptive Adjectives

The second type of vivid language is descriptive adjectives. **Adjectives** are words that describe nouns. They tell how many, what kind, or which one. The words, phrases, and clauses highlighted in the following list are all descriptive adjectives:

the **blue** socks

a **friendly** salesperson

two friends

those carrots

the boy **wearing the hat**

a dress **that she borrowed**

This kind of descriptive information, combined with specific details, helps create clear images in your reader's mind. Adjectives are especially important when we describe something, such as an object, a person, or a place. They provide information readers must have to be able to "see" what you saw. For example, notice how the writer of the following paragraph uses describing words and phrases to help you picture the subject:

Melanoma skin cancer can be deadly if it's not treated, so pay attention to the warning signs. The most important warning sign for melanoma is a **new** spot on the skin or a spot **that is changing in size, shape, or color**. Another important sign is a spot **that looks different from all of the other spots on your skin**. The ABCD rule is another guide to the usual signs of melanoma. A is for Asymmetry: One half of a mole or birthmark does not match the other. B is for Border: The edges are **irregular**, **ragged**, **notched**, or **blurred**. C is for Color: The color is **not the same all over** and may include **shades of brown or black, sometimes with patches of pink, red, white, or blue**. D is for Diameter: The spot is **larger than 6 millimeters across** (about ¼ inch—the size of a pencil eraser), although melanomas can sometimes be smaller than this. If you have any of these warning signs, have your skin checked by a doctor.

Adapted from "Skin Cancer Prevention and Early Detection." American Cancer Society. www.cancer.org. 2012. Web. 26 Feb 2012.

Adjectives are important not only for describing things, but also for making your ideas clear. In the following passage, the writer has included few adjectives:

Does a diploma guarantee you success? That depends. The need **for employees** is increasing, but many jobs require **skilled** workers. Earning a diploma usually gives you the training **necessary for success**.

Notice how the addition of a few adjectives makes the writer's ideas much clearer:

Does a **college** diploma guarantee you **long-term career** success? That depends. The need **for entry-level employees in many fields** is increasing, but many of these jobs require **trained and educated** people **with effective communication skills**. Earning a **college** diploma usually gives you training **in crucial reading, writing, and speaking skills necessary for professional success**.

TIP

Adjectives can also be used for persuasive purposes. Think of advertisements that use adjectives to convince you that you want or need something. The idea of eating a hamburger might sound good, but the thought of a *quarter-pound, juicy, flame-broiled* hamburger *topped with melted cheese, crisp lettuce, and ripe red tomatoes* really whets your appetite!

However, beware of overusing adjectives. You do not want to pile too many of them in front of your nouns because they will slow the pace of your sentences and bog down your writing with a lot of unnecessary information. In the following examples, many of the adjectives are merely adding extra words without adding any additional meaning:

TOO MANY ADJECTIVES:	She could see the vampire's glistening, white, sharp fangs gleaming. [*Glistening* and *gleaming* mean the same thing. *Sharp* is an unnecessary adjective for fangs.]
BETTER:	She could see the vampire's white fangs gleaming.

TOO MANY ADJECTIVES:	Many Americans exhibit negative, unsympathetic, rejecting feelings for mentally ill people.
BETTER:	Many unsympathetic Americans reject mentally ill people.

TOO MANY ADJECTIVES:	My grandparents were loving, caring, kind, and affectionate toward all of their children and grandchildren.
BETTER:	My grandparents loved and cared for all of their children and grandchildren.

If you're placing two or three adjectives in front of every noun, go back and carefully evaluate each of your describing words. Select only those that are truly essential. If you have a tendency to use too many adjectives, check your verbs. Your meaning will be clearer if you let your verbs do more of the work.

Exercise 4.4

On your own paper, fill in the blank in the following paragraph with a descriptive adjective (some suggestions: *pleasant, miserable, lazy*). Then, rewrite the rest of the paragraph, adding adjectives to describe each word in green.

Summer is a _____ season. The sun shines brightly. The days lengthen, and the air warms. Children get a vacation from school. People wear clothes and spend hours outdoors.

Strong Verbs

You learned in Chapter 3 that interesting writing relies on strong action verbs to express ideas. A **verb** is the part of speech in a sentence that expresses the subject's action or state of being. The more precise and descriptive the verb, the sharper the image it produces in the reader's mind. Read the following passage and notice how the bold-faced verbs add action and life to the information:

For many of us, focusing is a challenge. We **work** too many hours, **crowd** our lives with obligations, and **rush** from one thing to the next. We **multitask**, believing that we **can surf** the Internet, **listen** to a new CD, **watch** a DVD, and **read** this chapter—all at the same time. The truth is, the more we try to multitask, the more we **sacrifice** the discipline for in-depth study. According to recent research, multitasking **hurts** your brain's ability to learn. Also, what you learn while distracted by other things is harder to use and recall. In fact, even though technology **has expanded** your access and your abilities, your IQ **drops** by 10 points when you are distracted by e-mail or phone calls. Technology's stimulation **gives** your brain a squirt of dopamine, which can actually be addictive, and being constantly connected, research shows, **can cause** brain fatigue. Multitasking, say experts, **triggers** a brownout in your brain; there's not enough power to go around. Your stress level **can skyrocket** when you "fragment" your attention in dozens of directions at the same time.

Adapted from Staley, Constance. *Focus on College Success*, 3rd ed. Boston: Wadsworth, 2013. Print.

This next example, too, highlights all of the strong verbs:

> In 2012, Google, the Internet search engine company, **rose** to the top of Fortune magazine's annual "100 Best Companies to Work For" list for the third time. Why **is** the company **rated** so highly? Google **rewards** its employees with the highest salaries and the best benefits in the tech industry. In addition, CEO Larry Page **has worked** hard to create an informal corporate culture that **treats** employees like family and **encourages** fun and creativity. The company's "Innovation Time Off" policy **permits** engineers to devote up to 20 percent of their workweek to working on projects that interest them. Finally, the company **pampers** its employees with an unbelievable list of perks, including free gourmet food at 25 companywide cafeterias, a gigantic outdoor sports complex, and frequent speeches and performances by celebrities.

Boring verbs will contribute to boring writing. As you write, notice if you are relying on weak verbs, such as *to be* or *to have* verbs. Though these verbs have their uses, and you cannot write without them, you might be choosing them instead of more interesting alternatives. In the following examples, the dull verbs are italicized. Notice how each revision substitutes a more action-oriented verb:

WEAK VERB:	College has been a real challenge for me.
STRONG VERB:	College has challenged me.
WEAK VERB:	The wreck was a three-car collision.
STRONG VERB:	Three cars collided in the wreck.
WEAK VERB:	The whole pan of lasagna fell off the table and went all over the floor.
STRONG VERB:	The whole pan of lasagna fell off the table and splattered on the floor.
WEAK VERB:	It was in Colorado Springs that we went up the highest mountain in the western United States.
STRONG VERB:	In Colorado Springs, we climbed the highest mountain in the western United States.

In the following passage, the writer uses a lot of dull verbs:

> Distance learning courses are not for everyone. Successful distance learners have several characteristics in common. For one thing, they are people who have the ability to motivate themselves. Although there is usually no one set time to show up for class, successful distance learners are in the habit of checking their computers regularly for information about course assignments and deadlines. Then, they meet those deadlines. They have the self-discipline to get the work done even without teachers or classmates reminding and encouraging them. Students who excel at distance learning also have good reading comprehension skills, and they have a preference for learning by reading

and writing. In distance learning, much of the course content **is** in the form of reading material, so being good at absorbing information presented in text form **is** a trait of successful distance learners.

The writer is relying too heavily on weak *to be* and *to have* verbs. Note how the subject and the writing become more interesting with the substitution of more action-oriented verbs:

> Distance learning courses **do not suit** everyone. Successful distance learners **share** several characteristics. For one thing, they **can motivate** themselves. Although class **does not meet** at one set time, successful distance learners regularly **check** their computers for information about course assignments and deadlines. Then, they **meet** those deadlines. They **discipline** themselves to get the work done even without teachers or classmates reminding and encouraging them. Students who excel at distance learning also **comprehend** what they read and **prefer** learning by reading and writing. In distance learning, much of the course content **takes** the form of reading material, so successful distance learners **can absorb** information in text form well.

Many times, the best verb for the sentence is lurking within the sentence, masquerading as another part of speech, such as an adjective, a noun, or an adverb. Creating a more interesting sentence, then, becomes a matter of rearranging the words to put the action where it belongs, in the verb:

WEAK VERB:	I **had** a ferocious fight with a close friend. [The best verb for this sentence—*fight*—is being used as a noun.]
STRONG VERB:	I **fought** ferociously with a close friend.
WEAK VERB:	I **had** all of the clothes washed and hanging on the line to dry. [The most interesting verbs are hiding as two adjectives, *washed* and *hanging*.]
STRONG VERB:	I **washed** all of the clothes and **hung** them on the line to dry.
WEAK VERB:	Sparkling with color, our work **was** done. [The verb is disguised as an adjective.]
STRONG VERB:	Our completed work **sparkled** with color.
WEAK VERB:	There **was** a long stretch of road a mile long. [The best verb is hiding as a noun.]
STRONG VERB:	The road **stretched** for a mile.

Strong verbs are easiest to select, of course, when you're describing action, such as the events in a story. However, you can get into the habit of evaluating your verbs in everything you write, from e-mails to research papers.

In the following passage, note how the subject becomes more clear and interesting simply by substituting more vivid verbs:

Dull verbs:

The Internet supposedly has the answer to any question, but, unfortunately, researchers are in the position of having to verify much online information for accuracy. The Internet does have huge amounts of information, but a lot of it has errors or is partially or completely false. Before using any online source, a researcher is wise to make sure that it's correct.

Revised for more interesting verbs:

The Internet supposedly **can answer** any question, but, unfortunately, researchers **must verify** much online information for accuracy. The Internet **does store** huge amounts of information, but a lot of it **contains** errors and falsehoods. Before using any online source, a wise researcher **investigates** it to make sure that it's correct.

In the following example from the work experience section of a résumé, notice how the better verbs are not only clearer and more interesting but also more *persuasive*:

Dull verbs:

Waited on customers, did daily store reports, made billing statements, took payments on accounts, and called past-due accounts.

Revised for more interesting verbs:

Assisted customers, **generated** daily store reports, **prepared** billing statements, **collected** payments on accounts, and **investigated** past-due accounts.

As you try out more action-oriented verbs in your sentences, be prepared to experiment with the wording of the entire sentence. Often, you will need to rearrange, delete, and add words and phrases as you search for the best action word.

Exercise 4.5

In the following sentences, the best verb is disguised as another part of speech. On your own paper, rewrite each sentence so that a more interesting verb conveys the action.

1. Some people are scared of taking risks.
2. Microsoft has put a lot of research and testing into its software.
3. The coach's recognition of the players' abilities was a boost for the players' morale.
4. Epilepsy is a misunderstood disease throughout America.
5. This county now has 28 licensed day care centers and 41 registered homes serving 2,000 children.
6. Recently, journalist Geraldo Rivera had an interview with a serial killer.

7. She **has** an excuse for every one of her bad decisions.

8. No matter how rich or powerful you are, a drug addiction **is** destructive.

9. Using coupons **is** a way to save money at the grocery store.

10. My military training **was** effective in teaching me self-discipline, confidence, and teamwork skills.

A. Choose a piece of your own writing. Underline the verb in each sentence. Then, revise any dull verbs to make them more interesting and action-oriented. You may have to reword all or part of your sentences.

B. Choose a piece of your own writing that you have saved using a word processor. Use the program's "search" function to find *to be* verbs (*is, are, was, were*) and *to have* verbs (*has, have, had*). Revise any dull verbs to make them more interesting and action-oriented.

Figures of Speech

Figures of speech are the fourth type of vivid language that adds interest and clarity to writing. Three specific figures of speech—metaphors, similes, and personification—will create images in your readers' minds to help them understand your ideas. Metaphors and similes creatively compare two things in order to reveal their similarities. **Metaphors** are direct comparisons, and **similes** are indirect comparisons that use the word *like* or *as*.

Here are some examples of common metaphors and similes that we use in our everyday speech:

Metaphors

Last night, I ran into an **old flame** in the grocery store.
Her words were a **slap in the face**.
Those two are **peas in a pod**.
He is **my knight in shining armor**.
I hope to become an actor, but bartending is **my bread and butter**.
My brother is **the black sheep of the family**.
He's a **big fish in a little pond**.
She **has a lot of irons in the fire**.
My co-worker is a **real thorn in my side**.
His son is a **chip off the old block**.

Similes

We'll have to be as quiet **as a mouse**.
She was **like a bull in a china shop**.
Our teacher is **as old as the hills**.

When the power went out, I was **blind as a bat**.
My poor grandmother is **deaf as a post**.
The children were **like worms in hot ashes**.
She works **like a dog**.
That test was **as easy as pie**.
The box was large but **as light as a feather**.
His skin was **as cold as ice**.

Exercise 4.7

Many advertisements and song lyrics contain metaphors and similes. Working with one or two of your classmates, generate a list of five metaphors and five similes in print ads or TV commercials and five metaphors and five similes in songs.

These kinds of comparisons add descriptive interest to writing, too, by conjuring up pictures in readers' minds. Authors of fiction and poetry have long known the power of creative figures of speech to communicate ideas while delighting readers. For example, author Janet Fitch used many striking metaphors and similes in her novel *White Oleander:*

I climbed the roof and spotted her blond hair **like a white flame** in the light of the three-quarter moon. [simile]

I sat at the empty drafting table next to my mother's, drawing the way the venetian blinds sliced the light **like cheese**. [simile]

She sat down next to me, handed me her brush, and I brushed her pale hair smooth, **painting the air with her violets**. [metaphor]

The heat lay on the city **like a lid**. [simile]

The **horses were fine-tuned machines on steel springs**, shiny as metal, and the jockeys' satin shirts gleamed in the sun as they walked their mounts around the track . . . [metaphor]

From, Fitch, Janet.
White Oleander. Back Bay Books, 1999. Print.

Metaphors and similes can also be included in nonfiction writing to add descriptive detail. For example, notice how the following passage from a student essay is improved with the addition of a few original similes:

Shiny polyurethane plywood formed five sides of the cage, and the top was wire. I peered into the cage, scanning the floor. In one corner, a collection of tiny baby boa constrictors wiggled **like boiling spaghetti**. A combination of blood and mucus still covered the babies, which were still attached to small yolk sacs that fed them in their mother's body. The huge reptile, her markings **as clear and bold as an argyle sock** with many shades of black, tan, gray, cream, and orange, slithered gracefully around the base of the cage. When she spotted me directly above, she tried to strike.

As you try to include more metaphors and similes in your writing, beware of clichés. A **cliché** is a phrase that's no longer fresh or interesting because it has been overused. Clichés include similes such as:

as strong as an ox	as slow as molasses	as busy as a bee
as fit as a fiddle	watched like a hawk	sharp as a tack

Instead of including dull, hackneyed phrases that everyone's heard before, strive for creativity in your comparisons. Make intriguing connections that startle or delight your readers with their originality.

A third figure of speech that can add zest and life to your writing is **personification**. To *personify* means to describe an inanimate or nonhuman object as though it possesses human abilities or characteristics. For example, the curtains *whisper* in the breeze, the fan *hums*, the springs on the porch swing *complain*.

Again, as you experiment with personification, beware of clichés. Phrases such as waves *lap the shore, wind whistles,* and *daffodils dance* are boring because they're common and overused.

Exercise 4.8

Many advertisements and song lyrics include personification. Working with one or two of your classmates, generate a list of five examples of personification in print ads or TV commercials and five examples of personification in songs.

Exercise 4.9

A. On your own paper, create original, descriptive metaphors or similes by filling in the blank in each of the following sentences:

1. The clothes on the clothesline fluttered like _____.
2. The boy was as thin as _____.
3. The abandoned swing set was a _____.
4. The asphalt parking lot was as hot as _____.
5. Her anger was a _____.

B. Add a verb that personifies each of the following nouns:

6. The willow tree _____.
7. The ringing phone _____.
8. The daisy _____.
9. The truck's engine _____.
10. The fire _____.

Exercise 4.10

Evaluate the use of vivid language in the essay "Memories of My Father" that begins on page 212 of Appendix 1: Eleven Model Compositions. How does the writer use factual and sensory details, strong verbs, descriptive language, and figures of speech to create mental images for you as you read?

TIP

Refer to a dictionary and a thesaurus as you compose to help you find vivid verbs, adjectives, and specific nouns. Assemble a home reference library or bookmark online resources such as dictionary.reference.com and thesaurus.com. If you are composing using the Microsoft Word® program, use the Thesaurus tool under the "Review" tab.

Precise Word Choices

As you experiment with more vivid details, adjectives, verbs, and figures of speech to enliven your writing, carefully evaluate the words you choose for the meaning they convey. The English language contains over one million words, providing us with many fascinating options for communicating with others. However, this variety of choice can often increase the danger of selecting a word that does not accurately express an intended meaning. As Mark Twain said, "The difference between the right word and the almost-right word is the difference between lightning and a lightning bug." Words have various shades of meaning that we must take into account as we search for the language to best express our thoughts.

Imprecise words will "sound" like wrong notes in a musical performance. For example, examine these sentences from student writing:

Cigarette smokers let their smoke run free about the restaurant until it infests the lungs of innocent bystanders. [The writer has attempted to personify his subject, but the two verb choices do not accurately describe the action of cigarette smoke.]

A lovely sunset pierced through nature's shrouds. Twilight lingered, spotting the garden with a final glow. Night crept in to muffle the farmlands. The scent of flowers drifted on the breeze. Wildflowers showed their colorful dresses.

Imprecise word choices come in a variety of flavors. Sometimes a writer accidentally chooses the wrong word because he or she mistakes it for another word that sounds very similar. For example, "I said some things about his formal girlfriend that weren't true" (instead of *formal*, the writer means *former*). Or, in the same vein, a writer might substitute a word that sounds like the intended word choice: "Many unemployed people are idol all day" (the word should be *idle*). Sometimes word choices are imprecise because they don't match the rest of the composition. For instance, if you toss an informal slang term in the middle of a serious essay or report or use a very formal word in a more conversational document, those inappropriate words sound wrong. For example, a student writer included this statement in her research paper: "College graduates are lucky to *knock down* $20,000 a year." The phrase *knock down* is slang, too conversational for a formal document such as a research paper. In contrast, another student, in an e-mail to a fellow student, included the sentence "The members of our study group will convene at the library." The word *convene* seems too formal in that situation.

Another category of imprecise words is synonyms with subtle but different shades of meaning. Consider this list of words:

boat

yacht

canoe

schooner

barge

dinghy

steamer

ferry

Although all of these words refer to specific types of water transportation, they can't necessarily replace each other without significantly altering the meaning of the sentence. If you consult a thesaurus (a collection of synonyms) as you write, make sure you're selecting the word that most accurately reflects your meaning.

Finally, many imprecise word choices are ones the writer thought he or she knew, but didn't. Make sure you know the exact meaning of each word you select in order to avoid possible misunderstandings with your reader. When a student wrote the following sentence in an essay, she did not know the meaning of the word:

I would like to be efficient enough for garage mechanics to treat me like an adult, not a teenager.

Think about the mental picture an imprecise word choice can conjure up for your readers. Not only can it confuse them, but it can also leave them chuckling over a ridiculous mental image, like this sentence:

Rolling my eyes across the dusty floor, I stretched an eyeball as it stared into the attic.

Exercise 4.11

On your own paper, rewrite the following passage to replace each of the green words in the passage with a more precise choice:

I was awestruck when I got a speeding ticket today. I was on the highway in front of my residence when I saw the siren flashing behind me. I pulled up to the curb. A detective got out of his plain car and hiked up to my window. He asked me if I comprehended that I was succeeding the speed limit. I was scandalized by the acquisition. I insisted that I was cruising at the exact limit of 35 miles per hour. But then he accursed me of going 38 miles per hour. I couldn't believe it! Only three miles per hour above the limit and this lad had decided that I had perpetuated a major offensive. He treated me like a feline, and I became infuriated. By this time, a mob had gathered to watch. I argued with him, but he was unaffected. He preceded to furnish me with a ticket, which I excepted with reluctance. Then I lamented that I had debated with him. If I had treated him respectively, maybe he would have let me off with just a warning.

Rewriting for Vivid Language

When you need to write a paper, always give yourself enough time so that you can set aside your first draft for a day or two. Then, when you return to that draft, you'll be better able to spot places that need improvement. Go through your draft and, first, evaluate your nouns (people, places, and things). Are they as specific as they need to be, or could you substitute other words that would make your writing clearer? Then, go through the draft again and look at your verbs. Are the majority of them action-oriented? If not, replace them and rewrite the sentences if necessary. Next, find the adjectives in your sentences. Could you add more to help your readers create mental images? Finally, look for opportunities to insert a metaphor or simile or to use personification.

Notice how the following paragraph describing a scuba dive in Mexico is dramatically improved when revised to include all four types of vivid language:

First version:

On a trip to Cancun, my friend talked me into going chumming. "Chum" is made up of blood and fish parts. Sharks eat it. Too late, though, I knew I didn't want to be that close to man-eaters. I opened my eyes for a moment and saw the sharks. They swam around me, eating the chum, and I felt afraid.

Revised for vivid language:

On a trip to Cancun, my friend Dan talked me into going chumming. "Chum" is a combination of the blood, heads, tails, and entrails of fish, a meal especially appealing to sharks. Chumming involves placing this stinking, gory mess in a bucket and then taking it on a scuba dive in the ocean. When you release the chum into the water, a cloud of red spreads out into the clear water, attracting sharks to the irresistible scent of the blood. But 70 feet down in the chilly water, after we released this foul beacon, I suddenly realized that I didn't want to be that close to hungry man-eaters. It was too late. A swarm of silvery whitetip sharks moving gracefully though the water quickly surrounded me. At least 20 of them, all three to four feet long with glassy black dots for eyes, glided above my head. Seized by fear, I trembled as I watched them open their mouths, revealing rows of jagged teeth, to gobble the chum.

This revision adds facts (the name of her friend, the depth of the dive, the kind of shark, the number of sharks, the length of the sharks), sensory details (the smell and color of the chum, the temperature of the water, the color of the sharks' bodies and eyes), descriptive adjectives (*irresistible, foul, hungry, jagged*), strong verbs (*spreads, surrounded, glided, trembled*), and a figure of speech (*foul beacon*). Using more vivid language creates clearer, more interesting writing.

When you evaluate your writing to make sure that it includes the four types of vivid language, consider using a checklist like the following as a guide.

CHECKLIST FOR VIVID LANGUAGE

Use this checklist to make sure that you are including the four types of vivid language.

☐ Sentences include specific word choices.

☐ Sentences include adequate factual details and sensory details.

☐ Sentences include descriptive adjectives to create mental images and make ideas clearer.

☐ Most sentences include strong, action-oriented verbs.

☐ Clever or creative figures of speech (such as metaphors, similes, and personification) are used appropriately to make sentences more interesting.

Exercise 4.12

A. Use the checklist above to evaluate a composition you have recently written. If you revised this composition, what would you change to improve its sentences?

B. Use the checklist to evaluate a classmate's paragraph or essay. What improvements would you recommend?

SUGGESTED WRITING ACTIVITIES

Complete all of the steps of the writing process as you write one or more of the following compositions. As you write and revise, strive to include all four types of vivid language.

ACADEMIC WRITING

1. Write an e-mail to a new student who has asked you for advice about how to be successful in a specific course that you've already taken.
2. Persuade a high school graduate that he or she should attend your college.
3. Write instructions for registering for a class at the college you attend.

PROFESSIONAL WRITING

4. Give advice to job hunters who plan to apply for an opening at your place of employment.
5. Describe how a specific area of your workplace could be made more attractive.
6. Compare two different brands of a tool, piece of equipment, machine, or other item that you use to do your job.

PERSONAL WRITING

7. Describe the best-kept secret in your city or town, a place that more people should know about and visit.
8. Write directions to explain how to travel from your college's campus to your home.
9. Describe a relative, neighbor, friend, teacher, or spiritual leader whom you have adopted as your hero or role model.

PART III

Essential Characteristics of Effective Paragraphs

CHAPTER 5

Essential #5: Complete Paragraphs

Now that we've examined the kinds of words and sentences found in effective writing, we'll turn in the next three chapters to the characteristics of successful paragraphs.

As you learned in Chapter 2, a **paragraph** can be defined as a group of sentences that support one main idea. That idea is usually stated in a topic sentence, and the other sentences in the paragraph provide the details, facts, statistics, examples, reasons, or other information that explains and proves it.

When a paragraph is complete, it offers readers enough information to help them understand and accept the main idea. Good writing contains complete paragraphs that leave no doubt about the author's meaning because they provide sufficient explanation. Complete paragraphs anticipate and answer all of readers' questions and use *layers of development* to explain ideas.

Anticipating Readers' Questions

When you have a conversation with someone, that person can ask you questions if you say something he or she doesn't understand. These questions include: *What do you mean? Why do you say that? Can you be more specific? Can you give me an example?*

However, when you give readers documents that you've written, you usually will not be there when those documents are read. Whatever is on the page or computer screen must stand on its own. You will not be able to clarify or add to what's there. You will not be able to answer your readers' questions about anything that is unclear. If your readers are left with unanswered questions or feel that they don't have enough information to understand your ideas, your writing will not achieve your purpose or goal.

For example, the following paragraph attempts to explain how to cook a hamburger on a barbeque grill. Note all of the unanswered questions (in brackets) that arise as you read.

© Michael D Brown/Shutterstock.com

In conversations, we can ask questions when we don't understand. When we write, we must anticipate and then answer readers' questions.

To grill a hamburger, you first have to get the fire going. Remove the rack [On what?] and stack [How?] charcoal briquettes [How many?] in the center of the grill. Next, squirt charcoal lighter fluid [How much?] over the briquettes. Wait until the fluid soaks the charcoal [How long?]. Then toss in a lighted match. The flame will burn for a few minutes before it goes out. When this happens, let the briquettes sit for a while [How long?]. Don't squirt any more lighter fluid on the burning briquettes [Why?]. As the briquettes get hot enough [How do you know when they are?], spread them out with a stick so that they barely touch each other [Why?].

It would be difficult for the reader to complete this procedure successfully because so many important details are missing.

When we assume too much about our readers' knowledge, we risk omitting important information. Therefore, it is important to anticipate readers' questions and make sure that you answer all of them as you write. To do this effectively, you must take the time before you write to think about your readers' characteristics, their level of prior knowledge, and their needs. These three aspects of your audience, which are explained in Chapter 1 of this book, will help you make decisions about what you need to include. Ask yourself, as you write every sentence in your document, the following important question: *Will my readers need more information to fully understand what I'm trying to say in this sentence?* If the answer is yes, add the missing information to that sentence or include it in the next sentence.

As an illustration, let's say that you write the following sentence:

The car I drive is fuel-efficient.

If you ask yourself the question *Will my readers need more information to fully understand what I'm trying to say in this sentence?*, the answer would be yes. Even if your readers have some idea of what the term *fuel-efficient* might mean, they will need to know what you, the writer, mean when you use that term. In addition, they will surely wonder why that term describes your car. What specific information can you provide to explain why your car qualifies as fuel-efficient? You would need to add another sentence:

It gets 35 miles per gallon for city driving, and 39 miles per gallon for highway driving.

This additional, specific information helps the reader understand exactly what you mean by the term *fuel-efficient*.

Here's another example:

Crime rates are high in certain parts of the city.

This sentence probably triggers a number of questions in the reader's mind, including: *Which parts? How high are they?* and *What kinds of crime?* The sentences that follow this one need to answer each of these questions.

Exercise 5.1

On your own paper, write down the question that arises in your mind after you read each of the following sentences. Some of these sentences trigger more than one question.

1. A traditional wedding can be very expensive.
2. Smoking cigarettes can cause serious illnesses.
3. Adult learners differ from child learners.
4. The police have ruled out arson as the cause of the fire.
5. Using credit cards irresponsibly quickly got me into trouble.

Now let's look at how sentences within paragraphs raise questions for the reader. In the following example, unanswered questions are inserted in brackets:

Many people are using the Internet as a money-making tool. One effective way to earn cash is to sell things [like what?] on online auction sites such as eBay [how?]. Another way is to sell [where?] hand-made goods [like what?] to people who appreciate craftsmanship, artistic creations, or one-of-a-kind items. T-shirts, too, [what kind?] are a popular item to sell online. There are websites [what are some examples?] that allow individuals to set up their own store, create their own T-shirt designs, and sell their creations [what kinds sell well?]. Other people are actually earning a steady living sitting at their home computers and domain name flipping, blogging, and SEO reviewing [What are these? How do they work? How do they make money?].

Adapted from Fuller, John, and Stephanie Crawford. "Top Ten Ways to Make Money on the Internet." Howstuffworks.com. Web. 23 Jan. 2012.

By anticipating and providing answers to these questions, the writer would do a better job of helping the reader understand ways to make money on the Internet. The following paragraph, too, raises a number of questions that it does not answer:

> A person who is addicted to a particular substance (such as drugs, alcohol, or food) or activity (such as gambling, playing video games, or even exercising) will exhibit certain symptoms. One classic symptom is an inability to limit use of the substance or participation in the activity even when significant impairment is occurring. [What is an example? What does "significant impairment" mean?] Also, the person will exhibit a craving for the substance or activity. [What are the signs of a craving? What will a person with a craving do or say?] Another symptom is an increase in the amount or frequency of use, indicating a growing tolerance to the substance or activity. [What is an example? What does "tolerance" mean?] If the individual stops using the substance or engaging in the activity, symptoms of withdrawal occur. [What are some of these symptoms?] Finally, the addiction begins to interfere with the individual's work life, social life, and family life, causing a number of different problems. [How does the addiction interfere? What are some of the problems that result?]

> Adapted from "Psych Basics: Addiction."
> *Psychology Today*. Web. 5 Sep. 2011.

By providing answers to all of these questions, the writer will be much more likely to help the reader understand this important topic. As these examples illustrate, many statements require additional details and explanation to be understandable. Readers get frustrated when they have to "fill in the blanks." That frustration is understandable because filling in the blanks is the *writer's* job.

Exercise 5.2

As you read the following paragraph, what question arises in your mind after you read each sentence? List those questions on your own paper. For example, the question triggered by the first sentence is "Why not?" and the question triggered by the second sentence is "Why is it a smart choice?" Some of the sentences may trigger more than one question.

> [1] When high school seniors are deciding which colleges to apply to, they should not rule out their local community college. [2] Deciding to attend a community college to obtain the first two years' worth of college credit is actually a very smart choice. [3] Community college tuition is significantly lower than tuition at a four-year college or university. [4] Also, young people who choose to remain at home with their parents rather than moving to a college campus save even more money. [5] Despite the lower costs, however, most students will find that the education they receive at a community college is just as good or even better than a four-year college or university education. [6] One reason for this is the size of community college classes, which tends to be much smaller than the size of university classes. [7] Consequently, community college students often find that they can get more individualized attention and assistance. [8] An additional benefit of community colleges is the diversity of the student population. [9] Unlike four-year colleges and universities, where the majority of the student body has recently graduated from high school

and ranges in age from about 18 to 22, the community college includes a much wider range of students. [10] Interacting with a more diverse student population will provide an additional dimension of learning. [11] It will also better prepare students for success in their careers and personal lives.

TIP

After writing a draft, read each of your sentences, one by one, to a classmate, friend, or relative. Have that person ask you the question triggered by each of your sentences. Check to make sure that your next sentence or sentences answer that question.

Exercise 5.3

A. Find a piece of writing (in a textbook, a newspaper, a book, or a magazine) that you find difficult to understand. What questions do you have that the writer does not answer? List those questions on your own paper.

B. Select one of your recent writing assignments, and trade papers with a classmate. Read your classmate's paragraph or essay, and write down questions you have that the writer does not answer. List those questions on your own paper.

Exercise 5.4

Interview a classmate about an accomplishment that made him or her proud. Ask all of the questions in the following list to gather information and details. On your own paper, write down all of the *additional* questions you asked during the interview to fully understand what your classmate did and why he or she is proud.

1. What is an accomplishment that made you proud?

2. How did you achieve this accomplishment?

3. Why are you proud of this accomplishment?

Prewriting for Complete Paragraphs

TIP

A well-developed paragraph depends upon a clear topic sentence that includes the paragraph's topic and the point you want to make about that topic. See Chapter 2 (pages 16–17) of this book for more practice with writing effective topic sentences.

In Chapter 2, you learned that one of the four parts of a paragraph is the body, which offers support for the paragraph's main idea. Supporting a main idea does not mean simply repeating it over and over again using different words. Instead, the writer must offer *additional* information that will make his or her points understandable and more convincing to readers. When writers include explanation, they are developing the paragraph by making their thoughts clearer to their readers.

Sufficient development of your ideas begins in the prewriting step of the writing process. When you are generating ideas, spend a sufficient amount of time on this task to produce details you will need as you write. Think about your subject. Use two or more prewriting strategies (freewriting, brainstorming, clustering, and so on). Prewrite several different times, not just once. Make sure that you have written a clear topic sentence. Also, devote adequate time and effort to the task of organizing and outlining ideas. Include specific details, facts, and examples in your outline so that you will have them to refer to as you are writing.

▍ Exercise 5.5

Select one of the Suggested Writing Activities in the list on page 103. Use one or more prewriting techniques to produce ideas and details, and then organize those details in an outline. Finally, evaluate your outline. Will one or more parts of the outline need more details to completely answer readers' questions?

Writing Complete Paragraphs

During the writing step of the composition process, you make decisions about development with every sentence you write. Being able to evaluate how general each of your sentences is will help you determine when you need to add more details or explanations.

General and Specific Words and Sentences

When something is described as **general**, it includes or covers a wide range of different things. The word *animal*, for example, is a general word that refers to many creatures, from snakes to dogs to elephants. So, if we compare the word *animal* and the word *dog*, the word *animal* is the general word, and the word *dog* is the **specific** word because it refers to just one particular animal. If we compare the word *dog* to the word *poodle*, however, *dog* becomes the more general word because it refers not only to poodles but to all other kinds of dogs, too. Words are general or particular relative to what they are being compared to.

To understand the concept of general and specific, look at the diagram in Figure 5.1. The most general word in Figure 5.1 is *animals* because it refers to a wide variety of different creatures. At the next, more specific level, the three words name specific types of animals. The next level, which is even more specific, gives examples. The fourth, most specific level identifies two specific breeds of one kind of animal, dogs. The words get more specific as you move down the chart.

> *TIP*
>
> A diagram like the one in Figure 5.1 can be a useful tool for organizing your ideas during the prewriting step of the writing process.

▍ Exercise 5.6

On your own paper, create a diagram like that in Figure 5.1 for *transportation*, *academic subjects*, or *clothing*, or select another subject approved by your instructor.

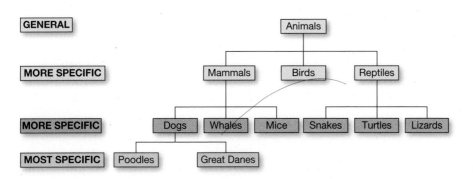

FIGURE 5.1

Just as words can be relatively general or specific, sentences can be general and specific. If you write a sentence like *The faculty and staff at my college are friendly and nice*, you have made a general observation about a group of people. What, exactly, leads you to conclude that these people are "friendly and nice"? Most likely, they say and do particular things. What are some of those particular things? Can you provide at least one specific example to help the reader understand what you mean?

Now look at another example:

I have a lot of homework to do.

The word *homework* is a relatively general term that includes many different activities. To help your reader understand what you mean by *homework*, you will need to give some more specific information about your assignments. Also, the phrase *a lot* needs further explanation. You could help the reader better understand your statement by adding the more specific information in the following sentence:

By tomorrow, I must complete 30 math problems, write a paper for my English class, and read a chapter in my business textbook.

Exercise 5.7

For each of the following general sentences, fill in the blank as needed and write another, more specific sentence that provides more information to help the reader understand the general idea. Write each pair of sentences on your own paper.

1. My friend _____ is beautiful [or handsome].
2. _____ is a hard worker.
3. My two younger brothers fight a lot.
4. My house [or apartment] is a mess.
5. Rush-hour traffic in this town is really bad.

Paragraphs contain both general and specific sentences. Some sentences express more general or abstract ideas, and other sentences provide more specific information to further explain those general ideas. For example, read the following paragraph:

¹ Brain research has shown that some emotional states help learning occur, and other emotional states actually interfere with learning. ² According to several studies, feeling happy or excited about the subject matter improves students' ability to think about and learn new material. ³ Teenagers, for example, readily soak up information about operating a vehicle and the rules of the road because they are enthusiastic about learning how to drive and obtaining a driver's license. ⁴ On the other hand, studies show that emotions such as anger, anxiety, and grief hinder the learning process. ⁵ New information that is absorbed through the senses must pass through the part of the brain that interprets emotions to get to the part that processes and stores the

information for future use. ⁶ When the learner is preoccupied with negative emotions or feels threatened, helpless, or incompetent with regard to the new information, the brain actually blocks that information from getting through to where the learning occurs. ⁷ To use one common example, students who doubt their ability to learn math and approach their study of math with fear and anxiety set up a mental roadblock that prevents the information from getting through and sabotages their own learning.

The first sentence of this paragraph is the topic sentence; it states a general idea about how different emotional states impact learning. The second sentence focuses on two specific emotional states (happiness and excitement) that help learning take place; therefore, it is more specific than the first sentence. The third sentence provides a specific example to illustrate the idea in the second sentence.

We can visually demonstrate these relationships between the sentences by noting the question that each sentence raises and then indenting the sentence below it to show that it answers the question with additional explanation or an example:

> ¹ Brain research has shown that some emotional states help learning occur, and other emotional states actually interfere with learning.

What are some of these emotional states?

> ² According to several studies, feeling happy or excited about the subject matter improves students' ability to think about and learn new material.

What is an example?

> ³ Teenagers, for example, readily soak up information about operating a vehicle and the rules of the road because they are enthusiastic about learning to drive and obtaining a driver's license.

Think of the indented sentences in this example as "layers" of additional information that help readers understand more general or abstract ideas. The box farthest to the left contains the most general sentence in the group. The second box is indented to show that the sentence it contains provides more specific information to explain the sentence in the first box. The sentence in the third box is the most specific in the group, so that box is the farthest to the right. With each **layer of development** that you add, you answer a question the reader might have; therefore, you strengthen your explanation and your chance of convincing your readers to accept your main idea. As you write each sentence, ask yourself, "*Is there an idea in this sentence that I should explain further or give an example for?*" If there is, add another layer, another sentence that clarifies the more general idea preceding it.

If we continue to arrange the rest of the paragraph about emotions' impact on learning into layers of development, you would see that the fourth sentence actually develops the second part of the topic sentence. Therefore, it is as general as the

> **TIP**
>
> The topic sentence should be the most general sentence in the paragraph.

second sentence. Then, each of the remaining sentences provides more explanation or examples for the one that comes before it:

⁴ On the other hand, studies show that emotions such as anger, anxiety, and grief hinder the learning process.

How?

⁵ New information that is absorbed through the senses must pass through the part of the brain that interprets emotions to get to the part that processes and stores the information for future use.

So how does this process affect learning?

⁶ When the learner is preoccupied with negative emotions or feels threatened, helpless, or incompetent with regard to the new information, the brain actually blocks that information from getting through to where the learning occurs.

What is an example?

⁷ To use one common example, students who doubt their ability to learn math and approach their study of math with fear and anxiety set up a mental roadblock that prevents the information from getting through and sabotages their own learning.

When you are writing, you need to be able to recognize relatively general sentences. These sentences will always need more explanation or development. Mature, sophisticated writing includes many rich layers of development provided to explain general statements. For example, read the paragraph on page 93. Its sentences have been rearranged and indented to show its many layers. The first sentence, which is the most general sentence in the paragraph, is the topic sentence. Then, each group of layers is colored a different shade of peach to show that these sentences are working together to explain one of the paragraph's relatively general supporting sentences.

In this paragraph, Sentences 2, 7, and 10 state the three ways that absences are harmful. The sentences that follow Sentences 2, 7, and 10 offer layers of development; they provide explanations, facts, and examples that help the reader understand each point.

TIP

Strive to provide two or three layers of development for each of the relatively general sentences you include to support your main idea. You will be more likely to answer your readers' questions if you do.

¹ Students often cut classes because they think that being absent will not have any negative effects, but absences are actually quite harmful in three ways.

What are these 3 ways?
How are absences harmful?

² For one thing, absences can result in a loss of understanding of the course content.

How?

³ Students are responsible for everything that is presented in class, whether they are there or not, and absences result in big gaps in information.

What's an example?

⁴ After missing an instructor's lecture on a specific topic, for example, a student may be able to recover some of the information by copying a classmate's notes, but a large portion of what that instructor presented cannot be recovered.

How is this harmful?

⁵ Therefore, the student won't be able to answer questions about this information when it appears on a quiz or a test.

⁶ A second negative effect of absences is missed opportunity for learning.

How do absences cause these missed opportunities?

⁷ Even if instructors post content such as PowerPoint presentations and other course material online for students to review outside of class, being absent deprives students of participation in class activities such as discussions, group work, and experiments.

How is this harmful?

⁸ Missing these opportunities for interaction, problem solving, and application of concepts can prevent students from achieving the deep learning that they need for other courses and in their careers.

⁹ The third way absences harm students is by putting them in danger of low grades, failing grades, or withdrawal from the course.

How do absences cause these problems?

¹⁰ Many instructors impose penalties for late assignments and grade their students on classwork activities that cannot be made up, so students who do not attend class lose points that factor into their final course grade.

¹¹ Many colleges have attendance policies that permit only a certain number of absences; when a student violates that policy, he or she will be withdrawn from the course and forced to take it over again.

Exercise 5.8

For each of the following paragraphs, work in a group with one or two of your classmates to rewrite the first few words of every sentence in boxes, like the examples on pages 91–93, to show the layers of development (the general-specific relationships between the sentences). Then, shade in each group of layers using a different color.

1. [1] If it's been a while since you've been to see a dentist, it's time to make an appointment for a check-up. [2] Like many people, you may be putting off a dental visit because you fear that the experience will be painful, but surveys of dental patients reveal that severe pain is actually rare. [3] Modern dentistry's equipment and methods have significantly reduced or eliminated the discomfort of most procedures. [4] Another reason you may be avoiding the dentist is the cost; however, paying for regular check-ups may save you thousands of dollars later on. [5] Regular dental care can prevent serious dental problems that could cost thousands of dollars to correct.

2. [1] If you need help paying for your college expenses, including tuition, fees, textbooks, supplies, and even living expenses, you need to know about four types of financial aid that might be available to you. [2] The first type of financial aid is grants awarded by federal or state governments or institutions. [3] Grants are gifts of money that do not have to be paid back, and they are typically awarded to students who qualify by demonstrating financial need. [4] One example of a grant is the federal government's Pell Grant. [5] The second type of financial aid is in the form of scholarships, which are gifts of money from institutions or private organizations. [6] Like grants, they do not have to be paid back; however, they may be awarded not based on financial need but on a high level of academic achievement. [7] The third type of financial aid is loans. [8] Students or their parents can apply to borrow funds at low interest rates to cover college expenses and then pay back the money after the student graduates or leaves school. [9] The federal Stafford loan is one loan program in which the federal government pays the interest accruing on the loan while the student is enrolled in school. [10] The fourth type of financial aid is the work-study program. [11] Students who participate in this program work a part-time job on campus to earn money to pay for their expenses.

Exercise 5.9

Select two of the following paragraphs in Chapter 6: gasoline prices on pages 118–119, generations on page 119, types of exercise on page 121, buying local foods on pages 122–123, and local libraries on page 123. For each paragraph, rewrite the first few words of the topic sentence and supporting sentences in boxes, like the examples on pages 91–93, to show the layers of development. Then, shade in each group of layers using a different color.

Types of Details

Layers of development can include many different types of information, including

- Facts
- Data and statistics
- Descriptive details
- Examples
- Stories or anecdotes
- Definitions of terms
- Reasons

The paragraph about emotions' impact on learning on pages 90–91, for example, includes facts and examples. The paragraph about financial aid on page 94 includes definitions, facts, and examples. The paragraph about attending a community college on pages 87–88 is developed primarily with reasons.

Exercise 5.10

The following paragraph has been arranged to show layers of development. Each group of layers is colored a different shade of peach to show that these sentences are working together to explain one of the more general supporting sentences. For each numbered sentence, identify the type of detail provided in that sentence. Choose from the list of types of details at the top of this page.

Anyone who is shopping for a house needs to consider purchasing his or her new home in the Whispering Lake neighborhood.   Topic sentence

[1] One reason you'll love Whispering Lake is the wonderful neighbors you'll have.

[2] The residents on my street, for example, are some of the friendliest, kindest, and most helpful people I know.

[3] When I moved into my house and pulled up with a loaded truck, several people who live nearby came over to help me carry in heavy furniture and boxes. Later that evening, when I was exhausted from hours of hard labor, another neighbor brought me a hot, homemade meal.

[4] Yet another reason to love Whispering Lake is its close proximity to schools, restaurants, stores, and the park.

[5] The elementary school is within walking distance, and the middle school is within bike-riding distance. A large shopping center only 0.8 miles from the neighborhood contains a grocery store, a Chinese restaurant, an Italian restaurant, and several specialty shops.

⁶ Whispering Lake is also a great place to live because of its natural beauty.

⁷ Huge, beautiful trees shade the sidewalks that meander through the neighborhood streets. Many residents are gardeners who fill their yards with flowers that we all enjoy. And of course, there is Whispering Lake itself, a sparkling body of water ringed with a wide walking trail.

⁸ If you're still not convinced, you need to visit the neighborhood and take a look at the pretty houses in a variety of different architectural styles.

⁹ The streets are lined with stately brick homes with white columns; farmhouses with long, inviting porches; and homes in the Victorian style, with bright colors and gingerbread trim.

¹⁰ Because our neighborhood is so lovely and pleasant to live in, citizens who completed a recent survey ranked it one of the top five most popular neighborhoods in our town.

Exercise 5.11

A. On your own paper, fill in the missing information in the first sentence by adding a specific class you are taking now or completed in the past. Then, for each numbered box, write a sentence to explain the sentence that comes before it.

My _____**1**_____ class has been a valuable experience for me.

First of all, I have learned a lot of useful and interesting information.

2

In addition, completing the assignments for the course has helped me develop some important skills.

3

Finally, I have met an interesting person.

4

B. On your own paper, fill in the missing information for the first sentence by adding the name and relationship of one of your relatives. Then, for each numbered box, write a sentence to explain the sentence that comes before it.

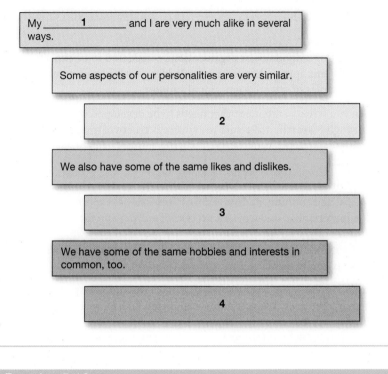

My _____**1**_____ and I are very much alike in several ways.

Some aspects of our personalities are very similar.

2

We also have some of the same likes and dislikes.

3

We have some of the same hobbies and interests in common, too.

4

Select one of the paragraphs in Exercise 5.11. Expand the paragraph with additional layers to write a complete, well-developed paragraph.

Information from Research

Some layers of development consist of information you discover through research, such as facts, statistics, quotations, and expert opinions. This information comes from other sources, such as magazine or newspaper articles, books, or websites. For example, in the following paragraph about helping an addict recover, sentences that could be developed with research are bold and numbered:

A person who is addicted to a substance or activity can conquer that addiction only by making a conscious choice to change and then committing to doing the hard work necessary to regain control of his or her life. However, a friend or relative can help get an addict on the road to recovery. **¹ First of all, the friend or relative must recognize the signs of addiction.** Then, the friend or relative must choose not to ignore those signs and accept the fact that an addiction has taken control of the person's life. **² The next step is to seek help and information from experts, either individuals or organizations that can provide good advice about how to handle the situation. ³ Armed with this knowledge, the friend or relative can select and use the best approach for bringing up the subject with the addict, getting him or her to acknowledge that a problem exists, and** recommending treatment. The final step is usually the most difficult because it can last for months or even years. ⁴ Providing ongoing emotional support, even during periods of relapse, will be necessary to help the addict as he or she recovers.

Here is a list of the information the writer should look for:

1. The signs of addiction
2. A list of individuals or organizations considered to be experts
3. Different approaches recommended by counselors or psychologists
4. Examples of effective emotional support

When you write a statement that needs to be developed with information you obtain through research, make sure the source is trustworthy so that the information is more likely to be accurate. Trustworthy sources usually have the following characteristics:

- The author is a respected expert with credentials such as college degrees, specialized training, and/or years of professional experience.
- The material has undergone a process of editing and fact-checking.
- Sources of the author's information are provided.
- The information does not significantly contradict any other reputable sources you've seen.

Many print sources—such as established magazines and newspapers—possess all of these characteristics. Websites, however, often lack many of these characteristics, so they are not always reputable sources of information.

When you include information from another source, always identify your source. Sometimes, you can do this informally by simply mentioning the source of the material in your sentence. For example, you might write, "According to the *Psychology Today* website, one symptom of addiction is the inability to limit use of a substance or participation in an activity even when significant impairment is occurring."

For many of the academic and professional documents you will write, however, you will need to **document**, or formally acknowledge, each of the sources you used according to specific guidelines. The two most common documentation systems are Modern Language Association (MLA) style and American Psychological Association (APA) style. Both of these systems are explained and illustrated in the Purdue Online Writing Lab website.

▌ Exercise 5.13

For each bold, numbered sentence, write the information you would look for to develop the idea in that statement.

Our state legislators should ban smoking in any vehicle in which one or more of the passengers is a child. One reason to outlaw smoking in cars is to reduce one of the main causes of vehicle-related injuries and deaths. ¹ Studies show that distracted drivers are a major cause of accidents. ² Evidence indicates that drivers who are fumbling around for and lighting cigarettes are more likely to be distracted, take their attention off the road, and run stop signs, run red lights, and hit other motorists or objects. Banning smoking while driving will eliminate accidents that harm young passengers. More importantly, though, drivers should not be allowed to expose children to secondhand smoke in a vehicle. [3] Research shows that the concentration of pollutants in secondhand smoke is much higher in the enclosed space of a vehicle than in a more open space. [4] While these toxins are dangerous to anyone who breathes them in, they are especially dangerous to children. [5] Children are far more sensitive to air pollution than adults are; consequently, they are more likely to suffer health damage when exposed to secondhand smoke. Because children cannot refuse to ride in the vehicle or remove themselves from the source of the smoke, the government should step in to protect them from this serious risk to their health.

Transition Words and Phrases

Effective writing includes clue words and phrases called **transitions**, which help the reader understand the relationships between sentences. Transitions such as *for example* and *for instance* usually indicate that the information to follow will further develop or explain the sentence that came before. Transitions such as *also, in addition, too, first/second/third, but,* and *however* usually indicate that the information will be as general as that in the preceding sentence rather than more specific. The following list contains some common transition words:

COMMON TRANSITION WORDS

above	consequently	later	then
after	conversely	like	therefore
also	during	likewise	third
although	finally	meanwhile	thus
another example, way, type, part, etc.	first	most importantly	to illustrate
	for example	next	to the left
	for instance	next to	to the right
as a result	furthermore	on the contrary	too
a second example, way, type, part, etc.	however	on the other hand	under
	inside	on top of	unlike
	in addition	one example, way, type, part, etc.	whereas
because	in back of		while
before	in contrast	outside	yet
below	in front of	over	
beneath	in like manner	similarly	
but	last	so	

Exercise 5.14

A. List all of the transition words that appear in the paragraph on the neighborhood on pages 95–96.

B. List all of the transition words that appear in the paragraph about helping an addict on pages 97–98.

Rewriting for Complete Paragraphs

A paragraph that lacks layers of development will not be effective. Because it does not provide enough specific information, it will leave readers wondering what the writer really means. For example, examine the following paragraph from a textbook:

> I have polled thousands of college instructors, and they consistently identify three behaviors that their most successful students demonstrate. Consider, then, these three rules as the foundation of your personal code of conduct. Rule 1 is to show up and commit to attending every class from beginning to end. Rule 2 is to commit to doing your best work on all assignments. Rule 3 is to participate actively. Commit to getting involved. College, like life, isn't a spectator sport.

Notice how the green parts raise questions they don't answer or are not explained or illustrated. Layers of development should be included to provide more information. Although you have some idea of the writer's meaning, his points become much clearer with the addition of layers of development in blue:

> I have polled thousands of college instructors, and they consistently identify three behaviors that their most successful students demonstrate. Consider, then, these three rules as the foundation of your personal code of conduct. Rule 1 is to show up and commit to attending every class from beginning to end. **Studies show a direct connection between attendance and grades. At Baltimore City Community College, a study found that, on average, the more classes students missed, the lower their grades were, especially in introductory courses. A study by a business professor at Arizona State University showed that, on average, his students' grades went down one full grade for every two classes they missed.** Rule 2 is to commit to doing your best work on all assignments. **Doing your best work means putting the time and effort into doing them correctly, making them look neat and professional, and always turning them in on time.** Rule 3 is to participate actively. Commit to getting involved. **Come to class prepared. Listen attentively. Take notes. Think deeply about what's being said. Ask yourself how you can apply your course work to achieve your goals and dreams. Read ahead. Start a study group. Ask questions.** College, like life, isn't a spectator sport.
>
> Adapted from Downing, Skip. *On Course*.
> Study Skills Plus Edition. Boston:
> Wadsworth, 2011. Print.

Here is another example of paragraph that lacks enough layers of development:

> One way you can improve the quality of your thinking is to recognize common errors in logic that interfere with sound reasoning. Most of these errors can be sorted into two categories: those that ignore issues and those that oversimplify issues. A logical error that ignores an issue distracts your attention from the argument as a whole. Errors that oversimplify issues resort to tactics such as drawing conclusions from insufficient evidence, reducing an issue to only two sides, using inaccurate comparisons, or insisting that one event caused another when the evidence is inadequate.

Notice how the green general or abstract parts are not explained or illustrated. Layers of development should be included to provide more information. Examples, in particular, would be especially helpful. Because readers don't get this information, they still don't know much more about errors in logic than they did before they read the paragraph. Notice how this same paragraph makes a lot more sense after the addition of just two examples (in bold print):

> One way you can improve the quality of your thinking is to recognize common errors in logic that interfere with sound reasoning. Most of these errors can be sorted into two categories: those that ignore issues and those that oversimplify issues. A logical error that ignores an issue distracts your attention from the argument as a whole. **For example, a student who earns a poor grade on an assignment says, "I can't make a decent grade in this course because the instructor doesn't like me." This argument keeps the student from facing the real issue: What was wrong with the assignment? What did the student do, or not do, that resulted in a poor grade?** Errors that oversimplify issues resort to tactics such as drawing conclusions from insufficient evidence, reducing an issue to only two sides, using inaccurate comparisons, or insisting that one event caused another when the evidence is inadequate. **For instance, a student misses several assignments in an algebra class and receives a midterm warning. The student says, "Either I do my algebra homework or my essays for the writing class, but I can't do both." Actually, the student can do both, as many students do. By acknowledging only two alternatives, the student engages in false reasoning and limits the possibilities for success.**
>
> Adapted from Kanar, Carol. *The Confident Student,*
> 7th ed. Boston: Wadsworth, 2010. Print.

To ensure that you are including sufficient layers of development in your own writing, try the following techniques:

1. **After you compose your first draft, you may want to separate and indent your sentences** (like the example on pages 95–96) so that you can clearly see how many layers of development you've included. Once you rearrange a paragraph, check to see if a sentence that is *not* followed by a layer of development contains any general or abstract ideas that need further explanation or illustration.
2. **Count the sentences in your paragraph.** Although there is no magic maximum or minimum number, your paragraphs are probably not adequately developed if they contain only four or five sentences each.
3. **Scan your drafts for the phrase *for example*.** This phrase often begins sentences that really help your reader grasp your ideas. If you never begin sentences this way, you may not be including the information in the form of specific instances or anecdotes that your reader will need in order to understand you.
4. **Consider using the checklist on page 102 to guide you in looking at specific features.**

CHECKLIST FOR COMPLETE PARAGRAPHS

Use this checklist during the rewriting step to make sure that you are answering all of your readers' questions and including sufficient layers of development.

☐ The information in the composition is appropriate for the intended readers' characteristics, their level of prior knowledge, and their needs.

☐ Layers of development explain or illustrate general or abstract sentences.

☐ Various details—such as facts, data, statistics, examples, and anecdotes—are included to explain general or abstract ideas.

☐ When appropriate, information obtained from other sources is included, and the sources are properly identified.

☐ Transition words and phrases help readers understand the relationship between the sentences.

Exercise 5.15

Select three paragraphs from reports or essays you've written. Rewrite each paragraph to show the layers of development. Are there sufficient layers of development?

Exercise 5.16

A. Use the checklist above to evaluate a paragraph you have recently written. If you revised this paragraph, what would you change to improve its development?

B. Use the checklist to evaluate a classmate's paragraph. What improvements would you recommend?

SUGGESTED WRITING ACTIVITIES

Complete all of the steps of the writing process as you write one or more of the following compositions. As you write, concentrate on anticipating and answering the reader's questions. As you revise, check for adequate layers of development.

ACADEMIC WRITING

1. Convince a fellow student to stop cheating on tests or plagiarizing.
2. Write an autobiography that you would include in your application to a college or university.
3. Compare two different career options that you have considered pursuing upon completion of your education.

PROFESSIONAL WRITING

4. Write to your supervisor to request one or more days off from work to prepare for an exam or to attend a specific event related to one of your classes.
5. Write to your co-workers to explain how you changed a process or a procedure to make it more efficient.
6. List and explain three qualities or skills that are required to do your job well.

PERSONAL WRITING

7. Persuade someone to
   - join a charitable or civic organization to which you belong.
   - participate in an upcoming event or activity (such as a fundraiser or an event like the Special Olympics).
   - donate money to an organization you support. (Explain how the organization's activities are beneficial, but also include additional reasons the group is worthy of support.)
8. Report on the activities of a civic organization or club in your city or town. What is this group doing to benefit your community?
9. Choose a hobby or sport in which you participate, and then do one of the following:
   - Explain the benefits of engaging in this activity.
   - Explain the materials or equipment a person would need to begin participating in this activity.

CHAPTER 6

Essential #6:
Coherent Paragraphs

In addition to being complete, effective paragraphs must also be coherent. *Coherent* means that the paragraph makes sense because its sentences are orderly and logically connected. In other words, the reader can easily follow the writer's ideas from one sentence to the next.

Coherence in a paragraph can be achieved by using methods of development to explain and support ideas and by using transitions to help the reader understand the relationships between sentences.

Methods of Development and Transitions

Chapter 5 discussed layers of development, which are the facts, data, statistics, details, examples, and anecdotes that a writer uses to explain and develop general ideas, abstract concepts, or opinions. This chapter covers some common patterns for arranging these layers to achieve coherence. These patterns, called **methods of development**, are familiar to readers, so they're effective for organizing and explaining ideas.

The next sections provide examples of some of the most common development methods: narration, description, illustration, process, comparison, cause and effect, division, classification, and argument. The explanation of each method includes a diagram of its main components. Think of each diagram as a kind of simple map. Have you ever sketched out a map, like the one on page 105, to show someone how to get from one place to another? You probably used lines, squares, rectangles, and other shapes to represent streets, buildings, and other landmarks. Likewise, the diagram for each method of development is like a map that uses lines, boxes, and arrows to show you a basic pattern for arranging the details in your paragraph.

The next sections also list transition words and phrases that are commonly used with each method of development. In Chapter 5, you learned that effective writing includes clue words and phrases called **transitions**, which help the reader understand the relationships between sentences. These words and phrases show

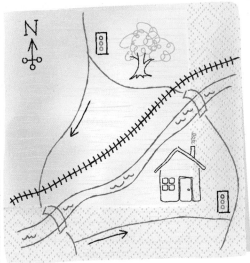

Like a map, a method of development can give you a pattern for arranging your paragraph's details.

how the new sentence relates to what came before. You can think of them like hooks that connect things, like those used with train cars. Along with clear methods of development, they provide coherence to paragraphs. In the following sections of this chapter, you'll learn how to use these words and phrases in your own paragraphs to help the reader follow your ideas.

Transitions are like hooks that connect a sentence to what came before it.

Narration

One way to develop an idea stated in a paragraph's topic sentence is to tell a brief story to explain or illustrate that idea. The events in the story are presented in chronological order, or the order in which they happened.

TOPIC SENTENCE

Event #1

Event #2

Event #3

Typical transition words and phrases indicate when the events in the story took place.

SOME TRANSITION WORDS AND PHRASES FOR NARRATION		
before	then	next
during	meanwhile	while
after	later	last
on Monday	as	at 2:00 o'clock

For instance, the following paragraph tells a story to explain the main idea, which is underlined. Transition words and phrases are highlighted in blue.

> **Last month**, I landed an interview for my dream job: assistant manager at a popular restaurant just three miles from my home. I was well qualified for the position, and I really wanted to be hired. Unfortunately, though, a series of interview mistakes cost me the job. My **first** mistake was not properly preparing. I had three days to get ready, and I had planned to rehearse my answers to common interview questions, but I kept procrastinating. **The night before the interview**, when I should have stayed home to practice, I accepted an invitation to go out with my friends. I told myself that I'd have some time to rehearse the next morning, right before my interview, but **then** I overslept. Rushing to get dressed, I discovered that the professional-looking blazer I usually wear to interviews had a stain on the front, so I had to scramble to find a different outfit. The dress I **finally** threw on was wrinkled and a little too tight. **By the time I arrived for my interview five minutes late**, I felt nervous and stressed, so I did not seem confident or competent. I stumbled through my answers to the restaurant manager's questions **while** tugging at my ill-fitting dress. I could see the doubt on the manager's face about my ability to handle the pressures of the job. Not surprisingly, she did not hire me.

Here's another example of narration used to develop the topic sentence:

> The ancient Greek storyteller Aesop wrote many fables, short stories that teach a lesson. One of them, "The Crow and the Pitcher," reminds us that "little by little gets the job done." **At the beginning of this story**, a crow is dying of thirst and searching for water. The bird finds a pitcher and sticks his beak into the pitcher's mouth. He can see some water left in the bottom of the container; however, he cannot reach it. In despair, he is about to give up, but **then** he gets an idea. He finds a pebble and drops it into the pitcher. He finds another pebble and drops it into the pitcher. Again and again, he drops pebble after pebble into the container. **As the crow continues his hard work**, the water slowly begins to rise closer and closer to the opening. **Finally**, it reaches the mouth, and the bird is able to drink. This story teaches us that important achievements often take time, effort, and perseverance.

TIP

More examples of narrative passages appear on pages 63 and 80.

More examples of narrative passages appear on pages 63 and 80.

Exercise 6.1

Read the paragraph below and then answer the questions that follow. Write your answers on your own paper.

Do you let anxiety about a test overwhelm you to the point that your mind goes blank and you perform poorly? Before a competition, many athletes use visualization to picture a positive outcome, and this technique works for students, too. The scenario you can mentally rehearse goes something like this: *On the day of the exam, I walk in fully prepared. I have attended all of my classes on time, I have done my very best work on all of my assignments, and I have studied effectively. Feeling confident, I first find a comfortable seat and take a few moments to breathe deeply, relax, and focus myself. Then, I concentrate on the subject matter of this test. I release all my other cares and worries. When the instructor walks into the room and begins handing out the exams, I feel excited about the opportunity to show how much I have learned. Next, I glance over the test and see questions that my study group and I have prepared for all semester. Alert and aware, I begin to write. As I work, I know the answers to all of the questions. After finishing, I check my answers thoroughly. I hand in the exam with a comfortable amount of time remaining. As I leave the room, I feel a pleasant weariness, and I am confident that I have done my very best.* Visualization exercises like this one not only improve your ability to take the test but also reduce associated fears.

Downing, Skip. On Course. Study Skills Edition.
Boston: Wadsworth, 2011. Print.

1. What is the paragraph's topic sentence?
2. List the major events in the narrative.
3. What transition words and phrases are used to indicate narration?

Choose one of the following topics and write a topic sentence and organization plan (outline or diagram) for a paragraph that uses the narration method of development.

1. How I broke a bad habit
2. How I improved a particular skill or ability
3. An accident I witnessed

Description

Sometimes, an idea needs to be explained with descriptive details. These details might include size, weight, dimensions, color, materials of construction, or the locations of different parts.

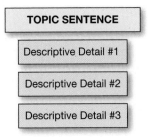

Typical transition words and phrases for description indicate the locations of things being described.

SOME TRANSITION WORDS AND PHRASES FOR DESCRIPTION			
above	under	beneath	over
below	on top of	inside	outside
to the left	in front of	in back of	next to
to the right			

The following paragraph uses description to explain the perfect job-interview outfit. The topic sentence is underlined, and the transitions are highlighted in blue:

> For women who are dressing for a job interview, the words *conservative* and *covered* should describe all aspects of their appearance. **Beginning with the head**, hair should be neatly arranged or pulled back, not falling over the face or constantly needing to be brushed away. **For the face**, makeup should be in subdued colors (such as grays and browns for eye shadow and soft pink or coral for lipstick). Avoid bright, distracting colors such as blue, green, and bright red. Earrings should be small and tasteful; small hoops or pearls, for example, are a good choice. Flashy or otherwise distracting necklaces should be avoided. **For the body**, the best clothing choice is a blouse worn under a gray, navy, or black suit or a blazer paired with pants or a skirt. **On the arms and hands**, bracelets should be avoided altogether, and rings should be limited to one or two. Shirts should not be so low cut that they reveal cleavage, and skirts should be knee-length so that they don't expose too much leg. **For the feet**, shoes should not reveal toes or have heels so high that balancing and walking are difficult.

Another example of a descriptive paragraph provides readers with information about the elements of a courtroom:

> The locations of the elements in a U.S. courtroom vary slightly, but the basic layout always includes seating areas for the trial's specific participants. The judge is seated on an elevated bench **at one end of the room**, with a seat for the law clerk **on one side of the bench** and a seat for the witnesses who will give testimony **on the other side**. A court reporter's desk is usually **right in front of the judge's bench**. The jury box, where the jurors who will decide the case are seated, is **on the right or left side of the room**. **In the middle of the room** are two tables: one for the defendant and his or her attorney, and the other for the prosecuting attorneys. **Behind them**, a bar divides all of the trial participants from the spectators, who sit in an area called the gallery.

> Information from "Courtroom Staff." U.S. Department of Justice. Web. 1 Feb. 2012.

TIP

Another example of a descriptive paragraph appears on pages 69–70.

Exercise 6.3

Read the paragraph below and then answer the questions that follow. Write your answers on your own paper.

> At a formal dinner, the place setting at your table will include a number of different plates, utensils, and glasses, each of which has a different purpose. In the middle of the place setting is a large plate on which other plates will be placed. A napkin will be set on top of this plate. To the left of the plate will be up to three forks in this order from left to right: fish fork, dinner fork, and salad fork. Above the forks will be

a small butter plate with a butter knife on top of it. To the right of the plate will be a series of additional utensils, which appear in this order from left to right if any of these foods is being served: salad knife, dinner knife, fish knife, soup or fruit spoon, and oyster fork. Above the knives will be up to five glasses, including a water goblet, champagne flute, red wine glass, white wine glass, and sherry glass.

Information from "Formal Place Setting."
The Emily Post Institute. Web. 3 Mar. 2012.

> **TIP**
>
> The drawing prewriting technique, which is explained on page xxv of this book's Introduction, is useful for generating ideas for descriptions.

1. What is the paragraph's topic sentence?
2. Draw a picture that shows the placement of the items in a formal place setting.
3. What transition words and phrases are used to indicate the locations of the items?

Exercise 6.4

Choose one of the following topics and write a topic sentence and organization plan (outline or diagram) for a paragraph that uses the description method of development.

1. Something (an animal, a vegetable, a costume, a craft or an artwork) that won an award
2. Someone who is dressed to do a particular job
3. A place that surprises, delights, or frightens (for example, a beautiful garden, a museum display, or a hospital room)

Illustration

Some topic sentences are best developed by presenting one or more specific examples to illustrate the main point.

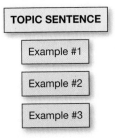

Typical transition words and phrases for illustration indicate that examples will follow.

SOME TRANSITION WORDS AND PHRASES FOR ILLUSTRATION	
for example	to illustrate
for instance	one example
another method	a second way

The following paragraph shows how a topic sentence (underlined) can be developed with specific examples. Transition words and phrases are highlighted in blue.

> <u>In classrooms, in job interviews, and during conversations with your supervisor, be aware that you can use body language to communicate your interest, attention, and respect.</u> **One example** is posture. Standing up straight while directly facing someone and sitting up straight while leaning slightly forward indicate that you are listening and interested. **Another way** of communicating your attention is making eye contact with the other person. **A third example** of attentive body language is using facial expressions and head movements to communicate your reactions to what the other person is saying. By smiling, frowning, widening your eyes, raising an eyebrow, or nodding or shaking your head to express different emotions, you are showing the speaker that you are listening and silently reacting to his or her message. Interestingly, this body language communicates these attitudes not only to the people with whom you interact but also to *yourself*. How you sit, stand, and move also signals to your own brain that you intend to pay attention and participate in the exchange.

Here is another paragraph that uses illustration to develop the topic sentence:

> Like most Americans, you probably think of George Washington, who led the American colonies to victory over Britain in the Revolutionary War, as a great man. And he was, but he didn't start out that way. <u>In fact, George Washington made quite a few serious mistakes in his early military career.</u> **For example**, when serving as a 22-year-old lieutenant colonel at the beginning of the French and Indian War in 1754, he ordered the British troops he commanded to build a fort in a meadow on low ground. When French and Indian forces surrounded the fort, they were able to fire down into the fort from the high ground they occupied, killing or wounding several of Washington's men. He was forced to surrender and then was demoted for his bad decisions. **Another example** occurred in 1758, when he was involved in an embarrassing "friendly fire" incident. The men in his unit, thinking they were firing on the French enemy, killed or wounded dozens of their own troops in another unit. Even by 1776, when Washington was an experienced military leader 44 years old, the mistakes that he and his generals made led to defeat in a series of battles, resulting in the loss of New York City to the British. Yet, these failures did not prevent Washington from going on to become an American hero. So, the next time you make a mistake, do as George Washington did—learn from it and overcome it.

Exercise 6.5

Read the paragraph below and then answer the questions that follow. Write your answers on your own paper.

> College students already know that mobile devices such as iPhones and iPads are useful for communicating and for surfing the Internet. They should also be aware of several iPhone and iPad apps that can help them achieve academic success. For example, several apps—such as dictionaries and encyclopedias—are

reference tools that can be handy sources of information when reading textbooks or writing papers. Another example is a voice-recorder app, such as iTalk and Voxie Pro, which will allow students to record class lectures or their study notes. Several additional apps, such as Google Docs, MindNode, and gFlash, provide tools for creating documents, mind maps or brainstorms, and flashcards that can then be shared with fellow students or study group members. Other apps, such as iStudiez Pro and Study Tracker Pro, are for keeping track of assignments and grades. Finally, a number of different apps can help students review and study subjects ranging from French to anatomy to history to astronomy. With these powerful and portable tools in the palms of their hands, students will find it easier to achieve their academic goals.

1. What is the paragraph's topic sentence?
2. How many examples does the writer present? What are they?
3. What transition words and phrases are used to indicate illustration?

Exercise 6.6

Choose one of the following topics and write a topic sentence and organization plan (outline or diagram) for a paragraph that uses the illustration method of development.

1. A specific quality of all effective teachers
2. Celebrities (athletes, musicians, or actors) who are good role models for children
3. Television commercials

Process

The **process** method of development includes an explanation of the steps or stages in a process or procedure. Process is a useful pattern when you need to explain to readers how something is done or how something works. For example, you would use process to explain how bees make honey or how an airport control tower works. Process is also used to give readers how-to instructions for completing a task, such as baking a cake or building a campfire.

Typical transition words and phrases for the process method of development indicate when each step or stage occurs.

SOME TRANSITION WORDS AND PHRASES FOR PROCESS		
first	next	finally
second	then	last
third	after	before

The following paragraph uses the process pattern to explain how to lift a heavy object properly. The topic sentence is underlined, and the transition words are highlighted in blue.

Many back injuries occur when people are trying to pick up something heavy. <u>To protect yourself from injury, follow the correct procedure for lifting a heavy object.</u> **First**, stand close to the object you need to lift, with your feet spread apart about shoulder width, and one foot slightly in front of the other for balance. **Then**, bend at the knees, not at the waist, and squat down. Keeping your back straight and vertical, tuck in your chin and firmly grasp the object. **Finally**, slowly straighten your legs, pushing yourself straight up without twisting your body. **As** you stand, keep the object close to your body to reduce strain on your lower back.

The next paragraph uses the process pattern to explain how jury duty works.

<u>The selection and service of juries for courtroom trials is accomplished in a process established by the Jury Selection and Service Act of 1968.</u> **In the first step of the process**, potential jurors are chosen from a jury pool generated by random selection of citizens' names from lists of registered voters, or combined lists of voters and people with driver's licenses, in the judicial district. **Next**, the potential jurors complete questionnaires to help determine whether they are qualified to serve on a jury. **After** reviewing the questionnaires, the court randomly selects individuals to be summoned to appear for jury duty. Being summoned does not guarantee that an individual actually will serve on a jury. **When** a jury is needed for a trial, the group of qualified jurors is taken to the courtroom where the trial will take place. The judge and the attorneys **then** ask the potential jurors questions to determine their suitability to serve on the jury and exclude anyone who may not be able to decide the case fairly. Those who are selected to serve get specific instructions about how to consider the evidence and conduct themselves during the trial. They listen to the information presented by the attorneys and **then** deliberate with the other jurors to reach a fair verdict.

Adapted from "Jury Service." United States Courts.
Web. 23 Mar. 2012.

TIP

Another example of a process paragraph appears on page 16, in Figure 2.1.

Exercise 6.7

Read the paragraph below and then answer the questions that follow. Write your answers on your own paper.

Do you struggle to concentrate when an instructor is lecturing in class or while reading and studying? If you do, you're not alone. Many students have trouble ignoring distractions and focusing their attention. However, you can improve your ability to focus and concentrate by using a technique to prevent and control common distractions. First, make a conscious, intentional decision to focus your attention on the lecture or the task you need to complete. At this point, you might want to make a deal with yourself. Say something like, "I'll think about my boyfriend later. Right now, I'm going to focus on the information this instructor is presenting." Next, clear away things (such as your cell phone) that you know will draw your attention. Turn off or put those things out of sight. Then, take a few minutes to give your full and undivided attention to thoughts (such as friends, future plans, or problems) that are likely to intrude as you try to concentrate. Consider freewriting about them for 5 to 15 minutes as a way of clearing them from your mind. When the class begins or you start your reading or study session, sit up straight so that your body will signal to your mind that it's time to pay attention. Force yourself to ignore noises and movements around you by not turning to look at them. Any time you find your mind wandering, self-correct by consciously re-focusing your attention. Finally, don't expect to achieve perfect concentration right away; like any skill, the ability to focus takes time and patience to develop. Practice all of these steps, and your powers of concentration will improve.

1. What is the paragraph's topic sentence?
2. How many steps are in the process the writer explains? What are they?
3. What transition words and phrases are used to indicate the steps in the process?

Exercise 6.8

Choose one of the following topics and write a topic sentence and organization plan (outline or diagram) for a paragraph that uses the process method of development.

1. How to perform a procedure you do at work
2. How to begin using Facebook, Twitter, or another social media website
3. How a(n) _____ works

Comparison

Sometimes, a writer needs to develop an idea by showing how two or more subjects are alike or different. **Comparison** involves examining the similarities and/or the differences between two subjects. A paragraph might do one or the other or both to explain a point to the reader.

As the diagrams on page 114 show, there are two ways to arrange the points of comparison you have chosen to include. You can present each point and explain how it applies to first one subject and then the other. Or, you can present all of the points as they apply to the first subject, and then discuss all of the points as they apply to the second subject.

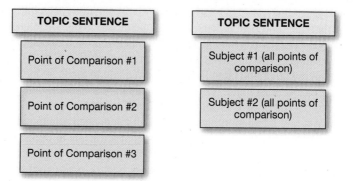

One set of typical transition words and phrases indicates similarities. Another set indicates differences.

SOME TRANSITION WORDS AND PHRASES THAT SHOW SIMILARITIES	
similarly	in like manner
like	likewise
too	also

SOME TRANSITION WORDS AND PHRASES THAT SHOW DIFFERENCES	
however	conversely
on the other hand	in contrast
but	yet
whereas	although
on the contrary	unlike

The following paragraph is an example of a comparison paragraph that is organized by the points of comparison to show the similarities between the two subjects. The topic sentence is underlined, and the transition words and phrases are highlighted in blue.

Some prescription drug manufacturers claim that the brand-name drugs they produce are better than the generic versions of those drugs. <u>The truth is that brand-name and generic drugs are exactly the same except for their cost.</u> **Both** brand-name and generic drugs are regulated by the U.S. Food and Drug Administration, which uses the exact same standards for brand-name and generic companies' manufacturing facilities. The quality, purity, and content of the two versions of prescription drugs are the same. The generic drug delivers the same amount of active ingredient in the same time frame as the original product. Generics are as potent as name-brand drugs. Their therapeutic effects are the same, and their side effects are the same. **The only difference between the two** is generic drugs cost a fraction of what brand-name drugs cost. So, the next time your pharmacist offers you a generic version of a drug, you can select that option with confidence.

Adapted from "Myths and Facts about Generic Drugs."
Public Citizen's Health Research Group. Web. 12 Feb. 2012.

The next example illustrates the pattern in which all points as they apply to the first subject are presented first, and then all points as they apply to the second subject are presented second. The topic sentence is underlined, and the transition words and phrases are highlighted in blue.

Effective reading requires knowing the difference between facts and opinions. You can think of a fact as an object, as in *objective*. *Objective* means not influenced by personal judgments or feelings. Facts exist externally. They are physical, observable things (like any object in the physical world). They exist separately from you and outside of you. They are independent of you. They can be verified—you can check to see if they are true. No matter what you do, believe, or feel, facts will still be facts. Consider an opinion, **on the other hand**, as having to do with a subject, as in *subjective*. *Subjective* means based on or influenced by personal beliefs, feelings, or tastes. Opinions are internal. They exist inside you (or me or someone else). They depend upon the person who holds the opinion. **Unlike** facts, opinions can't be verified by looking in dictionaries, encyclopedias, or newspapers. Because opinions are personal, they may be held by only one person, several people, or many people.

Adapted from Dole, Ivan, and Leslie Taggart.
Engage College Reading. Boston: Wadsworth, 2013. Print.

This paragraph explains all of the characteristics of facts first, and then it explains all of the characteristics of opinions.

Exercise 6.9

Read the paragraph below and then answer the questions that follow. Write your answers on your own paper.

Both charter schools and public schools are funded with state taxpayer dollars, so students do not pay to attend either one. Both types of schools are held accountable and have to show that their students are learning and making academic progress. However, charter schools and public schools differ in several key ways. Students who attend public schools are assigned to a specific school based on where they live. In contrast, students must apply to attend charter schools, which may or may not be near their homes, and acceptance to a school depends upon available space. Also unlike public schools, charter schools have greater flexibility in the way the schools are run. They often have a "theme," such as a special focus on math and science or on the arts, or they may emphasize certain types of instructional methods, such as project-based learning or online learning. Charter schools are free from many of the rules and regulations that affect public schools, so they can focus their attention and their resources on achieving academic excellence.

1. What is the paragraph's topic sentence?
2. How many points of comparison are there? What are they?
3. What transition words and phrases are used to indicate similarities and differences?

Exercise 6.10

Choose one of the following topics and write a topic sentence and organization plan (outline or diagram) for a paragraph that uses the comparison method of development.

1. A difference between men and women
2. Two brands of a product you want or need to buy
3. Two candidates for public office

Cause and Effect

Another way to develop ideas is to give the reasons why something occurred (examining **causes**) or to explain the consequences of something (exploring **effects**). The following diagrams indicate different patterns that may apply, depending upon the topic. The first diagram should be used for a topic in which the causes are separate and unrelated. The second diagram applies to a topic in which the effects are separate and unrelated. The third diagram indicates a chain reaction of events in which one thing led to another.

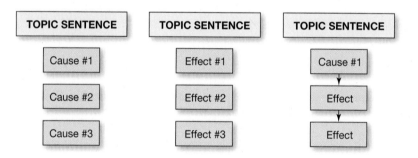

Typical transition words and phrases for cause and effect indicate causes or results.

SOME TRANSITION WORDS AND PHRASES FOR CAUSE AND EFFECT	
thus	as a result
one effect	so
therefore	another cause
because	consequently

The following paragraph explores the causes of the decision to drive drunk. The topic sentence is underlined, and the transition words and phrases are highlighted in blue.

With all of the news coverage of the damage caused by people who drive drunk, why do so many people continue to get behind the wheel of a vehicle when they're intoxicated? The decision to drive drunk has several major causes. **The main cause** is alcohol's effect on good judgment. When people become drunk, they believe that they are still capable of making good decisions and behaving responsibly, even when they aren't. **Therefore,** they make the choice to drive because they still believe they can handle it. **Another cause** of drunk driving is lack of awareness of the effects of alcohol. Some people think that they can have several beers or alcoholic beverages without becoming intoxicated. They may not feel as though they are legally drunk, but they are. **One last cause** is the hope of not getting caught. Some people know they shouldn't drive but do it anyway because they mistakenly believe that they have a slim chance of being stopped by the police.

This next example shows a chain-reaction relationship. Notice how there are no transition words and phrases, but several of the verbs in the sentences, which are highlighted in blue, indicate cause-and-effect relationships. The paragraph's topic sentence is underlined.

<u>Studies show that prolonged stress may damage memory</u>. When experiencing severe, chronic stress—for example, a chaotic work environment, an overload of responsibilities, or the death or illness of a loved one—the brain releases a hormone called cortisol. Cortisol **triggers** the body's fight-or-flight response, which **increases** the heart rate and **causes** adrenaline to pump throughout the body. Too much cortisol **seems to interfere** with cells in the hippocampus, the part of the brain responsible for practical, everyday memory. When the cells of the hippocampus are damaged, an individual has more difficulty recalling even basic information, like a friend's telephone number. Not surprisingly, people who do not handle stress well seem to be more likely to show significant memory loss with age.

TIP

Another example of a cause-and-effect paragraph appears on pages 90–91.

Flemming, Laraine. *Reading Keys*, 2nd ed.
Boston: Wadsworth, 2006. Print.

Exercise 6.11

Read the paragraph below and then answer the questions that follow. Write your answers on your own paper.

One of the most striking effects of using the drug methamphetamine, or meth, is the change in the physical appearance of meth users. Because meth causes the blood vessels to constrict, it cuts off the steady flow of blood to all parts of the body. Heavy usage can weaken and destroy these vessels, causing tissues to become prone to damage and inhibiting the body's ability to repair itself. Acne appears, sores take longer to heal, and the skin loses its luster and elasticity. Some users are covered in small sores, the result of obsessive skin-picking brought on by the hallucination of having bugs crawling beneath the skin, a disorder known as *formication*. In addition, stimulants such as meth cause tremendous bursts of physical activity while suppressing the appetite, an attractive combination for many people who began using meth to lose weight. But while contemporary culture may idealize slim figures, heavy meth users often become gaunt and frail. Their day- or week-long meth "runs" are usually accompanied by tooth-grinding, poor diet, and bad hygiene, which lead to mouths full of broken, stained, and rotting teeth. While a meth high makes users feel more confident, attractive, and desirable, the drug is actually working to make them unattractive.

From Frontline. "The Meth Epidemic,"
Frontline Website. Copyright © 1995–2012 WGBH
Educational Foundation. Reprinted with permission.

1. What is the paragraph's topic sentence?
2. Draw a diagram of the cause-and-effect relationships explained in this paragraph.
3. What are three words or phrases in the paragraph that indicate causes or effects?

Exercise 6.12

Choose one of the following topics and write a topic sentence and organization plan (outline or diagram) for a paragraph that uses the cause-and-effect method of development.

1. Reasons for your decision to enroll in college
2. An activity that benefits body, mind, and spirit
3. A natural or human-made process or problem that occurs in the form of a cycle

---

Division

Some ideas are best developed by explaining how something can be divided into smaller parts. Often, it's easier to understand a larger thing or concept by breaking it down into its components and examining each one in detail.

Typical transition words and phrases for division indicate the specific parts, areas, or sections of the thing or idea being divided.

SOME TRANSITION WORDS AND PHRASES FOR DIVISION	
one part	the second area
another section	the first portion

The following paragraph uses division to explain the cost of a gallon of gasoline. The topic sentence is underlined, and the transition phrases are highlighted in blue:

When you pump $30 of gasoline into your vehicle's tank, that money is divided up and distributed among several entities. **The biggest portion** of the cost of gas—about 65 cents of every dollar—goes to the crude-oil suppliers, the countries that get the oil out of the earth. **Another portion** of that dollar, about 14 cents, goes to companies that refine the crude oil, turning it into different types of fuel, including gasoline, kerosene, and heating oil. **The next portion**, about 8 cents of every dollar, goes to distribution and marketing. Fuel produced by the refineries has to be shipped to distribution points and then to gas stations. The price of transportation is passed along to the consumer. Taxes account for **a fourth part**, about 13 cents of every dollar. Federal and state governments each place excise taxes on gasoline, and there may also be some additional taxes, such as sales taxes and environmental fees. **The final portion**, a few cents of every dollar, goes to the service station that dispenses the gasoline to consumers.

Adapted from Bonsor, Kevin, and Ed Grabianowski.
"How Gas Prices Work." Howstuffworks.com 5 June 2006.
Web. 8 Mar. 2012.

The next example divides the American workforce into four generations:

For the first time in U.S. history, the American workforce is composed of four different generations. **The first group**, known as the "Silent Generation" or the "Traditionalists," includes those born from 1925 to 1945, who are now in their 60s, 70s, and 80s and mostly retired; however, some of them are still working part-time hours or are still serving in positions of high authority, such as government positions, chief executive officers, or law firm partners. **The next group**, the "Baby Boom" generation, includes the American citizens born after World War II between 1946 and 1964. Now in their 40s and 50s, many are well established in their careers and hold positions of power and authority. **A third group**, Generation X, was born between the mid-1960s and 1981. They are in their 30s and 40s and still climbing the career ladder. **The fourth group** is the Millennial Generation, also known as Generation Y. Born from 1982 to about the turn of the new millennium in 2000, the first Millennials are now in their 20s and just beginning to enter the workforce.

Information from Kersten, Denise.
"Today's Generations Face New Communication Gaps."
USA Today. 15 Nov. 2002. Web. 21 Feb. 2012.

Exercise 6.13

Read the paragraph below and answer the questions that follow. Write your answers on your own paper.

If you're reading and come across an unfamiliar word like *percutaneous*, a knowledge of word parts may help you decipher that word's meaning. A word can have up to three parts. All words have a root, which refers to the part of the word that conveys its basic meaning. For example, the root word *port* means "carry," the root words *nom* or *nym* mean "word," and the root word *bio* means "life." Some words have a second part, which is known as the prefix. A prefix is added to the beginning of a root word to change or modify its meaning. Examples include *ex-* ("out"), *re-* ("again"), *sub-* ("under"), and *un-* ("not"). The third part, the suffix, is added to the end of the word to indicate a certain part of speech. Some suffixes (such as *-able, -cy, -er, -or*) create nouns. Others create verbs (*-ate, -fy, -ize*), adjectives (*-able, -ible, -ive*), or adverbs (*-ly*). Break *percutaneous* into its three parts, and you could decode it by knowing that its prefix (*per-*) means "through," its root (*cutan*) means "skin," and its suffix (-*eous*) makes the word an adjective meaning "pertaining to." So, putting these parts together, *percutaneous* means "pertaining to something through the skin."

1. What is the paragraph's topic sentence?
2. How many parts does the paragraph explain, and what are they?
3. What two transition phrases does the author use to indicate the parts?

Exercise 6.14

Choose one of the following topics and write a topic sentence and organization plan (outline or diagram) for a paragraph that uses the division method of development.

1. Departments in the company you work for
2. Parts of a successful team
3. Parts of your day or your week

Classification

Classification places things in groups based upon qualities or characteristics they share. When we explain an idea with the classification method of development, we demonstrate how the subject can be thought of in terms of types or categories.

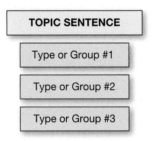

Typical transition words and phrases for classification indicate the different types, groups, or categories.

SOME TRANSITION WORDS AND PHRASES FOR CLASSIFICATION	
one type	a second group
another kind	the first category

This next paragraph uses classification to explain types of interview questions. The topic sentence is underlined, and the transition phrases are highlighted in blue.

<u>During a job interview, the interviewer will usually ask you two types of questions</u>. **One type** includes traditional questions that seek factual information about an applicant. This category includes questions such as *What makes you qualified for this position?* and

What computer programs can you use proficiently? **Another kind** of interview question includes the situational questions, which ask the applicant to describe various situations and circumstances he or she has encountered. The purpose of situational questions is to assess more complex skills such as decision-making skills, use of ethical reasoning, and problem-solving strategies. Questions such as *Tell me about a time when you had to accomplish a task with someone who was particularly difficult to get along with* and *Describe a situation in which you had to resolve a problem with no rules or guidelines in place* are situational questions. When preparing for an interview, applicants should practice answering both types of questions.

> Adapted from Solomon, Amy, et al. *100% Job Search Success*,
> 2nd ed. Boston: Wadsworth, 2012. Print.

Here's another example of a paragraph that uses classification:

Exercise can be classified into three types, depending on its effects on the body. **The first type** of exercise is aerobic exercise. It focuses on sustained movement of the body's large muscle groups, which increases the heart rate and improves cardiovascular fitness. Examples of aerobic exercise include jogging, running, dancing, and swimming. **The second type** of exercise is strength training. It focuses on building muscle power and endurance. Examples include weight lifting and working out using resistance machines. **The third type** of exercise is flexibility exercises, which increase the range of motion of muscles and joints. Flexibility exercises include stretching and yoga. An effective workout plan includes all three types of exercises.

> *TIP*
>
> Another example of a classification paragraph about types of financial aid appears on page 94.

Exercise 6.15

Read the paragraph below and then answer the questions that follow. Write your answers on your own paper.

Two kinds of skills that are essential to career success are hard skills and soft skills. The first type, *hard skills*, includes the skills that an employee must know to perform a specific job. For example, nurses need to know how to give an injection of medication, tax accountants need to know how to complete an accurate tax return, and engineers need to know how to use certain computer programs. These are the skills that students learn in the courses they take to complete their college degrees. The other type of skills is referred to as *soft skills*. A study commissioned by the U.S. government in the 1990s identified a list of soft skills that are necessary for career success. This list included taking responsibility, making effective decisions, setting goals, managing time, prioritizing tasks, persevering, giving strong efforts, working well in teams, communicating effectively, having empathy, knowing how to learn, exhibiting self-control, and believing in one's own self-worth. Workers who lack these skills will not only fail to advance in their careers but also risk losing their jobs.

1. What is the paragraph's topic sentence?
2. How many groups or categories does the paragraph explain, and what are they?
3. What two transition phrases does the author use to indicate the two categories?

▌ Exercise 6.16

Choose one of the following topics and write a topic sentence and organi-zation plan (outline or diagram) for a paragraph that uses the classifica-tion method of development.

1. Types of teachers or friends
2. Types of jobs
3. Types of goals

Argument

A final method of development involves explaining or presenting reasons to con-vince readers to accept the writer's opinion.

```
  ┌─────────────────┐
  │ TOPIC SENTENCE  │
  └─────────────────┘
        ┌─────────────┐
        │  Reason #1  │
        └─────────────┘
        ┌─────────────┐
        │  Reason #2  │
        └─────────────┘
        ┌─────────────┐
        │  Reason #3  │
        └─────────────┘
```

Typical transition words and phrases for argument are words that indicate the addition of another reason.

SOME TRANSITION WORDS AND PHRASES FOR ARGUMENT		
first	finally	furthermore
second	last	also
third	in addition	most important

The following paragraph uses argument to try to convince readers to change a behavior. The topic sentence is underlined, and the transition words and phrases are highlighted in blue.

If you've been in the habit of buying meat, produce, and other foods at your super-market, consider purchasing at least some of your foods at your local farmer's market instead. <u>Although they may cost a little more and require an extra stop on your shop-ping day, local foods will be worth the extra expense and inconvenience for three main reasons</u>. **The most important of these reasons** is taste. Because they don't have to be transported hundreds or even thousands of miles from the field to the supermarket, locally grown foods can spend more time developing naturally before they are harvested. Therefore, they are usually fresher and have more flavor and more nutritional value than supermarket foods. **Second**, buying locally grown foods supports your local economy. By buying food from local producers, your money will help support farmers and growers in your own community instead of those in other states or countries. **Finally**, buying and eating locally grown foods is good for the environment. Food grown near your home does not require as much energy to transport from field to table; consequently, buying local foods not only conserves natural resources but also contributes less to pollution that causes global warming.

This next paragraph, too, uses argument to convince the reader:

> According to the American Library Association, many states have had to cut funding to their public libraries due to reduced tax revenues. <u>People in those communities should do whatever is necessary to keep their local libraries open</u>. **First**, libraries are a great value. Libraries provide not only a vast array of print and audiovisual materials but also programs and services that patrons can use to expand their knowledge and skills and obtain hours of entertainment—all for free. **Second**, libraries offer resources that help people improve their communities by starting businesses, finding jobs, learning to speak English, and so on. **Third**, libraries play a key role in developing educated citizens who have the tools and information they need to maintain their freedom and their democratic government. By providing free and ready access to a wide range of ideas plus the latest news and information, libraries give their patrons the tools they need to make sound decisions.

> *TIP*
>
> Additional examples of paragraphs that present reasons appear on pages 20, 87–88, and 94.

Exercise 6.17

Read the paragraph below and then answer the questions that follow. Write your answers on your own paper.

> Don't ever drive a vehicle after you've been drinking. Most importantly, drunk driving will put your life and the lives of others in danger. Drivers who are impaired often lose control of their vehicles and cause accidents in which they, their passengers, and other motorists and their passengers are seriously hurt or killed. According to the Mothers Against Drunk Drivers (MADD) organization, this year, over 10,000 people will die in crashes caused by drunk drivers. If you mix alcohol and driving, you could be one of them. A second reason not to drive while intoxicated is to avoid the many penalties and punishments that await those who are caught. These penalties vary from state to state but can include suspension of your driver's license, expensive fines, seizure of your vehicle, criminal charges, jail time, and a steep increase in your auto insurance premiums. Finally, drinking and driving is a bad idea because being convicted of a drunk driving charge can rob you of opportunities for years or even the rest of your life. Many employers, for instance, will not hire you if you have a criminal record for driving drunk.

> Information from MADD.org.

1. What is the paragraph's topic sentence?
2. How many reasons are provided to convince readers? What are they?
3. What transition words and phrases are used to indicate each reason?

▌ Exercise 6.18

Choose one of the following topics and write a topic sentence and organization plan (outline or diagram) for a paragraph that uses the argument method of development.

1. A class that all students should take
2. An honor or award that someone you know should receive
3. A company or business (for example, a restaurant, an airline, or the circus) that should be boycotted

Prewriting for Methods of Development and Transitions

Writing coherent paragraphs begins in the prewriting stage of the writing process. After you've decided on the main idea you'll discuss in your paragraph, consider whether that main idea suggests a particular method (or methods) of development.

Choosing a Method

How do you know which method will best develop your idea? The topic sentence will often dictate which method you must use. Certain statements lead the reader to form an expectation about what will come next. For example, these topic sentences insist that you proceed with a particular method of development:

> You can housetrain your new puppy in just three days. [process]

> We must keep the store open on Thanksgiving Day. [reasons]

> College is very different from high school. [comparison]

> Every expression of love or affection that we give or receive fits into one of five categories. [classification]

> This drug produces several positive and negative side effects. [effects]

Other topic sentences, however, will allow you to select one or more different methods of development. For example, look at the following topic sentence:

> The Pittsburgh Steelers are one of the National Football League's most successful teams.

To further explain this idea, you could *illustrate* it by giving examples of the team's achievements, or you could *argue* the reasons for this statement.

This next example is also a topic sentence that could be developed with a variety of different methods:

> Music can relieve tension and stress.

The writer could use the *cause-and-effect* method of development to explain the effects of music on the mind and body. However, she could also develop this main idea by *narrating* a personal experience or by *illustrating* the idea with examples of people she knows who use music for relaxation.

Selecting an appropriate method before you compose gives you a map or guideline that will help you organize your ideas when you create your outline. If your outline shows how the details you will include fit the model for the method of development you selected, you will be more likely to use a recognizable pattern that will give your writing coherence.

Exercise 6.19

Working with one to three of your classmates, decide on the method of development that should be used to develop each of the following topic sentences. Choose from narration, description, illustration, process, comparison, cause and effect, division, classification, and argument. Record your answers on your own paper.

1. Grocery store brands of foods and products are usually just as good as name brands.
2. Reducing the amount of beef you consume has both personal and societal benefits.
3. I made a serious mistake when I was younger, but I learned from it.
4. Many crimes should be punished with community service instead of prison sentences.
5. The members of my generation tend to be hard workers (or family-oriented, or technologically savvy, or team-oriented, or civic-minded).
6. Bad bosses come in four different types.
7. Performing certain activities in the hour before going to bed will contribute to a good night's sleep.
8. A good camping spot has several key features.
9. The brain has three main parts.
10. My mother is beautiful, talented, and smart.

Exercise 6.20

Which method of development should be used to develop each of the following topic sentences? Choose from narration, description, illustration, process, comparison, cause and effect, division, classification, and argument. Write your answers on your own paper.

1. For many, single parenthood brings three specific types of hardships.
2. Children's television programs have changed dramatically over the last 30 years.
3. Last Saturday night, the emergency room was especially hectic.
4. Making good iced tea is simple.

5. Penalties and punishments for drunk driving should be much worse than they are now.
6. Organic foods may be more expensive, but they're worth the extra cost.
7. The iPhone 4 is much better than the iPhone 3.
8. Meditation is a useful relaxation technique.
9. The four different types of human teeth have distinct shapes and functions.
10. Celebrities are often bad role models for children.

Combining the Methods

Often, instead of using only one method of development in a paragraph, you'll use two or more in combination to fully explain your idea. For example, read this next paragraph about getting into debt by using credit cards.

> <u>Using credit cards irresponsibly quickly got me into trouble</u>. **When** I got my first credit card, I vowed that I would follow financial experts' advice and use it only for emergencies such as car repairs. **Before long**, though, I was using it to make everyday purchases, such as lunches and gas for my car. **Then**, I began using it when I wanted something, such as a new pair of shoes or concert tickets, but didn't have the money to buy it. I **soon** hit my $3,000 limit on that card. I was worried, of course. My monthly payments had increased to $100 per month, and I was not earning enough income to cover the additional expense. **So**, I applied for and got a second credit card. Although I tried not to use it as frequently as I used the first card, unexpected needs and wants were always popping up, and I never seemed to have the money for them. **In a little more than a year**, I was $7,500 in debt and unable to afford my monthly credit card payments at all.

This paragraph develops the underlined topic sentence with narration and cause and effect. It presents the main events in the writer's journey into debt and also explains the reasons for those events. Here is another example:

> <u>If you smell smoke or hear a smoke detector sound the alarm, you will need to get out of your house as soon as possible, but how you do that will depend on where you are</u>. **The first thing** you should do is scream "Fire!" to notify everyone else in your home. **Then**, if you are in the same room as the fire, get on your hands and knees because the least amount of heat and the cleanest air can be found close to the floor. **Next**, get out of the house by any means necessary. Throw a chair through a window if you have to. If you are in a different room than the fire, do not open the door of the room until you feel your room's door. If it feels hot, do not open it. Find another way out. **As** you are leaving, don't waste valuable time trying to collect keys, papers, clothes, or other personal belongings. Your life is far more important than anything you can carry out with you. **Once you are outside**, call 911 to report the fire and *do not go back inside for any reason*. If you cannot escape because there's no exit or because you are on an upper floor, use towels or blankets to stuff under the door to prevent smoke from entering the room and stay close to the floor. If possible, call 911

to report that you're trapped, or get someone's attention by waving a towel or sheet out a window.

This paragraph uses a combination of process and cause and effect to explain what to do if your home catches fire. In this next paragraph, try to determine the methods of development:

> <u>Vocalized pauses are extraneous sounds or words that interrupt fluent speech and sometimes distract listeners</u>. The most common vocalized pauses that creep into our speech include "uh," "um," "er," "well," "OK," and those nearly universal interrupters of American conversations, "you know" and "like." At times we may use vocal pauses to hold our turn when we momentarily search for the right word or idea. Because they are not part of the intended message, occasional vocalized pauses are generally ignored by those who are interpreting the message. However, when we begin to use them to excess, listeners are likely to perceive us as nervous or unsure of what we are saying. As the use of vocalized pauses increases, people are less able to understand what we are saying, and they may perceive us as confused and our ideas as not well thought out. For some people, vocalized pauses are so pervasive that listeners are unable to concentrate on the meaning of the message.
>
> Adapted from Verderber, Kathleen S., et al. *Communicate!*
> 13th ed. Boston: Wadsworth, 2010. Print.

This paragraph illustrates vocalized pauses by providing specific examples, and then uses cause and effect to explain how these pauses can affect communication. Can you determine the two methods used in the following paragraph?

> <u>Readers fall into two categories: active readers and passive readers</u>. Active readers control their interest level and concentration. They read with a purpose: They know what information to look for and why. Active readers constantly question what they read. They relate the author's ideas to their own experience and prior knowledge. On the other hand, passive readers are not in control of their reading. They lose interest easily and given in to distractions. They read the same way they watch television programs and movies, expecting others to engage them and keep their attention. Active readers control the process of reading; passive readers are unaware that reading *is* a process they can control.
>
> Kanar, Carol. *The Confident Student*,
> 7th ed. Boston: Wadsworth, 2011. Print.

This paragraph uses classification to group readers into two categories and then compares the characteristics of these groups.

▌ Exercise 6.21

Add transition words and phrases to the blanks in the following paragraphs to improve their coherence. HINT: Identify the method(s) of development used in each paragraph to determine the most appropriate transitions.

A.   Personnel in doctors' offices often will include a variety of health care professionals, including physicians, nurses, physician assistants, and medical assistants. Most people are familiar with doctors and nurses, but what's the difference between physician assistants and medical assistants? _____ difference relates to the two positions' duties and responsibilities. Physician assistants, or PAs, practice medicine under the supervision of a physician or surgeon. They examine patients, order diagnostic tests, diagnose the problem, provide treatment, and prescribe medications. Medical assistants, _____, can have administrative or clinical duties. Their duties vary from office to office, but they may update patients' medical records or files, schedule services, prepare patients for examinations, assist the doctor or physician assistant with treatments, sterilize medical instruments, or keep the office clean and stocked with the necessary supplies. _____ difference between the two positions is the educational requirements. Physician assistants usually obtain a bachelor's degree and then complete an accredited PA program that takes two years of full-time study and results in a master's degree. _____, medical assistants can learn to do their jobs through on-the-job training or completion of a one-year diploma program or a two-year associate degree program at educational institutions such as community colleges, technical schools, or vocational schools. _____ difference is licensure. Physician assistants must pass an exam to obtain certification from the National Commission on Certification of Physician Assistants (NCCPA), and they must be licensed by their state to practice. Medical assistants, _____, are not always required by their state to be certified or licensed.

B.   Every year, over a million teenagers drop out of high school. Reducing the number of teens who leave school requires an understanding of the three key causes of their decision and then using appropriate prevention strategies. _____ of dropping out includes all of the school-related reasons. According to a recent U.S. Department of Education survey, 51 percent of teens dropped out because they do not like school, 35 percent said they could not get along with their teachers, and 39.9 percent were failing. _____ of causes are job-related. Fifteen percent of teens had to get a job to help provide financial support for their families, and 14.1 percent said that they could not work and go to school at the same time. _____ of drop-outs' reasons are family-related. Fifty-one percent of teens who left school were pregnant, 13.6 percent became a parent, and 13.1 percent got married.

C.   To prevent these students from leaving, schools can use several strategies. They can begin monitoring students' attendance, grades, and test scores at earlier ages and _____ intervene to address these problems. _____, they can provide instruction in basic skills that might be preventing students from being academically successful. _____, schools can do more to help students transition from middle grades to high school. _____ students have entered ninth grade, schools should do everything possible to provide them with classes that match their interests and future goals so that they don't become bored. If life events such as financial problems or pregnancy threaten to interfere with their education, schools should supply alternates to the traditional school day so that the students will complete their education.

_____, schools can provide night or weekend classes for those who must work full-time.

Information from "Underlying Causes
of High School Dropout." George Family Connection
Partnership. Gafcp.org. Web. 26 Feb. 2012.

Writing Using Methods of Development and Transitions

To achieve coherence as you compose your paragraph, use your outline or diagram to guide you as you write. Your organization plan will remind you of the major components that you need to include if you are using a particular method of development.

As you compose each new sentence, think about how it relates to what came before it, and include appropriate transition words and phrases to indicate those relationships. You won't use a transition at the beginning of every sentence, but you will often need to include them to signal to readers that you are moving to a new event, detail, example, step, point, cause, effect, part, type, or reason.

Rewriting for Methods of Development and Transitions

To ensure coherence in a paragraph, carefully review your draft to check the match between your topic sentence and the method(s) of development you selected. Also, evaluate your use of transitions. Consider using a checklist like the following as a guide.

CHECKLIST FOR COHERENT PARAGRAPHS

Use this checklist to make sure that you are using methods of development and transitions to give your writing coherence.

 The paragraph's method (or methods) of development fit(s) the idea or opinion stated in the topic sentence.

 The details in the paragraph are arranged according to the standard patterns of the method(s) of development).

 Transition words and phrases indicate the relationships between sentences.

Exercise 6.22

A. Use the checklist on page 129 to evaluate a paragraph you have recently written. If you revised this paragraph, what would you change to improve its coherence?

B. Use the checklist to evaluate a classmate's paragraph. What improvements would you recommend?

SUGGESTED WRITING ACTIVITIES

Complete all of the steps of the writing process as you write one or more of the following compositions. Check your paragraphs carefully for coherence.

ACADEMIC WRITING

1. Tell the story of a historical event or discovery that you learned about in one of your classes.
2. Argue that your college should add a particular resource or service to help students.
3. E-mail one of your instructors to ask him or her to write you a letter of recommendation for a scholarship, a job, or your college application package. In your e-mail, describe the qualities that make you a good candidate.

PROFESSIONAL WRITING

4. Explain the components of good customer service. What do you expect from salespeople when you go to stores or businesses?
5. Describe a small business that is needed in your community.
6. Compare two different ways of accomplishing a specific task. Examine points of comparison such as time requirements, necessary resources, and quality of the finished product.

PERSONAL WRITING

7. Argue that a particular restaurant is the best one in your city or town.
8. Think of a product or service you need, and then compare or contrast two different brands or providers that offer it.
9. Persuade someone you know to stop doing something harmful (such as smoking, driving too fast, or driving while intoxicated).

CHAPTER 7

Essential #7:
Cohesive Paragraphs

In Chapters 5 and 6, you learned that an effective paragraph is *complete* and *coherent*. It must also be *cohesive*; that is, it must present and develop only one main idea. The word *cohesive* means "tending to stick together," so a **cohesive paragraph** is one in which of all of the sentences "stick together" by focusing on developing the one idea stated in the topic sentence. If a paragraph is cohesive, it does not include any unrelated information or sentences. In other words, it has *unity*.

When a writer includes information that does not belong in a paragraph, two problems result. First, non-cohesive paragraphs are difficult to follow. By definition, a paragraph is a unit that develops just one idea, so a paragraph that includes more than one main idea or jumps around from one idea to another within the paragraph unit will confuse and frustrate your readers. Second, non-cohesive paragraphs often do not completely develop the main idea. The unrelated information may take the place of layers of development that should be included to develop the writer's point, so that development is incomplete and inadequate.

Two types of non-cohesive paragraphs to be aware of are paragraphs that digress and paragraphs that ramble.

Paragraphs That Digress

To *digress* means to wander or stray away from your main topic or purpose. A non-cohesive paragraph that digresses is one that starts off just fine and begins to develop the main idea in the topic sentence, but then veers off course and begins to discuss an unrelated topic. This is a natural and common occurrence, for our brains are constantly producing a variety of thoughts. If you think about it, we digress frequently when we have conversations with others. Someone will say something that triggers a thought about another topic, and the conversation changes to focus on that topic. When we write, however, we cannot digress from the main idea in the topic sentence. We must pay attention as we compose so that we don't lose control of the supporting sentences in a paragraph.

The following paragraph is an example of a paragraph that digresses.

Like a car that veers off course, a paragraph that digresses leaves the path it should be on by including information unrelated to the main idea.

<u>To better manage your paperwork, you must begin by acquiring good equipment.</u> If you don't already have one, purchase a sturdy filing cabinet with at least two file drawers. In one of these drawers, you'll store all of your current files. In the other, you'll place paperwork you need to store. Along with the filing cabinet, also purchase a box of hanging files and a box of folders. The next step is to create your new filing system.

According to the underlined topic sentence, this paragraph will focus on the equipment needed to manage paperwork. The body of paragraph supports that main idea by discussing a filing cabinet and then files and folders. In the last sentence, though, it digresses from the idea of equipment and mentions a filing *system*. This is a new main idea that disrupts the paragraph's cohesion.

Here's another example of a paragraph that veers away from the main idea at the end:

Many words have two kinds of meanings: *denotative* meanings (their literal dictionary meanings) and *connotative* meanings, which are the positive or negative emotional associations that people make when they hear the words. <u>To understand connotative meaning, consider the names of vehicles we buy.</u> Automobile manufacturers carefully choose names for the vehicles they make and sell because they know that certain names cause us to associate good feelings and desires with the word and, by extension, with the vehicle. Automobiles with names that sound fast or powerful (such as Dodge Charger, Chevrolet Avalanche, and Nissan Titan) are appealing to drivers who value speed and strength and want to be perceived as people who have both. Other automobiles, such as the Ford Expedition, the Toyota Tundra, and the Nissan Frontier, are named to be attractive to those who desire a rugged or adventurous image. Still other automobiles, including the Buick Regal, the Lincoln Continental, and the Buick Park Avenue, appeal to people who value wealth and luxury. Another way that wealthy people show off their status is by wearing Rolex watches, designer clothes and shoes, and by consuming expensive foods like lobster and caviar.

This paragraph focuses on the connotative meanings of vehicle names. It does a good job developing the main idea with specific examples. However, the last sentence is not about vehicle names. By including this unrelated thought, the writer digressed from the main idea and disrupted the paragraph's cohesion.

In a third paragraph, the digression occurs earlier than the last sentence:

Every day when I attend classes, I see young men dressed in pants so baggy that the pants are in danger of falling down; young women wearing skimpy outfits that bare their legs, arms, backs, and shoulders or skin-tight jeans that expose their undergarments when they bend over; and people of both sexes wearing what looks to be their pajamas with flip flops. <u>This kind of attire is not appropriate for a college campus, so our college's administrators need to adopt a stricter dress code for students</u>. A new dress code that would ban these types of outfits would, first of all, make our campus safer. Students who are wearing pants that are too big for them are in danger of tripping and falling down stairs. Women who are exposing a lot of skin are not properly protected in classes like chemistry, where harmful chemicals are in use. A more specific dress code would also reduce distractions for those who are trying to concentrate and learn. Everyone knows how difficult it can be to stay focused on lectures and reading assignments. Some professors talk very fast and present ideas and information in a sophisticated way that can be difficult to follow. One way to cope is to ask permission to record those lectures and also to use an effective note-taking strategy.

In this paragraph, the writer begins with some background information followed by the topic sentence (underlined). He presents and explains one reason in support of this idea. After he presents the second reason, though, he forgets what he was writing about and digresses to a discussion of college lectures. As a result, he does not fully explain his main idea with several well-developed reasons.

Exercise 7.1

On your own paper, write the number of the sentence that states the main idea. Then, write the number of the sentence that digresses from that idea.

A. [1] The challenge of communicating in the workplace is learning how and when to share your ideas or concerns. [2] If you need to tell your supervisor about something that is not going well, it is important to remember that both timing and your attitude are extremely important. [3] For example, if you are a cashier at a carry-out restaurant, and the long lines during the lunch rush "stress you out," causing you to give customers incorrect change, it is best to wait to talk to your supervisor about the problem during a slower period. [4] At an appropriate time, you may want to ask if it would be possible to have someone assist you during busy periods. [5] And if you are able to explain that this would not only allow you to make fewer mistakes, but also allow the business to provide better service by making the line move more quickly, your supervisor will be more likely to take your ideas seriously. [6] Another proactive strategy would be to talk to your supervisor or another senior employee about how you could do your job more efficiently. [7] Listening is also a critical communication skill.[1]

B. [1] Watching movies on DVD at home is almost always preferable to watching them at a movie theater. [2] Renting and then popping in a $4 DVD is certainly cheaper than spending at least $10 on a movie theater ticket and then another $10 or more at the concession stand. [3] Watching at home is also more comfortable because, when I'm in my living room, I can lay back in my recliner or stretch out on the couch under a blanket. [4] In movie theaters, the only option is sitting up straight in a sometimes uncomfortable seat. [5] Even worse, I have several times had the bad luck to sit next to a total stranger who texts on his or her cell phone during the

---

[1] "Soft Skills: The Competitive Edge." U.S. Department of Labor. Web. 11 March 2012.

entire movie. [6] I, too, have a cell phone, but I turn it off when I enter the theater. [7] I wish that everyone would think to be more considerate of those around them by stepping out to the lobby to send messages or take calls, not just in movie theaters but also in most public places, such as restaurants and waiting rooms.

C. [1] You may not be saving any money because you never have big chunks of cash to stash away. [2] However, you'd be surprised by how much your savings will increase if you save even small amounts on a regular basis. [3] Increasing your savings will happen slowly but surely if you try some painless, effective ways to set aside a little money every day. [4] For example, one tried-and-true method is emptying your pockets of change every evening and dropping those coins into a jar. [5] Remember "feeding" your piggy bank when you were a kid? [6] Back then, saving money was fun. [7] As we age, unfortunately, we lose the sense of fun and adventure we had when we were young. [8] Another way to save money is to pay yourself a reward (which you then put in your savings jar) every time you do something beneficial, such as exercise, pass a test in one of your classes, or do a good deed for someone. [9] Using that technique, you'll not only be motivating yourself to do something that needs to be done, but you'll also be saving money. [10] A third way to increase savings is to get a debit card from a bank that will round up the amount of every purchase to the nearest dollar and then deposit the extra amount automatically in your savings account. [11] Using that strategy, you'll literally be saving money every time you buy something. [12] The little amounts here and there will hardly be noticeable to you, but they'll quickly add up.

Paragraphs That Ramble

A second type of non-cohesive paragraph results when the writer is not sure before or during composing what one idea he or she wants to discuss in the paragraph. This uncertainty produces a paragraph that rambles from idea to idea. For example,

[1] Children who are diagnosed with attention deficit hyperactivity disorder, or ADHD, exhibit a number of symptoms. [2] They are often immediately prescribed medication, like Ritalin, that calms them and helps them focus. [3] The medication has unpleasant side effects, such as insomnia and loss of appetite. [4] Drugs are not the only effective treatment option for ADHD patients. [5] Duke University Medical Center offers a program that uses behavioral treatments based on skills training. [6] Many children with ADHD have poor social skills; for example, they interrupt people instead of waiting for their turn to talk, and they easily use their temper. [7] Summer camps for ADHD kids provide them with therapy and skills training. [8] For years, researchers have been debating whether treatment with medication or treatment without medication is best.

The first sentence of this paragraph suggests that the paragraph will focus on the symptoms of ADHD. However, the paragraph goes on to state and partially develop a number of different ideas, including:

Medication and its side effects (sentences 2 and 3)

Non-drug treatments (sentences 4, 5, 6, and 7)

The debate about treatment (sentence 8)

The writer should choose one of these ideas for the paragraph and save the others for other paragraphs.

Here is another example of a paragraph that rambles:

> [1] The price of gasoline is affected by a number of different factors. [2] One of those factors is the demand, or the need, for gasoline. [3] The price of gasoline, just like any other product, goes up when more people want or need it. [4] The more people need gas to get to work or to go on vacation, the more the demand increases, so the more the price increases. [5] Gasoline prices in America seem high, but they're actually much higher in other countries. [6] To save money on gas prices, you could trade in your gas-guzzler for a more fuel-efficient car. [7] Americans should also invest more in technology that will make electric cars more affordable so that we don't have to rely so heavily on gasoline.

The first sentence of the paragraph indicates that the paragraph will focus on factors that affect the price of gasoline, and sentences 2–4 explain one of those factors. However, the writer begins to ramble in sentence 5, and the last three sentences of the paragraph introduce different ideas that are off the topic of factors that affect gas prices.

© Benoit Tessier/Reuters/Landov

Rambling paragraphs are like mismatched outfits.
They are composed of different parts that do not seem to fit together.

Here is one final example:

> ¹ A balanced diet will help you stay fit and reduce stress. ² Every day, eat a variety of foods such as fruit, vegetables, bread, cereal, lean meat, fish, poultry, and low-fat dairy products. ³ All are healthy foods that help the body deal with stress. ⁴ Eating regular meals in a relaxed setting will also help you reduce stress. ⁵ Avoid excessive sugar, salt, fat, caffeine, and alcohol, which can contribute to stress or nervous irritability.

The first sentence promises readers that the paragraph will focus on two benefits of a balanced diet. Sentences 2 and 3 remain focused on that idea, but sentence 4 moves on to the setting of meals, and sentence 5 introduces yet another idea about substances that contribute to stress. Notice how you didn't learn much about the writer's ideas in this rambling paragraph. Instead of developing those ideas, the writer included points that should be deleted or addressed elsewhere.

TIP

For more information about organizing the information in paragraphs, see Chapter 6.

Exercise 7.2

On your own paper, write the numbers of the sentences that do not relate to each paragraph's main idea, which is underlined.

A. ¹ <u>Facebook and LinkedIn are both online social networking sites, but their goals, their look and features, and their users all differ.</u> ² Facebook focuses on personal networking to begin or maintain relationships with friends, family members, and romantic partners. ³ LinkedIn, on the other hand, focuses on professional networking to connect with former co-workers, to make contacts that could help you be successful in a current position, or even look for a new job or recruit new employees. ⁴ LinkedIn was launched in 2003. ⁵ Millions of people all over the world are registered users of this site, which can be accessed in a number of different languages. ⁶ In 2011, the number of LinkedIn members surpassed the number of MySpace members. ⁷ Although Facebook is the number one social networking site, it has been criticized for failing to protect users' privacy and safety, for contributing to online crime, and for lowering worker productivity. ⁸ In fact, some workplaces ban the use of Facebook to prevent their employees from using it during work hours.

B. ¹ <u>Oncolytic viruses are viruses that target, infect, and destroy cancer cells but not normal cells.</u> ² Basically, these viruses, which can tell the difference between cancer cells and normal cells, enter a cancer cell, kill it, and then spread to adjacent cancer cells, killing them, too. ³ Many cancer researchers across the globe are busy investigating these viruses. ⁴ Research on mice with brain tumors has shown that animals treated with oncolytic viruses live much longer; some were even tumor-free when they died. ⁵ Some of the diseases being targeted with these viruses are lung cancer, liver cancer, melanoma skin cancer, brain cancer, and pancreatic cancer. ⁶ Cancer patients can choose many additional weapons in their fight against cancer, including surgery, radiation, chemotherapy, transplantation, and gene therapy.

C. ¹ <u>Our store's bakery department needs to add a third worker on Fridays and Saturdays.</u> ² The two of us employees who work on those two days do our very best to keep up, but the workload is always much heavier because of the many special orders for cakes that customers want to pick up on Fridays or Saturdays for their weekend events. [3] As you know, our store has a reputation for making cakes that are attractive and tasty, and we make cakes for all kinds of parties, wedding receptions, baby showers, and many other events. [4] My favorite cakes to make are the ones for children's birthday parties because they are usually a lot of fun to decorate. [5] Two bakery staff members cannot bake and decorate all of those special-order cakes and wait on our regular bakery customers, too. [6] Consequently, many customers have to endure long waits, and special orders are not always ready for pick-up when they should be. [7] They deserve better customer service than that. [8] One factor that is probably contributing to the problem is the layout of the food preparation area. [9] It's too cramped for two people to work there at the same time, so it reduces our productivity and efficiency.

In the following sections, you'll learn techniques to use during the prewriting, writing, and rewriting stages of the process to avoid writing paragraphs that digress or ramble.

Prewriting for Cohesive Paragraphs

Writing a cohesive paragraph starts at the beginning of the writing process, during the prewriting stage. Make sure that you select just one idea to develop in your paragraph, and then compose a topic sentence that clearly states this main idea. A firm grasp of your main idea will make it more likely that you will focus on that idea alone as you develop your paragraph.

A second way to ensure cohesive paragraphs from the beginning is to organize and outline your ideas before writing. Skipping the outlining stage increases the likelihood of writing paragraphs that lack unity and cohesion. Not only should you devote an adequate amount of time to organizing your ideas, but you should also check all of the details in your outline against your topic sentence to make sure that everything you're planning to include in the paragraph truly belongs there.

Exercise 7.3

Study the following outlines. On your own paper, give the writer of each outline advice about how to change the outline to avoid writing a paragraph that digresses or rambles.

1. **Thesis:** The Fisherman's Catch is an excellent restaurant.
   a. The food is delicious.
   b. The service is friendly and efficient.
   c. My wife and I ate there on our first date.
   d. The prices are reasonable.
   e. The owners are retired Chicago schoolteachers.

2. **Thesis:** The American Red Cross is one charitable organization that is worthy of support.

    a. Its activities help millions of people prepare for emergencies and get help when they become disaster victims.

    b. Clara Barton, a nurse, founded the organization in 1881.

    c. The vast majority of the money donated to the Red Cross goes to the organization's programs, not administrators' salaries or fundraising expenses.

    d. Other excellent charities include Habitat for Humanity and the American Cancer Society.

3. **Thesis:** When anger, frustration, anxiety, or other strong emotions threaten to overwhelm you, calm yourself using a deep-breathing technique.

    a. Draw in air through your nose while you count to five.

    b. Hold your breath while you count to five.

    c. Exhale through your mouth while you count to five.

    d. After exhaling all of the air in your lungs, count to five.

    e. Repeat the inhale-hold-exhale-hold cycle at least 10 times, and you should feel more relaxed.

    f. Both meditation and yoga emphasize breathing to reduce stress and achieve relaxation.

    g. Physical exercise—even as little as a 30-minute walk several times a week—can calm your mind.

Writing Cohesive Paragraphs

You can do several things as you compose your paragraph to make sure to achieve cohesion. First of all, as you write, use your outline as your guide. If you carefully crafted your outline to include only relevant information, follow that outline as you write each new sentence. If you decide while you're writing to include details or information not present in your outline, check that information against the main idea to make sure that it matches.

Second, refer back to your topic sentence often as you write. As you write each new sentence in the body of your paragraph, check it against your main idea to make sure that it directly relates to that main idea.

Finally, use methods of development when they are appropriate. In Chapter 6, you learned that methods of development are common patterns for organizing and explaining ideas. Consciously selecting and then adhering to a particular method may help keep you on track and prevent digressions and rambling.

Exercise 7.4

Each of the following topic sentences is followed by several supporting sentences. Select the supporting sentence or sentences that do not develop the idea in the topic sentence. Write your answers on your own paper.

1. After clocking in, all employees must follow the company's approved procedure for thorough hand-washing.

   a. Wet your hands with clean running water (warm or cold) and apply soap.

   b. Rub your hands together to make a lather and scrub them well; be sure to scrub the backs of your hands, between your fingers, and under your nails.

   c. Alcohol-based hand sanitizers can quickly reduce the number of germs on hands in some situations, but sanitizers do *not* eliminate all types of germs.

   d. Continue rubbing your hands for at least 20 seconds. Need a timer? Hum the "Happy Birthday" song from beginning to end twice.

   e. Rinse your hands well under running water. Dry your hands using a clean towel or air dry.[2]

2. Almost all foods sold at movie theater concession stands are bad for our health.

   a. Many of the snack choices, such as candy and soda, contain large amounts of sugar.

   b. Healthier snacks include fruit, a granola bar, or trail mix.

   c. Other foods are loaded with fat and cholesterol; two good examples are the melted butter that is squirted onto popcorn and the processed cheese sauce that is poured over chips to make nachos.

   d. Movie theaters serve huge portions of foods like popcorn and candy, but they also charge very high prices for those foods.

   e. Most of the foods sold at concession stands have little nutritional value, so they offer only "empty" calories that turn easily to fat.

3. To be truly motivating, a goal must have five different qualities that can be remembered using the acronym "DAPPS."

   a. An effective goal must be *dated*; in other words, it has a specific deadline.

   b. A motivating goal is also *achievable*; it may be challenging, but it's also realistic.

   c. A *short-term* goal is one that can be accomplished within a few weeks or months, whereas a *long-term* goal is one that may take years to achieve.

   d. Another characteristic of an effective goal is *personal* because it must reflect what *you* desire, not what someone else wants for you.

   e. A motivating goal is one that is *positive*, meaning that it focuses on what you *do* want instead of what you *don't* want.

   f. Finally, an effective goal must be *specific*; it should state the exact outcome you seek, such as an A or B in a course or a specific number of pounds you want to lose.

   g. Some people think that goals and dreams are the same thing, but they are actually quite different.[3]

---

[2]   "Wash Your Hands." Centers for Disease Control and Prevention. Web. 1 Apr. 2012.
[3]   Downing, Skip. *On Course*, 6th ed. Boston: Wadsworth, 2010. Print.

Rewriting for Cohesive Paragraphs

To ensure cohesion in your paragraphs, get in the habit of reviewing every paragraph as part of your rewriting stage of the writing process. Check each supporting sentence against the idea you state in your topic sentence and make sure that it directly relates to that idea. When you find sentences that don't seem to belong, delete them or move them elsewhere in the composition. If a paragraph digresses to another idea, consider dividing that paragraph into two paragraphs and adding more layers of development to both. Pay special attention to paragraphs that are relatively long, because they may not be cohesive. Check them carefully for digressions or too many different ideas.

Exercise 7.5

What advice would you give to the writer of the following paragraph? How could this paragraph be improved for better cohesion? The paragraph's main idea is underlined. After you read each sentence in the body of the paragraph, go back and reread the topic sentence. Ask yourself, "Does this body sentence explain or support the topic and point stated in the topic sentence?" If it doesn't, then it should be removed or rewritten.

[1] You are driving along when you see the dreaded flashing blue lights in your rearview mirror, and you realize that a police officer wants you to pull over. [2] <u>The encounter between you and the officer will go more smoothly if you remember to do several things.</u> [3] The first one is to stop as soon as you safely can by pulling to the right side of the road. [4] The most common reason for traffic stops is speeding. [5] If you can't stop right away, reduce your speed, acknowledge the officer's presence by waving or by turning on your hazard lights, and stop when it's safe to do so. [6] Most states have a "move over" law that requires motorists on four-lane roads to change from the right lane to the left if a law enforcement vehicle is stopped on the roadside. [7] After you stop, turn off the vehicle, and turn on the interior light if it's dark outside. [8] Stay in your vehicle, and keep your hands in sight, preferably on the steering wheel. [9] Wait to provide documentation (such as your driver's license and vehicle registration) until the officer requests it. [10] If you receive a ticket, accept it without complaining and listen carefully to the officer's instructions about how to handle it. [11] During the entire encounter, address the officer as "Officer" and speak to him or her with courtesy, civility, and respect. [12] Refrain from arguing with the officer there on the roadside; court is the appropriate place to debate the issue. [13] Following these guidelines could mean the difference between getting just a warning and getting a citation or even being arrested. [14] Police often set up roadblocks called "checkpoints" to verify drivers' sobriety, seat-belt use, and licenses.

When you evaluate a paragraph for cohesion, consider using a checklist like the one on page 142 as a guide.

CHECKLIST FOR COHESIVE PARAGRAPHS

Use this checklist to make sure that you are avoiding digressions and rambling and instead writing cohesive paragraphs.

☐   The paragraph includes a clear topic sentence.

☐   Every sentence in the paragraph develops the idea in the topic sentence.

☐   The paragraph does not digress.

☐   The paragraph does not ramble.

Exercise 7.6

A. Use the checklist above to evaluate a paragraph you have recently written. If you revised this paragraph, would you need to make any changes to improve its cohesion?

B. Use the checklist to evaluate a classmate's paragraph. What improvements would you recommend?

SUGGESTED WRITING ACTIVITIES

Complete all of the steps of the writing process as you write one or more of the following compositions. Check your paragraphs carefully for cohesion.

ACADEMIC WRITING

1. Explain why a particular book, film, television show, play, or album has been popular with audiences.
2. Compare two different instructors' teaching styles. Examine points of comparison such as their methods, their materials, and their assignments.
3. Explain how to set up for a specific process or procedure (such as a lab or an experiment).

PROFESSIONAL WRITING

4. Explain to a co-worker how to prepare for something (such an inspection, a special event, or an especially busy day).
5. Describe a workplace conflict you handled poorly and explain what you would change if you had the opportunity to deal with the conflict again.
6. Write a letter or an e-mail to respond to a customer's request for information.

PERSONAL WRITING

7. Write to an elected official to argue for a pay raise for teachers, firefighters, police officers, social workers, or another group of city or state employees.
8. Based on your experience, give readers some tips for avoiding potential pitfalls when using Facebook, e-mail, or Twitter.
9. Argue against an unpopular local ordinance (such as a curfew for young people, a zoning request, or a ban on a substance or activity).

Essential Characteristics of Essays and Other Multiparagraph Compositions

CHAPTER 8

Essential #8: Clear Organization in Essays and Other Multiparagraph Compositions

Before offering thoughts and ideas to readers for their consideration, writers must determine the most logical way to group those ideas together. If readers are presented with a jumble of random thoughts about a subject, they won't be able to make any sense of them or understand how the writer arrived at his or her conclusions. Therefore, an important part of the writer's job is to organize thoughts and ideas prior to writing and then maintain that organization while composing. A writer organizes by determining logical units in which to present information and opinions.

Organizing things into units is a task we're all familiar with. The clothes in your dresser drawers, for instance, are probably divided into different units. Most people place their socks in one drawer, undergarments in another, and shirts in still another. In this case, the units that determine where different items go are *types of clothes*.

However, when it's time to do the laundry, you probably reorganize your clothes using different units: *colors* of the clothes. Now you separate those same clothes into piles of whites, pastels, and darker colors.

You may have organized other things in your home into units as well. The food in your kitchen might be arranged according to *type of food* (different cabinets for canned goods, spices, and cereals). Your class notes, handouts, and assignments may be in a notebook that is divided into different sections according to *subject* (English, math, and study skills). The bills you need to pay might be arranged according to *due dates* (electric bill and phone bill this Friday, rent and car payment next Friday, and so on).

Just as you find units for things to help you understand and manage them better, you must put your ideas in units that will help your readers comprehend them. Each of these units should be addressed in a separate paragraph, which (as you learned in Chapter 2) is a group of sentences that state and support just one main idea. When you present your thoughts in logical units, readers can more easily follow your train of thought and grasp your meaning. Consequently, writers must spend some time determining the best organization plan for an entire composition before they begin to write.

A disorganized composition is like the jumble of items in the junk drawer in your home. An organized composition is like an orderly closet where like items are grouped together and easy to locate.

When a writer skips this important step and begins to write without planning ahead, the composition will often ramble or jump from thought to thought in a confusing way. At best, this disorganization causes readers to struggle more to understand the information. At worst, the reader will fail to understand at all and will feel frustrated and doubtful about the writer's thinking skills.

For example, read the following passage from a letter to the editor:

[1] After serving their country, many of our military veterans are having difficulty transitioning back to civilian life because we are not providing them with adequate assistance. About a million of them have been unable to find employment. Many lack adequate health care for physical and mental ailments directly caused by their military duties. Some are experiencing relationship problems due to the stress of reintegrating with their families after long absences. Too many of them are ending up homeless and living on the streets. We need to do a better job of forging partnerships between government agencies and private organizations to prevent this from happening to the brave men and women who put their lives on the line for us.

[2] Veterans sometimes have a hard time conveying to civilian employers how the skills they learned in the military apply to non-military positions. Of course, the Veterans Administration does offer some help, but its bureaucracy requires former soldiers to fill out tons of paperwork, and it moves slowly, so returning servicemen and servicewomen don't get the help they need when they need it. Providing mentors for veterans might help them return to civilian life more quickly and easily.

[3] Congress needs to allocate more money to providing services that help these people rebuild their lives. Many of the soldiers who went overseas and served in war zones are suffering from post-traumatic stress disorder, or PTSD; however, they are often unable to access the treatment they desperately need. In acknowledgment of their sacrifices and their heroism, we must provide them with the care they deserve now that they're home.

The writer did not organize her thoughts before composing; instead, she just wrote down details in the order in which she thought of them. As a result, the letter jumps around in a confusing manner. A list of topics discussed in each paragraph makes this clear:

Paragraph 1:   Four problems faced by veterans: lack of employment, lack of health care, family stress, homelessness
One solution to the problem: partnerships between agencies and organizations

Paragraph 2:   Problems faced by veterans: lack of employment and Veterans Administration bureaucracy
A solution to the problem: mentors for veterans

Paragraph 3:   A solution to the problem: more money for services
A problem faced by veterans: lack of health care

Because the writer did not determine her organizing units before beginning to write, the information is all mixed up and hard to follow. She begins in the first paragraph by listing several specific problems that veterans face as they transition to civilian life. But some of these same problems are mentioned again in the two paragraphs that follow, where the writer includes more specific information. Mixed in throughout all three paragraphs are sentences that propose various solutions to the problem.

To improve this letter, the writer should sort the details into the units listed above. But even then, she's still not ready to compose. The next step involves determining the logical order for these units. Should she present all of the problems first and then discuss all of the possible solutions? Or should she present one problem followed by an appropriate solution? In what order should she present the different problems? These are questions that need to be answered before composition begins.

Another example of a composition that lacks logical organization is this passage from a student's report on the causes of violent behavior in young people:

> Children who exhibit violent behavior have often been subject to abuse. Child abuse has a reciprocal effect, so abused children often grow into abusive adults. Most parents can control their anger, but some cannot manage it constructively. About 60 percent of child abuse cases involve substance abuse.
>
> Drug and alcohol use reduces self-control and often exposes children to violence, either as victims or perpetrators. Nearly four out of five high school students admit to drinking alcohol, and more than half of 12th graders say they've been drunk at least once. Alcohol is a major contributor to violent child behavior.
>
> Studies show that substance abuse and child abuse are linked. More than 9 million children are affected by parents who abuse alcohol or drugs.

This passage is quite difficult to follow because of its organizational problems and because general statements are not adequately developed with details and explanations. Listing the topics discussed in each paragraph reveals these problems:

Paragraph 1:   Child abuse cycle
Parents' substance abuse as a contributing factor

Paragraph 2:   Parents' substance abuse as a contributing factor
Children's substance abuse as a contributing factor

Paragraph 3:   Parents' substance abuse as a contributing factor

Clear units emerge from this list of topics:

Contributing factor #1:   The child abuse cycle
Contributing factor #2:   Parents' substance abuse
Contributing factor #3:   Children's substance abuse

The writer is offering three distinct causes of violent behavior in children, so the organizing units should be *causes of violent behavior in children*. To improve the reader's understanding of this information, the details need to be collected in the clear, logical units listed above, and the report should be rewritten to include three paragraphs, one for each of the three causes discussed.

Now that you understand the importance of grouping related information together, read the next sections about how to discover and arrange the best units for your ideas.

TIP

For more information about writing a paragraph that discusses only one main idea, see Chapter 7.

Prewriting to Organize Ideas

As you learned in the Introduction of this book, the prewriting stage of the writing process includes not only gathering ideas for a composition but also deciding on the main idea and the best order for the details to be included.

Before you proceed, flip back to Chapter 2 and review the form and features of an essay, which are explained and illustrated on pages 22–26. If you understand the required parts of a multiparagraph composition such as an essay, you can begin thinking about how to put your composition together during the very first step of the process.

The Thesis Statement

Before you can determine the appropriate logical units for your ideas, you'll need to decide on your main idea. What one major idea or opinion would you like your readers to understand or to adopt by the time they finish reading your composition? The answer to this question becomes your thesis statement. You learned in Chapter 2 of this book that the **thesis statement** offers your composition's main idea. It should include two components: the *topic* of your composition and the *overall point* you want to make about that topic. Here are some sample thesis statements:

TOPIC	OVERALL POINT
Participating in team sports	is beneficial for young people.
Williamsburg, Virginia,	is a wonderful vacation destination for families with children.
An effective complaint letter (one that produces action and resolution)	has several key components.

Your thesis statement, which should always be clearly stated in the opening paragraph of your composition, should possess the following characteristics:

- The thesis should be an idea or an opinion rather than a fact, but it should be specific enough that it can be fully explained in the composition.
- The thesis should be presented in one sentence that makes a statement and ends with a period. A thesis statement should not take the form of a question or a command.
- The thesis should be stated with confidence. Omit phrases such as *I think that* or *In my opinion* and just state your point.
- The thesis should not begin with phrases such as *In this essay, I'm going to. . . .* Beginning this way often results in a sentence that does not include the author's overall point about the topic.

Composing a clear thesis statement is the first step toward logical organization for your ideas because you have to know exactly what you're trying to explain or prove before you begin. As a matter of fact, a well-written thesis statement will often suggest the most sensible organization pattern.

▊ Exercise 8.1

On your own paper, first explain how each of the following thesis statements needs to be revised so that it includes the components and characteristics necessary for thesis statements. Then, revise each statement so that it possesses all of the characteristics listed on page 149.

1. The consequences of academic cheating
2. Something should be done about the problems in public schools today.
3. Can going to college help you determine your values and find inner direction for your life?
4. In this essay, I'm going to discuss my opinion about recycling.
5. Over 800 million people now have Facebook accounts.

Discovering Logical Units for Ideas

Once you have determined your thesis statement, you're ready to decide on logical units for presenting your ideas. How do you know what units to choose? Your topic and your thesis statement will sometimes dictate that your organizing units be specific reasons, events, examples, parts, steps, causes, effects, or categories. Other topics and thesis statements will require you to figure out the right units for arranging your thoughts.

For example, if you decided to organize your personal collection of DVDs, how would you arrange them? Many people would sort them according to *genre*, grouping discs together according to their type (drama, comedy, horror, documentary, and so on). However, that's not the only way to organize them. You could group them according to the *actors or actresses* who star in the films. Using that category, you would place all of your Johnny Depp movies in one area, all of your Denzel Washington movies in another, and your Angelina Jolie movies in another. Or you could arrange them from *most watched to least watched*. You could even organize them according to *length*. The category you chose would depend on your purpose.

As you are deciding on the right units, you need to understand the difference between natural and logical organization. Various examples in the following sections will demonstrate how a thesis statement can dictate that certain units be used or require writers to use their own powers of logical thinking to determine the most appropriate units.

Natural Organization

Some subjects organize themselves. If you are telling a story, for example, you will naturally arrange the events in chronological (time) order, from the first thing that happened to the last thing that happened. For instance, if your thesis is

I exhibited courage during my solo three-day wilderness trek.

you would tell the story of the main events during the trip. If your thesis is

> Mayor Mike Conn's campaign for reelection was beset by problems from beginning to end.

you would recount what happened during the campaign.

Even though narratives (stories) organize themselves, you will still need to determine how to divide your longer composition into smaller units. Often, it's appropriate to explain each main event or scene in a separate paragraph.

Another type of subject that will organize itself naturally is an explanation of a process or a procedure. Like a narrative, the steps in a process arrange themselves in chronological order, so you present each step in order from the first thing done to the last thing done. For example, read the following thesis statement:

> To take control of your spending and improve your financial health, follow three steps to create a budget that you will be likely to follow.

For this thesis, the major steps in the procedure would provide the logical units, and each step would be described in detail in a separate paragraph:

Paragraph 1:   Step #1: List all of your monthly income and expenses.
Paragraph 2:   Step #2: Subtract your fixed expenses from your monthly income.
Paragraph 3:   Step #3: Decide how you will divide up the amount that's left between luxury items (such as entertainment, eating out, vacations, and other non-necessities) and savings/investments that will help you achieve your longer-term goals.

Another example of a thesis statement that organizes itself is:

> The hiring process for police officers is lengthy and rigorous, with many stages.

Again, the major stages in the process provide the logical units, with each stage explained in a separate paragraph. For instance, the composition for this thesis could be organized into six units:

Paragraph 1:   Stage 1: Application
Paragraph 2:   Stage 2: First interview
Paragraph 3:   Stage 3: Criminal background check and reference check
Paragraph 4:   Stage 4: Second interview
Paragraph 5:   Stage 5: Polygraph test
Paragraph 6:   Stage 6: Psychological testing, drug screening, and physical agility test

Other explanations of procedures, however, require a little more logical thought. For instance, read this next thesis:

> Bicyclists who share the road with automobiles need to take steps to ensure their safety.

Let's say you generate the following list of ideas in support of this thesis statement:

- Wear a bicycle helmet. It is the law for persons under 18 years of age.
- Ride with the traffic flow.

- Ride in a straight line.
- Ride to the right if you are moving slower than other traffic, unless you are turning left, passing another bicycle or vehicle, or avoiding hazards.
- Stop at stop signs and red lights.
- Use a light, reflectors, and reflective clothing during darkness.
- Wear bright clothing during the daytime.
- Keep a safe distance from parked cars.
- Use proper hand signals when turning, stopping, or changing lanes.
- Use extra caution when it is raining, and allow extra time to stop.
- Cross railroad tracks at a right angle.
- Walk your bike when using a crosswalk.
- Do not wear headphones on both ears while riding.
- Keep your bike properly maintained so it is safe.
- Do not drink and ride.
- Ride defensively.
- Be alert for road hazards.
- Watch for cars at cross streets and driveways.

> Adapted from California Department of Transportation. "Bicycle Commuting and Safety." 2007. Web. 26 Mar. 2012.

Before you could write this essay, you would need to come up with organizing units. You might notice that some of these actions need to occur before getting on the bicycle, and others occur while riding. Therefore, possible units could include *steps to take before ride* and *steps to take during ride*. Then, you might break each of those larger units down into more specific steps:

1. Steps to take before ride
   - Dress in a helmet and bright and/or reflective clothing. (Paragraph 1)
   - Keep bicycle maintained and in good working order. (Paragraph 2)
2. Steps to take during ride
   - Obey all traffic signals and traffic laws. (Paragraph 3)
   - Remain alert for road hazards and other vehicles. (Paragraph 4)
   - Use hand signals to communicate with other motorists. (Paragraph 5)

Using this structure, you could sort most of the items in the brainstormed list into these units.

Exercise 8.2

For each of the following thesis statements, list the units (the specific main events in the story or the specific major steps in the procedure) that you would use to organize your ideas for the composition's body. Write these lists on your own paper.

1. Your test grades will improve if you use several strategies as you are taking the test.
2. The day I met _____ is still one of my most vivid memories. (Fill in the blank with the name of a person.)

3. Although I learned from my mistakes, my conflict with _____ was one that I handled very badly. (Fill in the blank with the name of a person.)

4. Becoming an organ donor is an easy process.

5. A college student who is undecided about his or her major and career goal should complete several steps to move closer to a decision.

Logical Organization

Many of the compositions you'll write will not organize themselves. Instead, you will have to use logic to determine the appropriate units, as well as the best order for those units. For example, read the following thesis statement:

> My criminology class is interesting and informative.

The logical units that would best organize this composition are *aspects of the class that are interesting* and *aspects of the class that are informative*. Aspects of the class that are interesting might include the instructor's dynamic public speaking and storytelling skills and/or the instructor's instructional methods (such as class discussions or activities). Aspects of the class that are informative could include specific examples of the useful knowledge and skills the writer is acquiring by taking the class. You would discuss these two groups in the order the adjectives are mentioned in the thesis statement.

Other thesis statements will clearly suggest the best type of units for grouping your ideas. Often, a word in the thesis will suggest a certain unit to use. Here is an example:

> Protecting yourself against identify theft will require you to develop several key habits.

This thesis statement indicates that *habits* will be the organizing units for the body. The writer must first determine which habits to present. Those habits could include creating secure passwords for online accounts, shredding documents with personal information on them, and protecting sensitive information such as social security numbers. After determining the habits to include, the writer would then need to decide on the order in which to present them.

Sometimes, the order may not matter. Other times, it *does* matter because of some relationship that exists among the organizing units. For example, consider this thesis statement:

> Buying a used, 10-year-old Chevrolet Nova was a very bad investment on my part.

The organizing units are clearly *reasons*, so the writer came up with this list:

1. Expense of repairs

2. Constant mechanical problems caused stress and worry about car's dependability

3. Inconvenience caused by breakdowns and periods of time with no transportation

If you study this list, you see a cause/effect relationship among the reasons emerge. The car's constant mechanical problems need to be discussed first, because this is the problem that causes the other two problems mentioned. Next, it would be logical to discuss how the mechanical problems led to breakdowns and periods when the car was in the shop for repairs and out of commission. Finally, it would make sense to explain how these breakdowns and repairs cost a lot of money. You might consider drawing out the relationship in a diagram to help you visualize it:

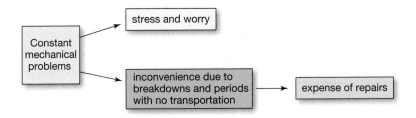

Sketching out your ideas in this way will help you decide on the right order for your paragraphs.

The thesis statements we've looked at so far have required one type of unit (events, steps, aspects, habits) for all of the body paragraphs. However, when you write academic or work-related reports with the purpose of informing readers about different aspects of a topic, you will often need to include more than one type of unit. For example, if you are writing to inform your readers about how to get started in a hobby that you enjoy, your organizing units might be:

Paragraph 1:   Equipment and supplies to purchase
Paragraph 2:   An effective layout for your workspace
Paragraph 3:   Sources of training or education for acquiring basic knowledge and skills
Paragraph 4:   Types of projects to start with

The important thing to remember is to avoid mixing different kinds of details together. Be sure to sort them into units that group related information together.

Exercise 8.3

For each of the following thesis statements, list the units you would use to organize your ideas for the composition's body. If there is a word in the thesis that gave you a clue about the best units, identify that word.

1. Keeping an automobile running well requires regular preventative maintenance.
2. Job hunters can use the Internet to find positions that match their goals and credentials.
3. Laser eye surgery may promise 20/20 vision, but patients should understand the risks of this surgery.
4. _____ should win the championship this year. (Fill in the blank with the name of a specific sports team.)
5. If you hire me, I will be an asset to your company.

Exercise 8.4

In the thesis statements listed for Exercise 8.2, which statements include a word that suggests the best units for the body? In each case, what is that word?

Exercise 8.5

What units of organization are used in the compositions that begin on pages 223 and 229 of Appendix 1: Eleven Model Compositions? Is there a word in each thesis that suggests the best units? In each case, what is that word?

Choosing Natural or Logical Organization

Neglecting to determine units for ideas is one way to ensure organizational problems. Another common way we create organizational problems is by trying to present ideas using a natural organization pattern when a logical pattern would be more effective. Telling a story, for example, is easy and comes naturally, so it can be tempting to present information as a chronological recounting of events. However, this form often buries the ideas in unnecessary details and prevents the reader from understanding them. The following essay provides an example:

My Best Job

I worked in retail sales for over 20 years, and I enjoyed it. I like working with the public, especially in jewelry sales. <u>My sales jobs were fun, financially rewarding, and socially enriching.</u>

Although many retail salespeople have to work flexible hours, I worked only Monday through Friday from 9:00 a.m. to 5:00 p.m., with weekends off. This was **a great schedule** for me, especially when my children were very young. Working on weekdays gave me the **opportunity to meet diverse, interesting people** as I helped them find what they were looking for.

Then, my employer required all employees to start rotating their schedules between day shifts and night shifts. I had to work sometimes until 10:00 p.m. and on Saturdays. However, **I made good money**, and **I liked my co-workers**, so I adjusted to the changes and stayed.

About a year later, though, the store I worked for began to struggle as the economy worsened. People had less money to spend, and sales declined significantly. Last May, the store finally closed, and I returned to college to study toward a degree in paralegal technology.

TIP

For more information about developing ideas in paragraphs, see Chapter 5.

TIP

When trying to determine the best organization plan for a composition, don't just select the first pattern that occurs to you. Consider different possibilities, then evaluate which one will help you best achieve your purpose.

The writer of this essay clearly states her thesis, which is underlined, in the opening paragraph. But then, instead of using the units *reasons I liked retail sales* to organize her information and discussing each one in a separate paragraph, she related the story of her history in this career field. She does briefly mention some of the reasons she liked her work; these reasons are highlighted in bold. However, this information is mixed in with a lot of seemingly irrelevant information that distracts readers from the essay's main point. This organization pattern also results in insufficient development of the writer's ideas, for she does not develop any of them with examples, facts, details, and other information that will help readers understand them.

Whenever you choose the narrative organization pattern, pause to consider whether it's the best method for arranging your ideas. If you're writing a report for your supervisor to explain why a piece of machinery malfunctioned, you might be tempted to tell the story of what happened the day it shut down. However, instead of using *events* as your organizing units, it might be more helpful to your reader if you present the information in units such as *causes for the malfunction* or *parts that were defective*. If you're writing to inform readers about a particular disease, don't tell the story of someone you know who has that disease. Instead, use the organizing units *causes, risk factors, symptoms, diagnostic tests,* and *treatments,* and devote at least one paragraph to each of those units.

▌ Exercise 8.6

For each of the following thesis statements, would natural organization or logical organization be the better pattern for the ideas in the composition's body? What units of organization would be best for each thesis? Is there a word in each thesis that suggests the best units? In each case, what is that word?

1. The risk factors for autism include male gender, a family history of autism, and parents' age.
2. San Jose, California, is one of the most family-friendly cities in the United States.
3. Dealing effectively with interpersonal conflict requires following five steps.
4. Meeting my fiancé changed my life for the better.
5. People who are grieving the loss of a loved one typically go through four stages.

Methods of Development

In Chapter 6, you learned about methods of development for paragraphs, which include narration, description, illustration, process, comparison, cause and effect, division, classification, and argument. These same methods can be used to organize the information in essays and other multiparagraph compositions, too.

Here is a list of model compositions in this book that are organized using one or more of these methods:

NARRATION

"I Drove Drunk and Killed Two Sisters," Appendix 1, page 219

ILLUSTRATION

"Memories of My Father," Appendix 1, page 212

PROCESS

"Don't Be a Victim," Chapter 8, pages 162–163

"Responding to Verbal Abuse," Chapter 10, pages 192–193

"Decision-Making and Problem-Solving," Appendix 1, page 214

"Avoiding Plagiarism," Appendix 1, page 231

COMPARISON

"Television vs. Real-Life Criminal Investigations," Appendix 1, page 227

CAUSE AND EFFECT

"The Drawbacks of Multitasking," Chapter 8, pages 166–167

"The Benefits of Club Membership," Chapter 10, page 193

"Why Americans Think (Wrongly) That Illegal Immigrants Hurt the Economy," Appendix 1, page 237

DIVISION

"Emotional Intelligence: Five Traits to Develop for Success in Life," Chapter 2, pages 26–27

"Soft Skills: The Competitive Edge," Appendix 1, page 223

CLASSIFICATION

"Bias in the News Media," Appendix 1, page 234

ARGUMENT

"The AAS Degree: Another Path to a Great Career," Chapter 2, page 23

"Going Shopping? Buy American," Chapter 8, pages 164–165

"The Drawbacks of Multitasking," Chapter 8, pages 166–167

"The Benefits of Club Membership," Chapter 10, page 193

Memo to Mr. Charles Morgan, Appendix 1, page 229

"In Defense of Police Pursuits," Appendix 1, page 239

COMBINATION OF METHODS (ILLUSTRATION, PROCESS, CAUSE AND EFFECT)

"Make the Choice to Harness Time's Power," Appendix 1, page 241

Outlining

Outlining involves reviewing the ideas and details generated during the prewriting step of the writing process, deciding which ones support or develop the thesis statement, and then organizing that relevant information into a plan to follow while writing the composition. During the organizing and outlining phase of the process, writers determine the overall structure for the composition and the best order in which to present their thoughts. Creating an outline of your ideas before you write will prevent you from:

- digressing from your main point.
- rambling or jumping from thought to thought in a confusing way.
- mixing different types of information together.
- discussing an idea in the wrong place.

Some inexperienced writers are in the habit of skipping the outlining step of the writing process. They argue, first of all, that outlining takes too much extra time. They figure that they'll save time by deciding on the best order for ideas as they compose. In reality, though, failing to organize before writing can actually *add* time to the writing step. When we don't spend time determining a plan of organization before we begin writing, we force our brains to do two challenging mental tasks (organize ideas *and* find the right language to express our thoughts) at the same time. As a result, composing is often slower and more frustrating. Separating the outlining stage and working out the organization of your ideas before you begin to write might actually save you valuable time in the long run.

Those who avoid outlining also argue that creating an outline is too difficult and complicated. It requires forcing ideas into a Roman-numeral system that is complex and hard to understand. As you will see in the following sections, though, there are several different types of outlines, both formal and informal, and you can develop a system that works for you.

Finally, people who don't outline proclaim outlines to be useless because they end up doing something different while composing anyway. However, just as a builder would never begin constructing a building without a blueprint, or plan, for the finished structure, a writer should not begin a composition without an outline. An outline is your best determination of the composition's overall structure, but that can change as you work. If, during construction, you find a better way to arrange something, then you can alter your initial blueprint to reflect your improvements.

Exercise 8.7

For each of the following thesis statements, identify the ideas in the brainstormed list that would support the thesis statement.

1. Our college's bookstore needs to make several improvements to its layout.
   - too many students allowed in at one time
   - not enough check-out lines at beginning of semester
   - aisles are too narrow
   - poor selection of snacks and drinks
   - store should open at 7:00 a.m. instead of 8:00 a.m.
   - supplies such as pens, paper, and notebooks should be moved to front of store
   - books on some shelves are too high to reach
2. Tanning in a tanning bed has a number of negative consequences.
   - too much exposure to ultraviolet light can cause premature wrinkling of skin
   - tanning can cause deadly skin cancer
   - a spray-on tan often looks just like a real tan

- the ultraviolet light in tanning beds can stimulate the body to produce beneficial vitamin D
- frequent trips to the tanning bed can damage the eyes
- it gets really hot in a tanning bed if you don't have a fan pointed at you
- tanned skin became fashionable in the 20th century
- when tanning oils and lotions are applied to the skin, they can accelerate the tanning process

3. Women's friendships and men's friendships tend to differ.
- women like to have conversations with each other, but men like to do things (e.g., play basketball or poker) with one another
- women and men use different communication and listening styles
- female friends talk to each other about their feelings and relationships, whereas male friends talk to each other about non-personal topics, such as sports
- women's childhood friendships are more likely than men's childhood friendships to last throughout their lifetimes
- female friends express intimacy by revealing personal, private details; male friends express intimacy by helping each other with tasks and chores
- women and men tend to approach problem-solving tasks in two very different ways

Formal Outlines

When most people think of an outline, they picture one that includes Roman numerals. This type of outline uses a combination of Roman numerals, letters, and Arabic numbers. The following outline, for example, shows a possible plan of organization and development for the body of an essay that develops a thesis statement mentioned earlier:

Thesis: An effective complaint letter (one that produces action and resolution) has several key components.

I. Specific details
  A. Provide names, dates, times
  B. Provide documentation
      1. Receipts
      2. Detailed account of events
II. Concise writing
  A. Don't include irrelevant information
  B. Avoid wordy sentences
III. A request for the action or result you want
  A. Be fair and realistic
  B. Ask for refund, replacement, repair, or needed change to a procedure
IV. A professional, businesslike tone
  A. Be firm and assertive in stating the problem and making your request
  B. Avoid insulting language and angry threats

In this type of outline, the Roman numerals correspond to the major organizing units, and the letters and Arabic numbers list supporting information and examples.

When using a Roman-numeral outline, follow these guidelines:

- The order for using numerals and letters to show the outline's subdivisions is: (1) Roman numerals, (2) capitalized letters, (3) Arabic numerals, and (4) lowercase letters.
- Indent each subdivided list so that the items align with each other.
- If you subdivide, include at least two different subtopics.
- Use topics in the form of short phrases. Capitalize only the first word, and do not use end punctuation.

This format is useful for separating ideas and indicating their relationships to each other. It also helps writers evaluate whether or not they are adequately developing each idea. However, writers do not necessarily need to use this more rigid form for planning compositions. Instead, they might choose a less formal approach.

TIP

To see a sample of a complete Roman-numeral outline, type "Purdue OWL Roman numeral outline" in an Internet search engine.

Exercise 8.8

Copy the following outline onto your own paper, filling in the blanks with appropriate ideas and details.

Thesis: Crime-proofing a house can be accomplished in a number of different ways.

I. _____
   A. Install deadbolt locks on all outside doors.
   B. _____
   C. _____
II. _____
   A. _____
   B. _____
   C. Hire a private security firm to maintain an alarm system.
III. Establish a neighborhood watch program.
   A. _____
   B. _____
   C. _____
IV. _____
   A. _____
   B. Leave the lights on when you go out.
   C. _____
V. _____
   A. Get a dog.
   B. _____
   C. _____

Informal Outlines

An outline is a tool that writers use to work out the best organization plans for compositions. Writers can choose from a variety of more informal outlines to help them accomplish this goal. An informal outline can be as simple and brief as a list of ideas written down in the order you plan to discuss them. You could number them or separate them with bullet points. Here's one example:

OPENING: Give background info about the importance of customer service at this store.

THESIS: Good customer service has three key elements.

BODY: Point 1: Being welcoming, friendly, and polite

Point 2: Good communication skills, especially listening skills

Point 3: The knowledge and skills to do the job efficiently and effectively

CLOSING: These skills will help you excel in your position here.

You could also organize your thoughts with the aid of a number of different diagrams. Here are two popular ones:

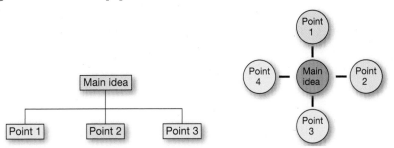

For those writers who prefer a more visual layout of their ideas, diagrams like these can be valuable tools for discovering and arranging logical units.

> **TIP**
>
> Always sketch at least an informal organization plan for everything you write, even academic and work-related e-mail messages.

Exercise 8.9

On your own paper, use at least two of the three different types of informal outlines to create outlines for each of the following thesis statements.

1. A good boss has several essential characteristics.
2. _____ is a rewarding hobby. (Fill in the blank with a specific hobby.)
3. _____ is a book/film/album/TV show that I would highly recommend. (Fill in the blank with the name of a specific book, film, album, or TV show.)

Writing to Organize Ideas

If you spend sufficient time organizing your thoughts and creating a formal or informal outline, you should have a useful guide or map to follow as you compose, and you can concentrate on finding the words that best express your ideas. As you write, consider using three specific techniques that will reinforce the structure of your composition and help readers understand the relationships among your ideas.

Make Connections to the Thesis Statement

Writers must make all of the necessary connections to help readers understand how the information in the body supports or proves the composition's main idea. Therefore, it's important to make an explicit connection between each unit within the body and the thesis statement. As you compose, do not move on to the next paragraph before you have directly tied that paragraph back to your thesis and explained how the information you've just provided supports your overall main point. In the following essay, the thesis is underlined, and the bold sentences demonstrate how these connections can be made:

Don't Be a Victim

The goal of a purse-snatcher or a mugger is to grab the goods and make a quick getaway, without being nabbed or having to fight. That's why these crooks pay attention to people's body language to help them identify potential victims. Certain types of body language reveal to a criminal that an individual is an easy target because he or she is unaware, afraid, or unlikely to defend himself or herself. <u>To avoid becoming the victim of a mugger, you must replace the body language that signals inattention or weakness with body language that will cause a predator to reject you as his or her next prey</u>.

Perfect mugging victims usually indicate with their bodies that that are not paying attention to or are unaware of their surroundings. For example, easy targets will look down or straight ahead while walking. They are often lost in thought or listening to music through headphones, limiting their ability to hear what's going on around them. Or, they may be talking on cell phones, which distracts them from noticing their environment, making it easier for a mugger to take their purse or wallet. In contrast, criminals will usually pass over people who are alert, aware, and taking in information about their surroundings through their eyes and ears. **So, if you are clearly paying attention to what's going on around you, you will be far less likely to be targeted by a thief.**

Likely victims also display body language that signals nervousness, fear, or a lack of confidence. They may have a slumped or stooped posture, hands stuffed into pockets, a worried or tense facial expression, a very fast walk, or an anxious look in their eyes. All of these types of body language send out the silent message that they are so timid or insecure, they could be easily overwhelmed by a robber. In contrast, people who communicate that they are confident and capable display a different set of behaviors. They stand up straight with their chins lifted. They walk with a long, purposeful stride. The expression on their faces is alert but relaxed and calm. They make direct eye contact with the people they pass. They project an air of being in control and ready for whatever may happen, so they are usually much less appealing to crooks. **By adopting this more confident, sure body language, you will be more likely to avoid victimization.**

Finally, how much people are carrying and how they're carrying it can factor into a pickpocket's decision to target them or not. People who are loaded down with several items, such as purses, tote bags, computer carrying cases, briefcases, grocery bags, or umbrellas, have made themselves slower, heavier, and unable to defend themselves with their hands. Furthermore, people who are carrying personal possessions in certain ways also attract the notice of muggers. For example, a purse being held only in one hand is fairly easy to snatch. A purse that is being clutched tightly with both hands indicates a nervous woman with valuables who would probably not put up a fight if the bag were wrenched away from her. On the other hand, a criminal is more likely to bypass a person who has left at least one hand free. **To make yourself less attractive to thieves, try not to burden yourself with too many things to carry when you must move around in public, and leave your hands free as much as possible.**

Any time you're out in public, someone may be sizing you up and trying to determine if you'll be the next target, so even if you don't feel as though you could resist or fight back, make yourself look as though you would. By doing so, you will probably prevent a mugging from ever happening in the first place.

Figure 8.1 provides a visual representation of the connections that an essay should make. The topic sentences show how the supporting points grow out of the idea or opinion in the thesis statement. The connecting statements at the end of each body paragraph explain how the information presented in the paragraph proves or supports the thesis statement. These techniques improve your essay's coherence by helping readers see how all of the parts are connected.

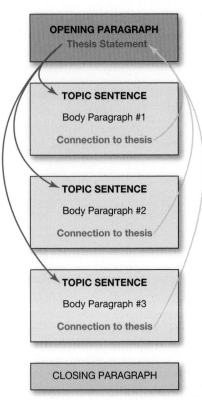

FIGURE 8.1

 Exercise 8.10

Examine an essay you've written recently. Did you tie the information provided in each of your body paragraphs back to your thesis statement? If not, what would you add to make these important connections?

Link Paragraphs

To follow your ideas, readers need to be able to understand the overall structure of your composition. You can help them do this by linking your body paragraphs in ways that reveal how each new paragraph is related to what came before it.

One effective way to link body paragraphs is to use **transitional words and phrases**. In Chapter 6, you learned that transitions show the relationships between sentences. They are also used to show the relationships between paragraphs. They include words and phrases such as *then, next, finally, consequently, as a result, in contrast, above, for example,* and *also*. In the essay below, notice how

Just as crossbars connect the parts of a table to stabilize it and make it more sturdy, the various techniques for linking paragraphs connect the different parts of your essay to reinforce its structure.

the bold, blue transitions indicate how the body paragraphs are related to each other and to the thesis statement. Each one signals the addition of another reason in support of that thesis.

Another effective way to link body paragraphs is to begin each one with clear references to what preceded it. These references can take the form of pronouns that refer to nouns mentioned earlier or synonyms for words mentioned earlier. A *synonym* is a word or phrase with the same meaning. In the essay below, notice how the bold, aqua words refer to the essay's topic using varied wording.

A final way to link body paragraphs is to refer back to an idea presented in a previous paragraph. In the essay below, notice how the phrases in orange refer to and reinforce points made in earlier paragraphs.

Going Shopping? Buy American

In the economic downturn that began in 2008, many American jobs were lost when numerous companies were forced to close their doors or significantly reduce their workforces. Even before then, many manufacturers had begun closing plants in the United States and moving them to foreign countries where the cost of labor is cheaper. To reverse this trend, improve the economy, and restore America's prosperity, we Americans must buy goods made by Americans in American plants. However, that's not the only reason to buy products manufactured in the United States. **Buying American-made products** is also good for all of us for a number of other reasons.

First of all, when you **buy goods made in the USA**, you are ensuring that these products are safe. The United States enforces safety standards that other countries do not. American consumer protection laws ensure that products are tested to make sure that they aren't poisonous, dangerous, or otherwise harmful. Safety standards in foreign counties are, in contrast, much lower. For example, millions of children's toys made overseas and shipped to the USA have been found to contain toxic levels of lead.

In addition to protecting your family, your choice to **purchase U.S.-manufactured goods also** helps protect Earth from environmental damage.

Manufacturing processes in America are much cleaner than those in other countries, which frequently produce heavy, even dangerous levels of pollution. By purchasing American products, you are contributing less to the smog, waste, and toxins that are spewing from foreign factories and harming our planet.

One final reason to **buy American** is a humanitarian one. In **purchasing U.S.-made products**, not only do **you help keep** *American* **workers employed**, but you also send the message to foreign manufacturers that you will not support companies that employ children or pay workers very little for their labor. Many other countries have no child labor laws or minimum-wage laws, so citizens there are often exploited and paid a few dollars a day for difficult and sometimes dangerous work. By refusing to buy products made in these countries, you are insisting that people everywhere be treated more fairly.

These are but a few of the many reasons to look more carefully at labels and ask more questions about product origins when you're shopping. You may pay a little more for the American-made version, but you'll sleep better at night knowing that you're doing what's right for your family, the environment, and your fellow humans.

Based on Lipscomb, Todd. "Top Ten Reasons to Buy American." MadeinUSAforever.com, 2007. Web. 31 March 2012.

Use Organizational Markers

Organizational markers are different systems for arranging information on the page. They include lists and headings. **Lists** line up information in a column and then add a visual feature such as numbering or bullet points (black dots) to help readers distinguish the items. **Headings** are mini-titles for smaller sections of a composition; they identify clearly and concisely the topic that will be discussed in that section. Headings are distinct from the rest of the text; they might be in bold print, underlined, or in a larger font size than the body text. This chapter, for example, uses bold headings of various sizes and colors to indicate section topics and to help readers understand the relationships between sections.

These markers help your readers visually separate ideas and quickly recognize their relationships to each other. Therefore, they aid readers' comprehension of the information. For example, the following passage uses bullet points to list tips for improving concentration while reading:

If you have trouble keeping yourself focused when you are completing academic reading assignments, try the following tips to improve your concentration and keep your mind from wandering:

- Read during the time of day when you are most alert.
- As you read, mark key ideas with a highlighter and write notes, summaries, reactions, or questions in the margins. Consider your reading experience a kind of conversation with the author, and interact with the text.
- As you read, think about how the information relates to your own opinions or experiences, or consider how the information will help you later when you achieve your career goal. Making these connections can make the information more meaningful and thus more interesting.

TIP

Read "Decision-Making and Problem-Solving" on page 214 of Appendix 1: Eleven Model Compositions to see an example of a composition that effectively uses headings and organizational markers.

- Work on improving your reading speed. Reading too slowly can make comprehension more difficult.
- If you're having trouble with a passage, try reading it aloud, especially if you're the type of learner who tends to remember what you hear.

Exercise 8.11

Read the essay below and then answer the questions that follow by writing your answers on your own paper.

The Drawbacks of Multitasking

¹ Busy modern Americans often try to multitask, or do more than one thing at a time. For example, we exchange text messages with a friend while simultaneously completing a class assignment, watching e-mail for new incoming messages, and listening to music. While driving our vehicles, we simultaneously talk on the phone and eat lunch. Many people believe that they have become good at multitasking because they do it so much. However, the truth is that no one is good at multitasking. When we try to do more than one thing at a time, everything we're doing—and we ourselves—suffer as a result. In fact, multitasking has four significant drawbacks that should cause us to stop it once and for all.

² The first drawback of multitasking is a reduction in the quality of every task we're trying to perform. Research has shown that switching back and forth repeatedly from one task to another might actually temporarily lower the IQ, which harms performance and therefore the finished product. So, if we try to complete a homework assignment while exchanging text messages, we are probably not producing work that's as high in quality as it would be if we turned the phone off until the assignment was done. In addition, studies show that anything we learn while multitasking is more difficult to recall later. This drawback alone should be reason enough to stop multitasking.

³ However, there are additional reasons. Doing two or more things at once also decreases efficiency and productivity. We might think that we're saving time by doing several things simultaneously, but that's a myth. In reality, we are usually *adding* time to tasks we are trying to complete because every time we switch from one thing to another, the brain needs a few moments to reorient itself to something different. The seconds lost in the readjustment periods add up, and we end up slowing ourselves down. The time we lose when we multitask is another good reason to vow to do just one thing at a time.

⁴ Multitasking affects more than just the quality, quantity, and speed of our output. Another drawback of multitasking is an increase in our stress levels. Dividing our attention between several tasks at the same time produces a feeling of busy-ness and creates a sense of urgency about getting everything done. This pressure can make us feel anxious and overwhelmed. Therefore, getting rid of a source of stress is a good reason to end our practice of multitasking.

⁵ When we multitask, the stress and the distractions lessen the pleasure we might otherwise experience in the process of completing a task. For example, we might not enjoy a phone conversation with a friend as much if we're trying to read e-mail at the same time because we can't really focus our full attention on that

conversation. When we stop multitasking, we can give our full attention to one thing and find pleasure in the performance of that task.

⁶ Therefore, if we want our work and our well-being to improve, we should adopt these sayings as our personal mantras to stop multitasking once and for all:

- One thing at a time.
- More is not better.
- Just say no (to simultaneous tasks).

1. What is the thesis of this essay?
2. What are the organizing units for the body of the essay?
3. What paragraph includes organizational markers? What are they?
4. What transitional words and phrases help readers understand how body paragraphs are related to each other and to the thesis statement?
5. Give one example of a sentence that ties a supporting point back to the idea in the thesis statement.
6. Give one example of a pronoun or a synonym that refers to a person, place, or thing in a previous paragraph.
7. Give one example of a phrase that refers back to an idea presented in a previous paragraph.

▌ Exercise 8.12

Select one of the model compositions in Appendix 1, which begins on page 211 of this book, and write your answers to the following questions on separate paper:

1. What is the thesis of the essay?
2. What are the organizing units for the body of the essay?
3. What techniques for linking body paragraphs does the writer use? Find specific examples in the composition.
4. Does the writer use organizational markers?

Rewriting to Organize Ideas

Even if you carefully crafted a detailed outline and then followed that outline as a guide as you wrote your first draft, you will still need to check that draft carefully for organizational problems. Review the overall structure of your composition. Do the units that you selected to organize the information in the body still make sense? Are they presented in a logical order? Are the details you included correctly sorted into appropriate units? Are paragraphs linked together in ways that help readers see their relationships to one another?

If you find problems, be willing to rewrite to eliminate them. Move paragraphs around to achieve better results. Move, add, or delete details. Add explanations as necessary.

The paragraphs on page 168 form the body of a report about organic foods, but they contain organizational problems. What advice would you give to the writer of these paragraphs?

When applied to foods, the term *organic* means that fruits or vegetables were grown without pesticides or chemical fertilizers, and that meat and dairy products come from animals raised without antibiotics or growth hormones. Many people are willing to pay extra for organic products because they believe these foods are better for health and better for the environment. Throughout most of human history, all farming was organic. In the 20th century, farmers began adding more chemicals to plant and animal products.

Organic foods are more expensive than foods produced by conventional farming techniques because organic farms tend to produce a smaller crop. So far, scientific studies have failed to produce evidence that organic foods are more nutritious than non-organic foods. However, many people believe that organic foods are safer than foods grown with conventional methods because they do not contain harmful chemicals. Organic farms use less energy and produce less waste.

Organic farms are less damaging to the environment than conventional farms. Because they do not use pesticides, they do not release these potentially harmful chemicals into the surrounding soil and water, where they can harm wildlife. The organic farming movement began in the 1940s, and today, the demand for organic foods continues to grow.

If you study these paragraphs, you see the following possible organizational units emerge:

Definition of the term *organic*

Reasons people buy organic foods

Cost of organic foods

Benefits of organic farming methods

History of organic farming

To improve organization, the writer needs to sort all of the details into the appropriate units and then evaluate each one for adequate development, adding more facts, examples, and other types of information as needed.

Exercise 8.13

The following paragraphs form the body of an essay with the thesis "Our public schools should not be closed in the summer; instead, our children should attend school all year long." Review the overall structure of this composition by considering the following questions: Is the information in the body organized with logical units? Are these units presented in a logical order? Are the details sorted correctly into each unit? Are paragraphs

linked together in ways that help readers see their relationships to one another?

On your own paper, write down the advice you would give the writer for correcting the organizational problems.

Every year, parents who work but can't afford day care or summer camps have to endure the stress of what to do with their kids during the summer months. They might have to impose on relatives for babysitting, or, in the case of older children, they might just leave the kids at home alone and unsupervised. Not surprisingly, many of these idle children get into trouble while no adult is there to watch over them.

Kids need to be learning all year round. Getting an annual break that's several months long can lead to a loss of retention of knowledge and skills gained that year. When children forget some or much of what they've learned over the summer, they have to go back and re-learn, losing valuable time.

The original reason for having summers off is no longer valid. A school calendar with summers off developed when many American families lived on farms, and the children were needed at home to help plant and harvest crops. Now, however, the majority of families no longer live on farms.

Summer vacations from school are hard on working parents. Those with young children have to pay child care expenses that can amount to hundreds of extra dollars for several months. This puts a strain on parents' finances.

Over time, school calendars continued to include summer vacations because schools without air conditioning were too hot during the summer months. Now, however, most schools have air conditioning, so there is no longer a reason for kids to be off from school for months at a time.

Our children's time would be better spent in school, improving their knowledge and skills, instead of running around unsupervised all day.

Some people say that our kids need a long break to rest, refresh, and re-motivate themselves after a long school year, but shorter breaks of two or three weeks throughout the year would achieve exactly the same purpose, and children wouldn't forget what they've learned.

When you evaluate the organization of a composition, consider using a checklist like the following as a guide.

CHECKLIST FOR CLEAR ORGANIZATION

Use this checklist to make sure that you are clearly organizing your ideas.

- ☐ The composition's opening paragraph includes a clear thesis statement that states the topic and the writer's overall point about that topic.

- ☐ The writer has used either natural or logical organization appropriately.

- ☐ The writer's ideas are organized into clear units.

- ☐ The units in the body of the composition are presented in a logical order.

- ☐ Each unit is clearly connected to the thesis statement.

- ☐ Each paragraph is linked in some way to what came before it.

- ☐ The writer has included organizational markers appropriately.

Exercise 8.14

A. Use the checklist above to evaluate an essay or multiparagraph composition you have recently written. If you revised this composition, would you need to make any changes to improve its organization?

B. Use the checklist to evaluate a classmate's composition. What improvements would you recommend?

SUGGESTED WRITING ACTIVITIES

Select one of the following activities and use all of the steps of the writing process to compose a multiparagraph composition. As you plan, write, and revise your composition, use this chapter's techniques for achieving clear organization.

ACADEMIC WRITING

1. Write a letter to a former teacher who positively influenced you or inspired you.
2. Write a composition to convince college instructors to use certain kinds of learning activities more often.
3. An alumnus of your college has donated $1 million for whatever the college needs. Write to your college's president to tell him how that money should be spent.

PROFESSIONAL WRITING

4. Persuade people to apply for a job at your place of employment.
5. Relate your work history. Include your places of employment and your job title and duties at each one.
6. Report on a professional organization for people working in the career field you wish to join. Explain the group's history, the group's goals, the group's activities, and the benefits of membership.

PERSONAL WRITING

7. Explain to a fellow student, friend, or relative how you lost weight, quit smoking, or made a good grade in a class.
8. Write to your city council to argue that the city needs to invest in something (such as a skateboard park, bicycle paths, or a dog park).
9. Interview an elderly relative about your family history and write a narrative for your children to read one day.

CHAPTER 9

Essential #9: Interesting Openings

In Chapters 5, 6, and 7 of this book, you learned about the parts and features of effective body paragraphs. Another type of paragraph in an essay or multiparagraph composition is the **opening paragraph,** which is also known as the *introduction* or the *introductory paragraph*. Unlike body paragraphs, which develop the main ideas that support the thesis statement, the opening paragraph provides necessary background information to prepare the reader for the thesis statement. It also gets the reader interested in the topic and main idea. Therefore, the elements and the structure of the opening paragraph differ from those of a body paragraph.

A good opening paragraph is critical to the success of your composition. First impressions are important because readers often judge a composition based on its first few sentences. If reading the document is optional, your audience may decide on whether or not to proceed based on what the opening paragraph contains. When your readers are *required* to read the composition, they may form certain opinions about the worth of your ideas or opinions based on those crucial opening statements.

Prewriting for Effective Opening Paragraphs

Many writers compose the body of their compositions *first* so that they will know exactly what they need to introduce to readers. Whether you write the opening paragraph before or after composing the body, the process should begin with prewriting. Just as you use prewriting strategies to generate ideas for the body of your essay, you can use the same prewriting strategies to produce ideas for the opening. For example, you could brainstorm a list of possible details to include. You could freewrite to explore what needs to be included and what techniques to use. You could talk to a friend or classmate and discuss various ways to begin.

Whatever method you use, you'll need to be aware of the three purposes of the opening paragraph so that you can be sure to address each one as you write.

Just as you form a first impression during the first moments of meeting someone new, readers form a first impression about a composition based on the opening paragraph.

Purposes of the Opening

Every effective opening serves three specific purposes:

1. It states your thesis.
2. It provides background information to prepare your readers for your thesis.
3. It gets readers interested in your composition.

State Thesis

The first purpose of the opening is to state your composition's main idea, or thesis. The thesis is the sentence that identifies the one idea or opinion you want your reader to know or to believe after reading your paper. Stating your thesis in your opening paragraph focuses your readers' attention on that point. Chapter 2 of this book explains thesis statements in more detail.

Where should you state your thesis? You could announce your main point in the first sentence of your opening paragraph; however, you'll often find that you'll need to prepare your readers with some background information first. They may need some explanation of the situation or issue to help them understand the point you're making in the thesis. If that's the case, the thesis is more appropriately placed later in the opening paragraph.

Give Background Information

Another purpose of the opening paragraph is to provide readers with any necessary background information they need to understand the topic or main point.

TIP

How long does an opening paragraph need to be? The answer is: *As long as it needs to be to achieve all three purposes for opening paragraphs.* Some opening paragraphs will be relatively brief, perhaps five or six sentences. Others will need to be longer.

The kind of background information you'll include depends on your subject. Some common types of background information include:

- Historical detail
- A description of the current situation or circumstances
- An explanation of your topic's relevance or importance
- Definitions of terminology

One type of background information is historical detail that helps the reader understand the past. For example, in an essay that advocates reintroducing the wolf into certain wilderness areas, you may need to explain the animal's past history in those areas, including an explanation of why it does not populate that area now. In a letter to convince a friend to join a grief support group with you, you might summarize the events that have led you to propose this suggestion.

Another type of background is a description of the current situation or circumstances of an issue or problem. In other words, you might need to give your reader information about what is happening now. For instance, an e-mail to your supervisor about an equipment problem should explain the current status of the equipment. In an essay advocating that public school students wear uniforms, you should explain why schools are considering this change.

Background can also include an explanation of your topic's relevance or importance. Why should the reader be interested in this subject? Why is it meaningful? How many people does it impact, and in what ways? For example, in a paper about the health risks of smoking cigarettes, you might want to provide statistics about the number of people who are suffering from smoking-related illnesses. In a letter to your local newspaper's editor about the need for a traffic light at a busy intersection, you might want to note how many motorists are affected, as well as how many accidents have occurred at this location in recent months. When establishing your topic's significance with data, make sure that the information comes from a reputable, accurate source. Also, always be sure to identify the sources of your information.

A final type of background information takes the form of definitions of terminology. To avoid confusion or misinterpretation, you'll want to make sure that your reader knows the meaning of significant words associated with your topic. For instance, if you write an essay to convince readers that they need a "living will," you will need to define what that is. If you write to oppose "factory farms," you'll need to explain the meaning of that term.

TIP

See pages 97–98 of Chapter 5 for more information about including information from other sources.

Exercise 9.1

For each of the following thesis statements, list the background information you would need to provide to help prepare your reader for the thesis.

1. The United States should require citizens to vote just as Australia requires its citizens to vote.
2. Anyone who is looking for a new romantic partner in online dating sites needs to be aware of some potential pitfalls.
3. _____ is overrated. (Fill in the blank with a specific person, place, or thing.)
4. Our city needs to invest in building a skateboard park for our teenagers.
5. Memorial Day is a day that people should observe rather than ignore.

Interest the Reader

If you're going to achieve your purpose for writing, you have to get your readers to read your entire composition. They are more likely to do so when they are interested in the topic or main point. Therefore, a third purpose of the opening paragraph is to capture readers' attention and make them want to know more about your topic and your main point. The next sections will explain and illustrate several effective techniques for sparking readers' interest.

Exercise 9.2

In each of the following opening paragraphs, the thesis statement is underlined. Does each paragraph get you interested and make you want to read the entire composition? Why or why not? Does each opening include a clear thesis statement? Does it provide enough background information?

A.   Letters are one form of written communication. People have been writing letters for a variety of different reasons for a very long time. Love letters, application letters, and thank-you letters are some of the different types of letters. Sometimes people write letters when they want to complain about something. <u>An effective complaint letter (one that will produce action and resolution) has several key components.</u>

B.   In 2008, three-year-old Brandon Salisbury was playing in a sandbox in the backyard of his home in Boise, Idaho. His mother was there with him, but when the phone rang, she ran inside the house to grab it. In the moment or two she was gone, her neighbor's dog—an animal that was part German Shepherd, part wolf—trotted into the yard and pounced on her son. Before Brandon's mother could reach her screaming child, the dog had crushed the boy's throat, killing him. This story illustrates why many states have banned or severely restricted ownership of "exotic" pets such as wolf hybrids, venomous snakes, chimpanzees, bears, and tigers. Our state does not. Your neighbors can possess wild animals as pets after obtaining a permit. Do you want a loose animal like the one that killed Brandon to wander into your yard one day? I know I don't. <u>State law should be changed to identify inherently dangerous animals and to prohibit people from keeping these animals as pets.</u>

C.   A lot of people need a new organ to replace a defective one. So, they are on waiting lists for donated organs, and they will die if they don't get the organs they need in time. Are you an organ donor? <u>You should be.</u>

Techniques for Writing Interesting Openings

To get your reader interested in your composition, you can use several different techniques:

- Tell a story
- Ask questions
- Connect to readers' goals or needs

- Begin with a quotation
- Give an example
- Explain the general topic and narrow to a specific point
- Surprise or shock the reader

Tell a Story

We all enjoy hearing stories. Narratives, real or fictional, usually generate immediate interest in a subject. Therefore, stories can be a good technique for drawing in readers. For example, read the following opening paragraph from a student's essay about the importance of wearing a helmet while riding a bicycle. The thesis statement is underlined.

> Five-year-old Johnny is riding his bicycle. He pedals up a hill, turns around, and pushes off. Suddenly going way too fast, he panics. He loses control of his speeding bike, hits the curb, and flies through the air. His head strikes the ground, knocking him unconscious. His parents rush him to the hospital, where the doctor admits him to watch for a possible concussion. His parents later receive a hospital bill for $3,000, but that's cheap compared to what the accident might have cost if Johnny hadn't been wearing a helmet. Many children are injured in bicycle accidents, but those who wear helmets are more likely to avoid serious damage. <u>Parents should insist that their children wear helmets, which reduce the likelihood of injuries and expensive medical treatment.</u>

This opening engages readers' interest by telling a suspenseful story about a little boy's bicycle accident. In this next example, the opening paragraph captures readers' attention by telling the story of famous entrepreneur Milton Hershey. The thesis statement is underlined.

> In 1876, Milton Hershey tried to start a candy business in Philadelphia, Pennsylvania. Although he worked hard for six years, his company failed. Hershey moved to Denver, Colorado, and went to work for another candy maker. Then, striking out on his own again, he opened a candy business in Chicago and another in New York City. Both failed. In 1885, he returned to his hometown of Lancaster, Pennsylvania, and—refusing to give up—joined forces with a business partner and scraped together enough money to open a fourth candy-making company. This time, he was successful, becoming the world's first mass producer of chocolate bars that are still enjoyed today. Hershey's life story is like that of many entrepreneurs who create and build businesses, and a study of these people reveals that that they have some traits in common. <u>Successful entrepreneurs tend to possess three essential characteristics: a strong work ethic, persistence and determination in the face of obstacles, and a willingness to take risks.</u>

Information from "Milton S. Hershey."
The Hershey Company. Web. 14 Mar. 2012.

A story in an opening paragraph can be true, fictional, or hypothetical, but it should always adhere to two important guidelines. First, it should be brief. Resist the urge to include a lot of descriptive details. Instead, concentrate on the events in the story. Second, the story should logically illustrate or clearly relate to your composition's main idea.

Exercise 9.3

Select one of the following thesis statements, and write an opening paragraph that uses a story to get readers interested. In your opening paragraph, also include any background information needed to prepare readers for the thesis.

1. _____ is the most talented person I know. (Fill in the blank with the name of a person.)
2. Children experience several negative effects when their parents divorce.
3. Our city council needs a stronger law to get pet owners to keep their animals on leashes when in city parks.

TIP

Never begin a composition with phrases such as *In this paper I am going to . . .* or *This essay will prove that. . . .* Readers will be yawning before they finish your first paragraph.

Ask Questions

Another technique for arousing readers' interest involves asking questions to get them thinking about your topic. This method encourages readers to participate by mentally answering the questions you pose. For example, the following opening draws the reader in with questions. The thesis statement is underlined.

> When you attended high school, what time did your school day begin? Do you remember feeling sleepy, dazed, or even irritable in your first-period class? Many students do, and researchers are finding out that schools' early start times may be to blame. Studies are revealing that adolescents experience major benefits when their day starts a little later. <u>Delaying high schools' start time to 8:30 a.m. results in a significant improvement in students' alertness, mood, and motivation.</u>

> Info from http://www.sciencedaily.com/
> releases/2010/07/100705190532.htm

Here is another example of an opening paragraph that asks questions to get readers thinking. The thesis statement is underlined.

> What are the advantages of driving a hybrid vehicle like the Toyota Prius, the Ford Fusion, or the Honda Insight? Because these cars run on a combination of gasoline and electricity and typically travel about 50 miles on just one gallon of gas, their main benefit is obviously fewer trips to the gas station and, therefore, significant savings. However, they offer other very important advantages. If everyone in America drove one of these hybrid vehicles, studies show, we would be able to import 70 percent *less* oil from foreign sources, and this change would produce benefits that range from greater national security to a reduction in pollution and greenhouse gases that cause global warming. <u>For these and other reasons, every U.S. motorist should seriously consider switching from gasoline-powered cars to hybrid cars.</u>

When you begin a composition by asking questions, follow three guidelines. First, keep each question brief and to the point. Second, don't ask too many questions. Readers are not reading your paper to be quizzed on a topic. Ask a few key questions to get them interested and involved, but then move on to providing some answers. Finally, make sure that your questions are directly related to your topic and main point.

Exercise 9.4

Select one of the following thesis statements, and write an opening paragraph that uses one or more questions to get readers interested. In your opening paragraph, also include any background information needed to prepare readers for the thesis.

1. Military service is an excellent choice for many high school graduates.
2. Crime-proofing a house can be accomplished a number of different ways.
3. People who are planning to buy a new vehicle should consider the _____ . (Fill in the blank with the name of a specific vehicle.)

Connect to Readers' Goals or Needs

Another very effective way to get your readers interested involves connecting your topic to your readers' goals or needs. Readers are interested in information or ideas that are relevant to their lives, so they will want to read your composition if you help them understand how they can directly benefit from doing so. In the following example, the writer explains how the topic relates to readers' desires. The thesis statement is underlined.

> You regularly lie in a tanning bed because you believe that having bronzed skin will make you look more attractive. Surely, though, you also want to remain healthy, avoid serious diseases, and look young as long as you can. If you want all of these things, too, you must stop exposing yourself to the harmful ultraviolet rays in tanning beds. <u>By lying in a tanning bed, you are significantly increasing your risk of cancer, and you are also ensuring premature aging of your skin, which will look old and wrinkled much earlier than normal.</u>

In the next example, the writer shows readers how they have directly benefited from NASA research. The thesis statement is underlined.

> Most of us modern Americans use filtered water, nonstick pots and pans, and sunglasses that block harmful ultraviolet rays. We appreciate the convenience of wireless headsets, Bluetooth technology, and cordless tools such as DustBusters and battery-powered drills. We enjoy being able to have long-distance telephone conversations with friends and family members in other states or countries. We feel comforted knowing that our smoke detectors will alert us if a fire starts and that medical body scanners will help our doctors diagnose what ails us. If you have used any of these inventions, you can thank this country's space program. All of these technological advancements are the inventions of researchers at the National Aeronautics and Space Administration (NASA) who were searching for ways to solve problems related to sending vehicles and people into outer space. However, the spin-off products that result from our space program and improve the lives of everyone here on Earth are just one of the many reasons that NASA should continue to receive funding to pursue space travel. <u>NASA and its projects are definitely worthy of U.S. citizens' continued support.</u>

Using this technique will require you to understand who your readers are. In Chapter 1, you learned to consider your audience's characteristics. Performing this analysis of your readers will be important to using this opening technique effectively.

▌ Exercise 9.5

Select one of the following thesis statements, and write an opening paragraph that connects to readers' goals or needs to get them interested. In your opening paragraph, also include any background information needed to prepare readers for the thesis.

1. _____ is easy if you follow three steps. (Fill in the blank with a specific procedure.)
2. _____ is a great place to vacation. (Fill in the blank with the name of a specific place.)
3. Every homeowner should invest in a home security system.

Begin with a Quotation

Using a quotation is another way to get your readers interested in your ideas. The best quotation is a short, clever, and thought-provoking statement. Quotations are often the words of a famous person, but you can also quote people you've known or refer to sayings that aren't attributed to any one individual. For example, you could refer to old sayings such as "Absence makes the heart grow fonder" and "The best things in life are free." The following example of an opening paragraph that begins with a quotation starts with the word of a famous philosopher. The thesis statement is underlined.

> Ancient Chinese philosopher Confucius said, "Choose a job you love, and you will never work a day in your life." This is good advice for anyone, but it may be even more important for college students who are undecided about their majors and career goals. Deciding on the job you will love may seem difficult, but it will become easier if you guide your thoughts in a certain direction. Making a career choice should involve an honest and in-depth consideration of three things: (1) your talents and your weaknesses; (2) your preferences about working conditions, compensation, and benefits; and (3) your long-term goals and how hard you're willing to work to achieve them.

In the next example, the opening paragraph begins with an old saying whose origin is unknown. The thesis statement is underlined.

> According to one old saying, "Sticks and stones may break my bones, but words will never hurt me," but that saying simply isn't true for most people. It would be great if we truly could form a mental shield that prevents ridicule, insults, name-calling, criticisms, threats, and other forms of humiliation from affecting us, but most of us don't have that power. Words _can_ hurt. Verbal abuse hurts people mentally and emotionally by causing them fear, anxiety, and depression; by robbing them of their self-esteem and sense of safety and security; by causing psychological abnormalities; and by warping their outlook on life and damaging their future relationships with others. Anyone who is suffering from verbal abuse must respond and take steps to put a stop to this potentially serious problem.

An effective quotation needs to be related to your topic. It either concisely summarizes your point or leads to your main idea. When including a quotation, always identify the speaker in order to properly credit that person.

> ## TIP
>
> Good sources of quotations include print books such as *Bartlett's Familiar Quotations* and online sources such as Brainy Quote, Bartleby.com, and ThinkExist.com. These sources are usually organized by topic or by author. When using online sources, check the wording and source of the quotation in several sites to verify their accuracy.

Exercise 9.6

Select one of the following thesis statements, and write an opening paragraph that uses a quotation to get readers interested. In your opening paragraph, also include any background information needed to prepare readers for the thesis.

1. Conquering a fear of _____ is possible by following several steps. (Fill in the blank with a specific fear.)

2. Good friendships are essential for not only our psychological health but also our physical health.

3. My _____ life story is a fascinating tale. (Fill in the blank with a specific person, e.g., uncle's, grandma's, friend Kara's.)

Give an Example

Giving an example involves describing how a specific situation or person illustrates your main idea. A concrete example often engages readers' interest immediately. This first model paragraph offers specific people who illustrate the idea in the thesis statement, which is underlined:

> My grandparents just celebrated their 50th wedding anniversary. They married in 1960, raised three children, and went through all of life's usual ups and downs, but they are still a devoted and loving couple all of these years later. People often ask them why, when so many marriages end in divorce, their relationship has been such a success. They reply that were lucky to have the three ingredients for a good marriage. <u>Two people who want to stay happily married, they believe, need to have mutual respect, shared values and goals, and genuine enjoyment of each other's company.</u>

A second model paragraph begins with an example of specific country. The thesis statement is underlined.

> In many Western European nations, such as Germany, the high school curriculum is not one-size-fits-all, with an emphasis only on academic studies. Instead, students select one specific track depending on their goal. Teenagers who want to attend a liberal arts university enroll in one set of courses. Teenagers who want to attend a technical college take a different set of courses. Teenagers who want to go straight to the workforce take courses that prepare them to be successful in that goal. In contrast, U.S. high schools are still emphasizing academic subject matter and doing little to prepare many of their students for the workplace. As a result, America's youth unemployment rate is much higher than the rate in

countries that do a better job of preparing students for different career pathways. <u>To better serve all of their students, high schools in America should copy the Western European model and offer a choice between academic education and vocational training.</u>

When beginning with an example, stick to the details that are relevant to your main idea. Resist the urge to include information, however interesting, that does not relate to your topic.

▌ Exercise 9.7

Select one of the following thesis statements, and write an opening paragraph that gives an example to get readers interested. In your opening paragraph, also include any background information needed to prepare readers for the thesis.

1. Our college's attendance policy needs to be changed.
2. _____ was one of America's best (or worst) presidents. (Fill in the blank with the name of a specific U.S. president.)
3. Keeping an automobile running well requires regular preventative maintenance.

Explain the General Topic and Narrow to a Specific Point

For some topics, it will be interesting for readers to learn more about how your main point arises from some broader issue or topic. So, another technique for opening paragraphs is to begin with a discussion of a general subject, gradually narrowing to your specific point about one aspect of this subject. Using this technique, you orient readers by showing them the "big picture" before zeroing in on the one idea or opinion on which you will focus. This first example provides an overview of different rehabilitation methods in prison before zeroing in on just one of those methods. The thesis statement is underlined.

For centuries, prisons have been trying a number of different methods in an attempt to rehabilitate inmates and encourage them to reject criminal behavior when they are released and reenter society. Prison programs have usually included some form of psychological counseling, substance abuse programs, and mental health treatment programs. Some offer spiritual development programs. Others have tried work programs characterized by hard labor for little compensation. All of these different approaches do help to rehabilitate lawbreakers to some extent. However, the best rehabilitation tool is actually education. Studies have shown that inmates who expand their education while they are incarcerated are significantly less likely to return to prison after they are released. <u>Prison education programs are a wise use of taxpayers' money because they give inmates the knowledge and skills they need to pursue a productive career pathway, the self-esteem to believe that they can better themselves, and a different outlook on life that leads them to make better choices.</u>

Figure 9.1 shows how this technique can be illustrated visually, using an upside-down triangle.

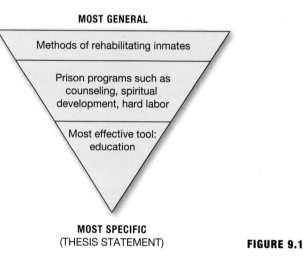

MOST GENERAL

Methods of rehabilitating inmates

Prison programs such as counseling, spiritual development, hard labor

Most effective tool: education

MOST SPECIFIC
(THESIS STATEMENT)

FIGURE 9.1

This technique is often used in work-related writing, where it's appropriate to explain an overall situation to readers to prepare them for your specific main idea. For example:

Since this company was created, it has required its salaried employees to work eight hours per day, five days a week, for a total of 40 hours per week. This work schedule has been standard among many companies and businesses in this country; however, some of them are beginning to see the value in offering other options. One of the most popular alternatives is a four-day work week in which employees are on the job 10 hours per day for four days. Switching our employees to a four-day work week would have a few disadvantages, but the benefits for both employees and the company far outweigh the drawbacks.

Exercise 9.8

Select one of the following thesis statements, and write an opening paragraph that explains the general topic and narrows to a specific point. In your opening paragraph, also include any background information needed to prepare readers for the thesis. If necessary, fill in the blank with your own topic.

1. The U.S. government should invest more in the development of _____.
   (Fill in the blank with a specific thing.)
2. My employer's (or my college's) policy about _____ is not fair.
   (Fill in the blank with a specific policy.)
3. _____ is one celebrity who is a bad role model for young people.
   (Fill in the blank with a specific celebrity's name.)

Surprise or Shock the Reader

Perhaps one of the best ways to pique your readers' interest is to surprise or shock them. You can achieve this several ways: with startling statistics, with a fascinating

or unusual fact, or with an attention-getting quotation. The following example begins with a surprising fact. The thesis statement is underlined.

> According to the U.S. Environmental Protection Agency, the average American
> throws away 4.5 pounds of garbage every day. That adds up to over 1,600 pounds of
> waste per person per year. Not surprisingly, U.S. landfills are running out of space, and
> finding places for new ones is problematic because no one wants to live near a dump.
> One way to solve this problem is to reduce the amount of trash generated so that
> landfills don't fill up as fast. Trash reduction requires recycling. When paper, plastic,
> glass, aluminum, and other materials are collected and recycled, they don't wind up
> consuming valuable space at the dump. <u>Recycling has always been optional for our
> city's citizens, but it's time to follow the examples of cities like Seattle and San Diego
> and make recycling mandatory for all residences and businesses.</u>

This next example begins with a shocking statistic. The thesis statement is
underlined.

> According to the Educational Testing Service, at least 75 percent of today's college
> students admit to having cheated when they were in high school. In the 1940s, only
> 20 percent of college students said they had cheated in high school. Parents and educa-
> tors need to understand the reasons behind this alarming increase in dishonesty among
> our youth. <u>Rampant cheating in high schools has several key causes.</u>

If you use this technique, make sure that the statistics or facts are related to
your topic and directly lead to the point you make in your thesis statement.

Exercise 9.9

**Select one of the following thesis statements, and write an opening para-
graph that surprises or shocks readers to get them interested. In your
opening paragraph, also include any background information needed to
prepare readers for the thesis.**

1. All high school students should be required to take a class that teaches
   them how to manage their personal finances.
2. College athletes and professional athletes are overcompensated.
3. The legal drinking age should remain at 21 years old.

Combine the Methods

The various techniques for interesting readers can be combined, as the following
opening paragraph from a student's letter to her senator illustrates:

> Our state's motto is "Iowa: A Place to Grow," and we do seem to live in a progressive
> and prosperous state. However, our problems with homelessness mock that motto. All
> over our state, people aimlessly wander the streets. They crowd into inadequate homeless
> shelters. Many live in cars and abandoned buildings. Many are suffering from mental and

physical illnesses. Should we dismiss them as bums and vagrants, people who don't matter? When we encounter them, should we look the other way and refuse to admit that we have a problem? The 14,000 homeless people in Iowa deserve a chance to "grow," but they can't without our help. <u>Our state's citizens must commit to supplying the resources and services that will provide our homeless citizens with the affordable housing, counseling, medical care, and job training that will get them off the streets and into a better life.</u>

This opening paragraph combines three different attention-getting techniques: a quotation, questions, and surprising statistics.

Exercise 9.10

What technique (or techniques) for interesting readers is used in the opening paragraph of each of the following essays?

1. "The AAS Degree: Another Path to a Great Career" on page 23 of Chapter 2
2. "Emotional Intelligence: Five Traits to Develop for Success in Life" on pages 26–27 of Chapter 2
3. "Going Shopping? Buy American" on pages 164–165 of Chapter 8
4. "The Drawbacks of Multitasking" on pages 166–167 of Chapter 8
5. "The Benefits of Club Membership" on page 193 of Chapter 10

Exercise 9.11

In a small group with your classmates, discuss three different ways to interest the reader in each of the following thesis statements.

1. A championship football team always has talented players, dedication, and a good coach.
2. Renting a house and buying a house have both advantages and disadvantages.
3. When choosing a family pet, consider the required expense, maintenance, and time involved in the animal's upkeep.
4. Young people who drop out of school before age 18 should lose their driver's license.
5. To comply with the Americans with Disabilities Act, the doors, restrooms, and elevators in this building will have to be modified.

Exercise 9.12

Select one of the compositions in Appendix 1: Eleven Model Compositions, which begins on page 211, and write a different opening paragraph for that composition.

TIP

Every time you receive a graded composition back from an instructor, use the comments and suggestions to set some goals for your future papers and to determine how you will achieve those goals. For example, if your instructor identifies openings as one of your weaknesses, resolve to write a paper with a better opening next time, perhaps by reviewing the techniques for interesting openings before you begin to write.

Rewriting for Interesting Openings

After composing your opening paragraph, reread it to make sure that it achieves all three purposes of openings. Does it include your thesis statement? Does it provide necessary background information? Does it use a technique to get the reader interested in the topic and main idea? If it's lacking any of these elements, revise it to improve it.

What changes would you recommend for the following opening paragraph?

> In this paper, I'm going to present the reasons for the decrease in crime in the United States. <u>Fewer crimes are being committed because of a decrease in hard-core drug usage, better policing, and an increased number of criminals serving time in prison.</u>

This opening includes a clear thesis statement, which is underlined. However, it lacks background information. At the very least, the writer needs to explain how much the crime rate has decreased and define the time period of this decrease. Also, the writer needs to use a technique for getting readers interested in the subject. If the statistics that need to be added turn out to be surprising, they may serve the double purpose of providing background information while also getting readers interested. Another way to begin would be to give an example of a specific community that has experienced a dramatic drop in crime rates. One final needed change is to revise the first sentence to eliminate "In this paper, I'm going to . . ." That's the most boring way to begin a composition.

When you evaluate the opening paragraph of a composition, consider using a checklist like the following as a guide.

CHECKLIST FOR INTERESTING OPENINGS

Use this checklist to make sure that your opening paragraphs are interesting and effective.

 The composition's opening paragraph includes a clear thesis statement.

 The writer has included sufficient background information to prepare readers to understand the thesis statement.

☐ The opening paragraph gets readers interested in the composition's topic and main idea.

Exercise 9.13

Reread the opening paragraphs in Exercise 9.2. What advice would you give the writer for improving opening paragraphs A and C?

Exercise 9.14

A. Use the checklist on page 185 to evaluate an essay or other multiparagraph composition you have recently written. If you revised this composition, what changes would you make to improve its opening paragraph?

B. Use the checklist to evaluate a classmate's essay or other multiparagraph composition. What improvements would you recommend?

SUGGESTED WRITING ACTIVITIES

Select one of the following activities and use all of the steps of the writing process to compose a multiparagraph composition. Experiment with different techniques for the opening paragraph until you find the one that works best.

ACADEMIC WRITING

1. Write an editorial to persuade your fellow students to run for an office in your college's student government organization.
2. Explain the physical, mental, and psychological (or emotional) effects of a common problem for college students (such as sleep deprivation, binge drinking, or prolonged stress).
3. Describe the most important qualities of an effective leader. Select current or historical leaders to illustrate your ideas.

PROFESSIONAL WRITING

4. Write a proposal to suggest changes that would make your workplace environment more pleasant.
5. Explain to your supervisor the team you would assemble and the tasks you would assign each team member in order to complete a big project.
6. Write a letter of application to explain your qualifications for a job you want and to request an interview.

PERSONAL WRITING

7. Write a letter to introduce and sell an item you made yourself (e.g., a craft, a food item, or an artwork).
8. Write to an elected official to argue that the fee or fine for something (such as a driver's license, a passport, a library fine, or a parking ticket) is too high.
9. Write an editorial to persuade voters to elect you (or a candidate whom you support) to an office (such as mayor, city council member, or county commissioner).

CHAPTER 10

Essential #10: Effective Closings

People are accustomed to clear endings. We don't like to hang up the phone until both speakers have said goodbye. We expect a song to wrap up with a final long note, a crescendo that builds to a resounding climax, or repetition while the tune fades. We like our movies and books to end with all of the loose ends tied up and all of the characters getting the rewards or punishments they've shown they deserve.

Readers, too, expect clear, satisfactory endings in compositions. They want to feel a sense of closure when they finish reading. In other words, they want thoughts and ideas to be wrapped up neatly and logically.

Writers, therefore, cannot end a composition with their last body paragraph. Instead, they need to provide one final paragraph to provide closure. This paragraph is known as the **closing paragraph** or *conclusion*. It should not simply repeat or summarize what's already been said. On the other hand, the closing is not the place to introduce any new ideas. This chapter will present five techniques for writing effective closings.

Prewriting for Effective Closings

Always write the body of your composition before writing your closing paragraph. After you've presented all of the information and explanation in support of your thesis statement, you will be able to select the type of closing that most logically follows. The next sections of this chapter explain and illustrate five common ways of ending a composition.

Use one or more of the prewriting strategies described in the Introduction of this book to generate possible ideas. You may even want to write more than one closing and then choose the one that provides the most satisfactory ending.

Techniques for Writing Effective Closings

Writers can choose from five common techniques for concluding their compositions:

1. Describe effects or consequences
2. Make predictions
3. Recommend action
4. Complete a circle
5. Ask questions

These are not the only possible strategies; you may come up with others that more logically and effectively fit the composition you have written. However, one or more of these techniques will often be suitable.

Just as a knot secures the strands of a rope, a closing paragraph ties together all of the information presented in the composition to provide a satisfactory ending.

Describe Effects or Consequences

One of the most effective ways to end a composition is to describe the effects or consequences of your ideas. These effects could be short term, long term, or both. When using this technique, you would complete the body of your composition and then ask yourself this question: "I have now convinced the reader to accept the idea or opinion I presented in my thesis statement. What are the effects or consequences of accepting this idea or opinion?"

For example, in an e-mail that describes the company's required hand-washing procedures for employees who handle food, your closing paragraph could explain the effects of following this procedure:

> Your compliance with this policy is appreciated. By adhering to this requirement, we will increase customer confidence, reduce complaints, and ultimately increase the company's profits and our own job security.

Another example is from a student's essay about a special celebration in his culture. His thesis statement is "Our Hmong New Year celebration has special meaning for the people of my culture," and his essay describes the specific elements of this celebration and their importance. He closes his essay with this paragraph:

> We have adopted many of the traditions of mainstream America and celebrate many of the holidays of this country. However, it's important for us to preserve this one annual celebration that is unique to our culture. The events and customs of the Hmong New Year help keep us connected to our families, our community, and the religion of our heritage.

Make Predictions

Another effective way to conclude a composition is to make some predictions for the future. These predictions should arise naturally out of the information presented in the composition.

For instance, in a letter to a representative in Congress about the poor condition of a road near your home, you might end with the following paragraph:

> If this road is not repaired as soon as possible, accidents and injuries will continue to occur. We should not let this happen when we recognize the problem and can do something about it.

This next example is from an essay that explains the benefits of researching your family history. The writer explains that studying one's genealogy provides the following: (1) important health information, (2) joy and entertainment (by making history come alive), and (3) better self-understanding due to knowledge of one's roots. The writer concludes her essay with this paragraph:

> Thanks to the Internet, genealogy research has become much easier. With websites such as Ancestry.com, Usgenweb.org, and Archives.com just a few clicks away, many more people will undoubtedly be able to experience the benefits of knowing their family tree.

Recommend Action

A third way to close your composition is to recommend that readers take some action in response to their acceptance of your main idea. You could suggest that they write a letter, join a group, make a donation, volunteer their time, or change a behavior. For example, in a review of a new film, you could recommend that the reader go see this film.

The following example is from a letter to the editor of a newspaper. The writer advocates the election of a particular candidate to the local school board. After describing the candidate's qualification and merits, she concludes with:

> Please consider the future of the schools in our county and do your part to elect a professional, experienced educator who understands the needs of our children. Our school system is facing tremendous challenges in the coming years, and we need dedicated people who can help us deal with these challenges. Cast your vote for school board candidate Robert Reynolds, who is one of those people.

An e-mail message offers another example of a closing that recommends action. After describing and evaluating the features of three different fax machines, the writer ends with a paragraph that states his recommendation about which machine his department should purchase:

> Because the Intellifax 615 has the same features as the other two fax machines but costs less, it is clearly the best buy. It should serve the Legal Department's needs well, so I recommend that we purchase it.

Complete a Circle

Another good technique for wrapping up a composition involves referring to something you mentioned in the opening paragraph of your composition. In this way, you circle back and close a loop, leaving the reader feeling as though the ending is tied neatly to the beginning. One example comes from a student's essay advocating uniforms for public school students. The writer begins his essay with a story about John, a high school senior shot and killed by another student who stole his expensive athletic shoes. To conclude the paper, he circles back to his beginning:

> If he had been wearing a uniform, John would not have been murdered for his shoes. Instead, he would have lived to benefit from a school that promoted self-esteem and equality for all of its students through the removal of economic class distinctions. He would have lived to complete his education in a place that chose a standardized dress code to create a safer atmosphere for success.

Another example comes from an essay about the traits of successful entrepreneurs. On page 176 of Chapter 9, you read an opening paragraph about Milton Hershey, founder of Hershey chocolate. The essay's writer went on to explain the three common traits of entrepreneurs, and then ended her essay by referring to the example at the beginning of the paper:

> Milton Hershey possessed these three common traits of entrepreneurs, and it's fortunate for us that he did. Because of his willingness to work hard, refuse to give up, and take risks, we are all able to enjoy delicious, affordable chocolate today.

TIP

For more about techniques for effective opening paragraphs, see Chapter 9.

Ask Questions

One final technique for ending a paper involves asking the reader questions. These questions encourage your readers to continue thinking about your topic even after they have finished reading your composition.

For instance, an essay that recommends adding security guards, video surveillance cameras, and metal detectors at a local high school closes with this paragraph:

> These additional security measures would cost money, but aren't they worth it? Shouldn't the safety and well-being of our young people be one of our most important priorities?

In an essay about the effects obesity, the writer discusses the health risks and the social, psychological, and economic impacts of being extremely overweight. Then, he concludes with the following paragraph:

> The World Health Organization predicts that obesity will soon replace the current most significant causes of poor health: malnutrition and infectious diseases. How can we continue to do nothing to slow and reverse the rising rates of obesity? How can we let this solvable problem become our next public health crisis?

Exercise 10.1

What technique (or techniques) for closing paragraphs is used in each of the following essays?

1. "The AAS Degree: Another Path to a Great Career" on page 23 of Chapter 2
2. "Emotional Intelligence: Five Traits to Develop for Success in Life" on pages 26–27 of Chapter 2
3. "Going Shopping? Buy American" on pages 164–165 of Chapter 8
4. "The Drawbacks of Multitasking" on pages 166–167 of Chapter 8

Exercise 10.2

Write two different closing paragraphs for the following essay. Identify the technique you selected for each closing. The essay's thesis statement is underlined.

Responding to Verbal Abuse

According to one old saying, "Sticks and stones may break my bones, but words will never hurt me," but that saying simply isn't true for most people. It would be great if people truly could form a mental shield that prevents ridicule, insults, name-calling, criticisms, threats, and other forms of humiliation from affecting them, but most people don't have that power. Words *can* hurt. Verbal abuse hurts people mentally and emotionally by causing them fear, anxiety, and depression; by robbing them of their self-esteem and sense of safety and security; by causing psychological abnormalities; and by warping their outlook on life and damaging their future relationships with others. Therefore, verbal abuse should not be tolerated. Anyone who is suffering from verbal abuse must respond and take steps to put a stop to this potentially serious problem.

The first step in dealing with verbal abuse is to set clear limits for the abusive person. Explain to the person that what he or she is doing is inappropriate and unacceptable to you. Of course, this requires you to care for yourself enough to refuse to put up with abuse from others, no matter who they are. Once you are able to recognize that you are a person who deserves supportive and healthy relationships, refuse to accept blame, accusations, and put-downs that are designed to hurt you or control you. Tell the abusive person that you will walk away from him or her any time a comment or statement crosses the line. If you are subjected to threats or outbursts that could trigger physical violence, don't hesitate to call the police to intervene.

If insisting on boundaries does not end the verbal abuse, the next step in dealing with the problem is to seek out help and support. Get psychological counseling to understand how your own beliefs and behaviors may be perpetuating an unhealthy situation. Confide in loving and supportive friends and relatives who will bolster your self-esteem and help you find the strength and courage to stand up for yourself. Surround yourself with people who will help you remember that you deserve loving, happy relationships. By reaching out to people who care, you should be able to take steps to free yourself from verbal abuse.

However, if the first two steps do not stop the abuse, end the relationship. No spouse or lover is worth being subjected to ongoing verbal attacks. If the abuser does not value you enough to treat you with kindness, then that person does not deserve you.

Exercise 10.3

Write two different closing paragraphs for the following essay. Identify the technique you selected for each closing. The essay's thesis statement is underlined.

The Benefits of Club Membership

Now that you're in college, you have undoubtedly become aware of the many announcements about campus club meetings on flyers, posters, and signs and in college newsletters. Have you seen an ad for a particular club that relates to your field or study or one of your interests? If you have, you may have concluded that you don't have the time, energy, or courage to attend a club meeting and learn more about the group, but you should reconsider. Getting involved in a campus club is an excellent decision for three reasons.

First, joining a campus club is likely to improve your social life. Club membership gives you an opportunity to meet people who share your interests and goals. For example, you can join a club for students who want to work in the same career field that you've chosen. Or, you can join a club for people who have a certain passion for something, such as films, community service, astronomy, or martial arts. Some of the club members you meet may wind up becoming good friends or supportive study partners.

Second, getting involved in a campus club can help you improve your future job opportunities. For instance, you might expand your job qualifications. Participation in a club gives you the opportunity to increase knowledge and skills—such as teamwork skills, organizational skills, and project management skills—that are valuable for any workplace. If you become an officer of the club, you will undoubtedly develop your leadership skills, too. These are the kinds of abilities you can list on a résumé. Also, your club's advisor may turn into a mentor or someone willing to help you network with people in your field when you complete your education and begin looking for employment.

Finally, club membership will enrich you personally. You'll gain more in-depth knowledge about a field or subject that interests you. Also, you may be presented with opportunities to raise others' awareness about the field or subject.

Select one of the compositions in Appendix 1: Eleven Model Compositions and write an alternative closing paragraph for that composition. Identify the technique you selected for your new closing.

Rewriting for Effective Closings

When you evaluate the closing paragraph of a composition, consider using a checklist like the following as a guide.

CHECKLIST FOR EFFECTIVE CLOSING PARAGRAPHS

Use this checklist to make sure that your closing paragraphs are effective.

☐ The writer avoids merely repeating or summarizing information or ideas presented in the body of the composition.

☐ The composition's closing paragraph provides a clear sense of closure by tying together the information presented in the body in a satisfactory way.

☐ The writer has used an effective technique for concluding the composition.

A. Use the checklist above to evaluate an essay or other multiparagraph composition you have recently written. If you revised this composition, what changes would you make to improve its closing paragraph?

B. Use the checklist to evaluate a classmate's essay or other multiparagraph composition. What improvements would you recommend?

SUGGESTED WRITING ACTIVITIES

Select one of the following activities and use all of the steps of the writing process to compose a multiparagraph composition. Experiment with different techniques for closing paragraphs until you find the one that works best.

ACADEMIC WRITING

1. Report on an innovative technique or product in your field of study. Who is using it? How is it being used? What are the benefits of using it?
2. Explain how to prevent something bad (such as heart disease, a fire, or an injury).
3. Select a current controversial news topic (on politics, crime, sports, or entertainment) and persuade someone to agree with your opinion about this topic.

PROFESSIONAL WRITING

4. Write a letter of recommendation for one of your co-workers who is seeking a promotion.
5. Write to your company to suggest that your current workplace be moved or that another store, branch, plant, or facility be opened in a specific location.
6. Write to your supervisor or company president to suggest ways to attract more and better-qualified candidates to apply for job openings.

PERSONAL WRITING

7. Write a letter to praise a manufacturer or business for one of its products or services.
8. Write a description of your city, town, or county for the "Visitor Information" section of your local Chamber of Commerce's website. Your goal is to attract new visitors to your community.
9. Write to the superintendent of your public school system to propose one or more solutions to a problem (for example, violence, bullying, low academic standards, promotion of students with poor academic skills).

CHAPTER 11

Essential #11:
Sensitivity and Tact

Let's say you arrive home one day to find the following note taped to your front door:

Dear Neighbor:

Your stupid dog is a menace to this neighborhood. He barks all of the time and uses my yard as his toilet. I'm pretty sure he dug up some of my flowers, too. Any moron knows that dogs have to be kept on a leash. Tie up the mutt, or I'll call the dog pound to pick him up.

Sincerely,
I. M. Irate

What would be your reaction to this note? You'd probably be angry and defensive, even if your neighbor's accusations are true. Is this note going to convince you to tie up your dog? Probably not. Because Mr. Irate insults you and your dog with words such as *stupid, menace, moron,* and *mutt*, you won't be inclined to do what he wants, even if his request is valid.

Writers should always strive to state their ideas and opinions with confidence and assertiveness. However, we must also take care to avoid offending or insulting our readers, for doing so will cause them to reject our ideas without even considering them. Instead, we must make sure to state our ideas with sensitivity and tact, always tailoring a composition to a specific audience.

© Yuri Arcurs/Shutterstock.com

Angering, offending, or insulting your readers will prevent them from considering your ideas.

Prewriting: Match Your Points to Your Reader

In Chapter 1 of this book, you learned that a careful consideration of your audience should always be a part of your prewriting process. An analysis of your readers is especially important when your purpose for writing is persuasive. An argument can often be supported with many different reasons. If you are going to convince your readers to make some change in how they think or act, you will need to make sure that the reasons you select to support your thesis statement are reasons that your *reader* (rather than yourself) will find persuasive. You will write with greater sensitivity and tact if you include only those points, ideas, and arguments that are directly relevant to your reader.

Choosing the right reasons to include requires you to think first about your reader's needs. In the case of the loose dog letter, perhaps the reader doesn't even know that his dog disturbs his neighbors. Therefore, one of his needs is simply information about the problem. He also may not be aware of the leash law.

Another factor to consider when determining the right reasons is your reader's priorities. One of the two reasons offered in the loose dog letter assumes that the reader is a law-abiding citizen who would not want to break the leash law. The other reason assumes that the reader does not want his pet to wind up in the dog pound. However, neither of these reasons is well explained, and the second one is presented in the form of a threat. Many people will become defiant in response to threats, so that is not the best way to persuade. Plus, there may be other, more convincing reasons to include. For example, the neighbor probably wants to keep his pet alive and out of harm's way, and he doesn't realize the danger the dog is in when he roams the neighborhood. Mentioning that the dog could be hit by a car or picked up by someone who believes that he's a stray might be a good argument to include.

By tailoring your reasons to your specific readers and what *they* think is important, you stand a better chance of convincing them to accept your main idea. As a second illustration, consider writing an e-mail to your supervisor to propose a change in a work procedure. To decide on the reasons you should present, first consider your reader's characteristics. She's in a position of authority and responsibility. She wants to make cost-effective decisions that will satisfy the company's customers. She wants the workplace to run smoothly and efficiently. So, what arguments are going to convince her to make the change you propose? Use arguments that point out how your proposal will help her fulfill her goals by saving the company money, generating more business, or delivering your product or service faster or more efficiently to your customers. Your reader is less likely to be swayed by arguments that focus on benefits to employees, unless you explain how those benefits will lead to increased productivity, profits, and happier customers, her three main priorities. It's not that you shouldn't mention the lighter workload and reduced stress that the change will bring to you and your co-workers. You just want to place the most emphasis on the points that match your reader's major goals.

When matching points to a specific reader, it's a good idea to consider whether or not that particular individual will be most affected by logical arguments, emotional arguments, or a combination of the two. **Logical arguments** are based on hard evidence such as facts, statistics, and results of research studies. For example, if you want to convince your reader to buy a certain brand of paper towels, you could explain how that brand's physical makeup results in greater absorbency and strength, or how it's a better buy than other brands because you get more towels for less money. These are the logical arguments that support your recommendation.

In addition, you can add **emotional arguments** to your appeal. If your reader has children, for example, you can argue (as many advertisements currently do) that buying this specific brand of paper towels makes the reader a better mother because the quick, easy cleanup will prevent her from getting upset about the messes her kids make. Emotional arguments target a reader's needs for love, friends, fun, power, and influence. As you're deciding on the most appropriate points to include, identify each one as either logical or emotional to help you find the most appropriate arguments for your specific audience.

TIP

Academic and professional writing should almost always rely solely on logical arguments.

▌ Exercise 11.1

Following each thesis is a list of reasons that support it. For each of three different audiences, list the letters of the reasons that would be best suited to that audience.

A. Thesis: Regular swimming would be an excellent addition to your fitness plan.

    a. Improved cardiovascular health

    b. Improved physical appearance (weight loss, muscle tone)

    c. Expanded social life

    d. Low-cost activity

    e. Increased endurance and flexibility for other sports

    f. Family-oriented activity

        1. A group of senior citizens

        2. A single mother

        3. A teenager involved in high school athletics

B. Thesis: The City Council should purchase a historic house in the downtown district and turn it into a museum.

    a. Preservation of local history and architecture

    b. Symbolic of citizens' pride in their heritage

    c. Increased revenue for the city

    d. Increased tourism

    e. More jobs in the downtown area

        1. The owner of a business in the downtown area

        2. A member of the City Council

        3. Readers of the city's local newspaper

C. Thesis: Your pet cats should be spayed or neutered.

    a. Lower upkeep costs (fewer mouths to feed, fewer veterinary bills)

    b. Less hassle (time and inconvenience required to care for and find homes for kittens)

    c. Reduction in the number of animals euthanized at the local animal shelter

    d. Lower license fees

    e. Lower taxes

    f. Health benefits for the cats

        1. A family that keeps cats as pets

        2. A cat breeder who sells kittens at the local flea market for extra cash

        3. Humane society members

Exercise 11.2

For each thesis statement, list three reasons that would be persuasive to the identified audience.

1. Thesis: Dr. Daniel Jones is a pediatrician whom I highly recommend.
Audience: Parents with young children

2. Thesis: The 7-point grading scale for this class should be replaced with the 10-point grading scale.
Audience: An instructor

3. Thesis: The salaries of our city's firefighters should be increased.
Audience: City Council members

Writing with Sensitivity and Tact

As you are composing your draft, you will write with greater sensitivity and tact if you make concessions to opposing arguments and avoid offending or insulting readers.

Make Concessions

The audience for a composition is never readers who already know the information or who already agree with the writer's viewpoint. Writing for these groups would be "preaching to the choir"; in other words, it would be a waste of time and effort. Because we usually write to inform our readers or to convince them to believe what we believe, we can assume one of two things about them: (1) they haven't yet made up their minds or formulated an opinion about the topic, or (2) they support the opposing viewpoint, which is why we need to write to persuade them to change their minds. In either case, our readers are likely to have at least a few preconceived ideas and opinions about the topic before they begin reading. Most issues are complex, with multiple viewpoints and valid arguments on two or more sides.

Keeping all of this in mind, you can write more successful compositions if you offer your readers **concessions**, or acknowledgments of preexisting opinions, disagreements, and objections. By briefly mentioning these opposing viewpoints, you indicate that you understand both sides of the issue, and you can show how the arguments for your side are stronger. For instance, consider the loose dog letter at the beginning of this chapter, which does not include any concessions. What arguments might the neighbor provide to support his decision to let his pet run loose? He might believe that chaining or locking up an animal all day is cruel. He might not be able to afford a fence or a dog pen. He may think that the animal is street-savvy and stays away from road traffic. He may think that the animal is well behaved and doesn't bother anyone. In a letter that seeks to convince this neighbor to confine his pet, you would want to address and overcome each of these concerns. In the following examples, the concession is underlined:

> You might believe that locking up an animal all day is cruel. However, allowing your pet to get hit by a car or picked up by strangers who think it's a stray is just as cruel to the animal.

> I realize that many fences and dog pens are expensive, but they are no more costly than the fees you would have to pay to release your dog from the pound or the veterinary bills you would have to pay if your pet was hit and seriously injured by a car.

Obviously, you have to consider your reader carefully to include appropriate concessions. Just as you match your supporting points to your readers' goals and priorities, you must match your concessions to your readers' most likely objections. You have to anticipate their arguments and, as you write, acknowledge but also refute those objections.

At this point, you may be worried that concessions may weaken your argument because they will reinforce your readers' arguments or provide new arguments they haven't yet considered. However, the advantages of concessions outweigh the disadvantages. First, including concessions will demonstrate that you understand the whole issue, not just one side. As a result, your readers will judge you to be a credible source of information and remain more open to

TIP

To fully understand the opposing viewpoint, debate your topic with someone who disagrees with your thesis statement. Your opponent's arguments will help you know what concessions to include in your composition.

your ideas. Second, concessions help you establish your goodwill toward your readers by acknowledging their viewpoint. Offering a concession is the written form of listening to your readers and giving them a chance to have their say. Consequently, your audience will be more likely to consider your views. Finally, concessions are valuable because they allow the writer to respond to and refute specific objections. After acknowledging a particular concern or disagreement, the writer can very thoroughly present all of the evidence that argues against it. This will help readers understand how each of their particular concerns might be addressed.

To understand the effects of omitting concessions, read the following excerpt from a letter written by a student to her senator:

> Homelessness in the United States has become a major problem. Thousands of Americans, many of whom are mentally ill, are wandering the streets with nowhere to go. Our government must do more for these unfortunate people.
>
> First of all, the government can start by giving them alternatives to sleeping on the street. Build more temporary shelters and more low-cost housing for the homeless.
>
> Second, after the government has helped these people get off the streets, it should find them jobs. New government programs could provide education and on-the-job train- ing. For those unable to do physical labor, the government could find jobs that aren't very strenuous. For example, they could work as secretaries or something like that, or they could work with children or the elderly.
>
> In conclusion, the government must do more to solve this major problem. We have to take care of those who need help.

One quick reading of this letter reveals the writer's total lack of consid- eration for the reader. The senator who received this letter undoubtedly had some valid objections to these proposals. For instance, what about money? How would "the government" pay for all of these shelters and housing? Wouldn't a tax increase be necessary? Wouldn't his constituents be likely to oppose such an increase? Where would "the government" get the resources (the money, the materials, and the manpower) for the new programs the writer proposes? Finally, how is the government supposed to provide jobs? And since when is working with the children or the elderly not strenuous? If the people who get the jobs are suffering from mental illness, will they be able to hold down jobs? Should they be working with children or the elderly?

The lack of concessions in this letter, along with the lack of adequate de- velopment of ideas, shows that the writer really doesn't understand the whole issue. Also, because the writer makes no effort to address any of the reader's concerns and disagreements, the senator probably did not seriously consider any of these proposals.

If you still fear that concessions will undermine your arguments, make sure that you adhere to the following guidelines to reduce the potential dangers:

- **Keep concessions brief.** Mention the argument or objection, but don't elaborate. The more detail you include, the greater the chance that you might strengthen your readers' opposition. Usually, a brief one-sentence statement will sufficiently acknowledge the argument. Then, move on im- mediately to refute it with your own evidence and explanations.

- **Don't end with concessions.** Concessions are more effective when you present them at the beginnings of your paragraphs and then go on to prove them invalid with your own ideas and evidence. When you end a paragraph with a concession, you're leaving the reader with that contrary thought rather than your viewpoint. Match the concessions you need to make to each of your supporting points, and then thoroughly refute each one with a fully developed paragraph.
- **Signal the beginning and the end of a concession.** Certain transition words signal to the reader when a concession begins and ends. Common words and phrases used to introduce a concession include the following:

TIP

For more information about developing paragraphs, see Chapters 5 and 6.

Admittedly,	Of course,
It's true that	I agree that
Granted,	I concede that
Yes,	I understand that

Follow your concession with another clear transition to signal that you will now refute that point. These transitions include words and phrases such as *however, but, nevertheless,* and *on the contrary.* The following passages provide effective examples of concessions, which are underlined. Transition words and phrases are blue:

> **Of course**, many people argue that the single lifestyle is better than marriage because single people remain completely free to make all of their own decisions and choices. **Actually**, **though**, single people are often forced to live without the deeply satisfying companionship that comes with marriage, so they tend to experience more frequent feelings of loneliness.

> **It's true that** one or two years of mandatory military service for all young Americans would ensure that the United States would always have plenty of soldiers for this country's defense. **However**, many in the military now currently oppose requiring military service because they believe that the military functions much better with a volunteer force than it would with thousands of people who were forced to be there.

Exercise 11.3

With a group of your classmates, write a concession for each of the points in the following outlines.

1. **Thesis:** No college courses should be required for a degree; a student should create an individual program of study by selecting courses he or she wants to take.
   a. Students should not be forced to take courses that are too difficult or beyond their intellectual abilities.
   b. Students should not be forced to take courses in subjects they won't need for their careers.

  c. College is too expensive to force a student to take courses in subjects he or she does not want to take.

  d. Students would enjoy their educations more if they took only classes they found interesting.

2. Thesis: The U.S. Congress should pass a law that limits senators and representatives to serving no more than two terms in office.

  a. The writers of the Constitution did not intend for political office to become a career.

  b. A career politician tends to focus on what he or she should do to get reelected rather than on what's best for the country.

  c. Absolute power corrupts politicians.

  d. A more frequent turnover of government servants would allow more citizens to directly participate in the governing of our country.

  e. A more frequent turnover would encourage the exchange of beneficial new ideas.

Exercise 11.4

Write a concession for each of the reasons you listed in Exercise 11.2.

Avoid Offending or Insulting Readers

Can you remember the last time someone insulted either you personally or a group to which you belonged? Your first reaction was probably to become defensive, maybe even angry. Your next reaction was probably to completely reject all of the ideas and opinions of the person who insulted you. Readers experience the same reaction when they are offended by the writer of a composition.

As writers, then, we must take care to avoid insensitive language, for no matter how brilliant our ideas are, an insulted reader will dismiss them without consideration. Thus, the composition will not fulfill its purpose. Of course, avoiding offensive and insulting language is sometimes easier said than done. When we feel very strongly about an issue, the emotions that we're feeling—such as anger, fear, grief, irritation, frustration, or lack of fairness—cause us to choose language that reflects these strong feelings. We must be aware of this tendency and watch for three specific types of insensitive language—name-calling, statements that create a condescending or dismissive tone, and emotionally loaded terms—that threaten the success of the compositions we write.

Name-calling

The first type of insensitive language is **name-calling**, or using derogatory labels to name or describe individuals or groups. Writers use this technique in an attempt to cast doubt upon or to destroy the credibility of an opponent's ideas by personally attacking that individual or his or her character. In reality, though, this most blatantly insensitive tactic

Negative emotions such as anger and hurt form a shield around your reader that none of your ideas will be able to penetrate.

© Rubberball/Mike Kemp/Getty Images

usually produces the reverse effect. Name-calling only brands the *writer* as immature or hostile.

In the following examples, the name-calling is highlighted:

Gun nuts want us to believe that the Second Amendment to the U.S. Constitution protects their right to own small arsenals of pistols and rifles.

The Bible thumpers who oppose same-sex marriages aren't concerned about violating the civil rights of their fellow citizens.

Thanks to shyster lawyers who'll do anything to make a buck, drunk drivers are escaping punishment and continuing to endanger other motorists.

The shopping mall's rent-a-cops need to do something about the big group of thugs who hang out in the food court on Friday nights.

You cannot build up yourself or your argument by tearing down someone else. You will only damage your own credibility when you resort to childish attacks upon others. Instead, focus on exposing the flaws in *ideas*, not in the people who believe in them.

⬛ Exercise 11.5

Rewrite each of the following sentences to improve its tact and sensitivity.

1. The close-minded rednecks and hicks in our town are refusing to acknowledge the benefits of a multicultural society.
2. The rich snobs and fat-cat politicians in Congress have no understanding of average Americans' economic struggles.
3. Obviously, a bunch of nerds and geeks wrote this instruction manual; consequently, none of us can understand it.
4. Tree-huggers like Dana think that we should all be recycling, riding bicycles to work, and growing our own food in our backyards.
5. When a dead-beat dad gets behind on his child support payments, his driver's license should be revoked.
6. People involved in beauty pageants for little girls are child abusers. Parents who encourage their kids to parade around in skimpy outfits and strike sexy poses should be ashamed of themselves.
7. This college should not lower its standards for the muscleheads who are here on athletic scholarships.

Condescending or Dismissive Language

A second type of insensitive language includes rude statements that state or imply that readers or their ideas are ignorant, uninformed, illogical, or ridiculous. Such statements indicate that the writer's attitude toward the reader is arrogant or condescending. Sometimes, the writer uses mocking statements or sarcasm to indicate disdain for readers' opinions. These tactics create the impression that the writer is "talking down" to readers. A writer will *never* convert readers to his or her opinions by implying that readers or their intelligence are somehow inferior. The following statements include examples of insensitive phrases, which are highlighted:

You're crazy if you think that smoking marijuana should be legal.

Do you ever wonder what happens inside an ambulance? Do you believe that paramedics simply move sick or injured people from one place to another? Well, think again!

Didn't you learn anything in your high school civics class? One of the most important privileges of democracy is the right to vote.

You honestly think that Sharon Blevins will lower our taxes if she's elected governor? If you believe that, you'll believe just about anything.

The convicted felon claims that he is innocent. Yeah, right. And I'm the pope.

Often, simply removing the condescending statement will take care of the problem.

Exercise 11.6

Rewrite each of the following sentences to improve its tact and sensitivity.

1. You obviously never bother to keep yourself informed about what's going on in the world; otherwise, you'd know that the United States sends billions of dollars in aid to foreign countries.
2. Let me try to put this in a way that will make sense to you. Lengthening the school day would be a total *disaster*.
3. You actually think that legalization of marijuana will lead to an increase in cocaine and heroin use? Oh, *please*. That argument was proven wrong ages ago.
4. If you tan in a tanning bed, you'll probably get skin cancer. Honestly, a five-year-old could understand that tanning beds are really dangerous.
5. If you think you're going to get me to believe that buying a used car is preferable to buying a new car, you'd better think again.
6. Opponents of seat-belt laws say that they limit our personal freedom. You've got to be kidding me. The only thing they limit is your chance of dying in a wreck.
7. Once you are *finally* able to understand the problem, you'll be able to see that a "flat-tax" income tax system is much fairer than the current tax system.

Emotionally Loaded Words

Many words have two types of meanings: denotative meanings and connotative meanings. The **denotative meaning** of a word is its literal dictionary definition.

The **connotative meaning** of a word refers to the positive or negative feelings that people attach to that word.

For example, the words *inexpensive* and *cheap* have roughly the same denotative meaning, but the two words have different connotative meanings. If you use the word *inexpensive* to describe a couch, you are probably suggesting that it's a good deal. If you describe that same couch using the word *cheap*, though, you suggest not only that its price is low but also that its quality is poor. Some readers will even attach the extra meanings of "tawdry" or "shoddy" to that particular adjective. As another example, compare the words *assertive* and *aggressive*. Favorable connotations are usually attached to the first word, whereas the unfavorable suggestions of "pushy" and "overbearing" are attached to the second word.

You do want to state your ideas and opinions with confidence and assertiveness so that your readers will believe you. However, using words that have strong emotional connotations can be annoying or offensive to your readers, especially if they hold the opposing viewpoint. As the examples in the last paragraph indicate, emotionally loaded words can be adjectives. For a few more examples, notice how the synonyms in the following list change from positive to negative:

I am thrifty. You are frugal. He is a tightwad.

I am concerned. You are anxious. He is paranoid.

I am spiritual. You are religious. He is a zealot.

I am gentle. You are passive. He is a wuss.

I am strong-willed. You are stubborn. He is inflexible.

I am curious. You are intrusive. He is antisocial.

I am well-read. You are informed. He is a know-it-all.

Thomas, Clint. "Perception." *Words in Edgewise: The Writing, Truisms, Falsisms, and Philosophy of Clint Thomas.* Web. 25 July 2010.

Like adjectives, verbs can also be emotionally loaded. For example, read the following statement:

That cashier cheated me out of $8 and then lied to the manager about it.

Cheated and *lied* are both emotionally loaded verbs with negative connotations. Here is another example with an emotionally loaded verb:

Greedy Americans who bring frivolous lawsuits are destroying this country.

In this sentence, the verb *destroy* has a strongly negative connotative meaning. In addition, the adjectives *greedy* and *frivolous* have negative connotations, so this brief statement contains three words that will probably offend any reader who has initiated a lawsuit. Here is one last example:

I'm sick of lazy co-workers who fake being busy when the boss is around but otherwise waste time doing nothing.

The verbs *fake* and *waste* and the adjective *lazy* are all emotionally loaded, making this statement insulting.

On a final note, remember that all vulgar, sexist, and racist language is also emotionally loaded and offensive. Never include curse words, gender-related insults, or racial slurs in academic or professional writing.

Exercise 11.7

Rewrite each of the following sentences to improve its tact and sensitivity.

1. Credit card companies prey on young people by making it easy for them to bury themselves in debt.
2. The fat chick who waited on our table gave us terrible service.
3. Illegal aliens put a tremendous burden on this country's hospitals, schools, and prisons.
4. Greedy advertisers are brainwashing innocent children on a daily basis.
5. Corporations, banks, and the crooks on Wall Street are robbing us all blind.
6. Mary was a woman, but she still turned out to be a very fine doctor.
7. You failed to qualify for a loan because of your bad credit score.
8. Your company's claims about your products are all just a big pack of lies.

Exercise 11.8

Find a piece of writing that you believe to be insulting or insensitive to some readers. What improvements would you recommend to the writer?

Exercise 11.9

Evaluate the sensitivity and tact of the compositions that begin on pages 229 and 239 of Appendix 1: Eleven Model Compositions. Answer the following questions for each composition by recording your answers on your own paper:

1. Describe the intended audience.
2. Does the writer include the reasons that will best persuade that audience?
3. Does the writer include concessions?
4. Does the writer avoid offensive or condescending language?
5. Does the writer use any emotionally loaded terms? What are they?

Rewriting to Improve Sensitivity and Tact

As you reread your drafts, make sure that you have included concessions where appropriate and avoid insensitive language. If necessary, revise your draft to more carefully consider your reader. Note how the letter about the loose dog improves dramatically when revised for more sensitivity and tact.

Dear Neighbor:

I wanted to let you know that your pet has been running loose in the neighborhood when you're not home. As I'm sure you're aware, the law requires owners to keep their dogs on leashes. I know you want your pet to be safe, but when he's running loose, he's in danger of being hit by a car or being picked up by animal control officers. If you'll give me a call, I'll tell you about some inexpensive products I've found that keep my pets in my yard.

Sincerely,
I. M. Irate

When you evaluate the sensitivity and tact of a composition, consider using a checklist like the following as a guide.

CHECKLIST FOR SENSITIVITY AND TACT

Use this checklist to make sure that you are writing with sensitivity and tact.

☐ The reasons offered to support the thesis statement match the audience's characteristics, needs, and goals.

☐ The writer has included concessions to opposing arguments.

☐ The writer refrains from offending or insulting the reader by avoiding name-calling, condescending or dismissive language, and emotionally loaded words.

Exercise 11.10

What advice would you give the writer of the following passage? How could he improve sensitivity and tact?

Wimpy environmentalists are crying big fat tears because a bunch of head-hunters in Brazil are chopping down some trees to make a little extra spending money. These fruitcake Chicken Littles believe if we chop up jungles there won't be any more air and we'll all die. Hogwash! They can PAVE the darn rain forests for all I care.

Anger, Ed. "Pave the Stupid Rain Forests!"
Quoted in McDonald, Daniel, and Larry W. Burton.
The Language of Argument. New York:
HarperCollins, 1996. Print.

Exercise 11.11

A. Use the checklist on page 208 to evaluate an essay or multiparagraph composition you have recently written. If you revised this composition, what changes would you make to improve its sensitivity and tact?

B. Use the checklist to evaluate a classmate's essay or other multiparagraph composition. What improvements would you recommend?

SUGGESTED WRITING ACTIVITIES

Select one of the following activities and use all of the steps of the writing process to compose a multiparagraph composition. Check your drafts to make sure that you have written with sensitivity and tact.

ACADEMIC WRITING

1. Argue that something at your college was a waste of money.
2. Compare Democrats and Republicans.
3. Argue that something (for example, child beauty pageants, gas-guzzling vehicles, or smoking in all public places) needs to be banned.

PROFESSIONAL WRITING

4. Write a letter to your company president requesting a specific benefit for employees (e.g., longer vacations, a 401K plan, flextime, and so on).
5. Convince your company or supervisor to stop doing business with a particular vendor or supplier.
6. Write to convince your supervisor that a certain job applicant should be hired for an available position.

PERSONAL WRITING

7. Write a letter or speech to motivate or inspire high school graduates.
8. Convince your parents, your husband, your boyfriend, your wife, or your girlfriend to buy you something.
9. Write a letter to convince a television station not to cancel your favorite show.

APPENDIX 1

Eleven Model Compositions

As you read the following model compositions, notice how each one demonstrates all or most of the 11 essentials of effective writing.

Model Composition #1

Memories of My Father
by Marty A. McNeely

[1] Recently, someone asked me, "If you were to be able to retrieve one item, attitude, or feeling from your childhood, what would that one thing be?" Although I'm now in my early forties, that question was not a difficult one. Age and experience has taught me that things—tangible things—are just that, and if I really wanted some "thing" from my childhood, I could probably find it, or a close substitute, in a store or on the Internet. Regarding youthful attitudes, I can't think of any worth retrieving; my current and most important attitudes have been developed throughout my adult life. But there are feelings that I do miss, so my answer results from a mixture of nostalgia and the longing for a dear departed parent. More than anything from my childhood, I'd want to retrieve feelings I experienced with my father when I was a young boy.

[2] One of these feelings is pride in what he taught me. My father was a gentle man, always soft-spoken yet direct, firm but fair, slow to anger but quick with a smile. He taught my sister and me that only our labors would provide us the fruits we sought and that, above all, we are all children under the canopy of God's heaven. I always knew where he stood on a subject, either by the way he voiced his support or by the way he remained silent while others criticized. He rarely worried about how others perceived him, but I believe he found great solace, when, in the later years of his life, he asked if I felt he'd done a good job raising me, and I responded that I hoped people thought half as well of me as they did of him. Although he was a farmer's son who completed his high school education well into his adulthood, he taught me more than any college professor ever could. I learned how to sharpen a knife, drink a beer, fix a flat bike tire, and treat others and myself respectfully, not by listening to his lectures, but instead by simply following his example.

[3] Another particular feeling that I would retrieve from my youth is the contentment I felt when we spent time together, especially when we went fishing on Saturday mornings in the spring and summer. He would wake me up around sunrise and, without much more than "it's time," set me to action. We had a 16-foot outboard boat that he pulled with an old Chevrolet truck. I would gather our fishing rods—one for me but two for him, which I found to be almost superhuman at the time—a small orange-and-tan plastic Plano tackle box (the kind that has an interior tray that raises up and back when the lid is opened), an oar, a net, a cricket box, a cooler, and various other items I was responsible for. Being so small at the time, I was astounded at how my dad could carry the outboard motor from its mount in the basement, lift it to the transom, and hold it in place while I tightened it down, securing it to the boat. As if following some unwritten ritual, we stopped at a local convenience store, iced down several Pepsi-Cola drinks in the cooler, bought a couple packs of crackers and maybe a candy bar for later, then proceeded to John's River for a day of fishing. Those were some of the happiest days of my youth, and the abundance—or lack—of fish didn't matter.

[4] A final example illustrates that my fondest memories are of times that blended companionship with caring guidance. I recall one evening when I was actually quite young. My dad had always preferred to grow a large garden in the summer, both to provide my family with plenty, but, I firmly believe, to also teach my younger sister and

me the value of hard work. We routinely had five-gallon buckets of fresh green beans to string and break as our dad would sometimes supervise, sometimes help. I had just begun to become curious about the existence of Deity, and, as I broke beans with my dad, a strong evening thunderstorm so common in the South began to brew. As we talked about church and God, I found it curious when he said that God was everywhere at once. I asked if God was with me at school, on the bus, on the playground, etc., all of which my dad answered in the affirmative. Just as I asked if God were on the back porch with us and my dad said "yes," a bolt of lightning struck a tree in the neighbor's yard. Years later, my dad still laughed at how I shot up from my seat, exclaiming that God could stay out on the porch with him, but I was going in the house with mama.

[5] My father passed away very unexpectedly one July night in 2004, leaving me with questions yet to ask and things left unsaid, but moreover with a profound appreciation for who he was and what he meant to me, both in my youth and as a man. Some people become collectors of dolls, stamps, shot glasses, or any other number of "things," but I prefer to collect memories, particularly of times and of people near and dear to my heart and recollection. Material belongings come and go; they can be replaced with little or great effort. It is, however, much more beneficial to me that, as I age, I collect feelings of days long gone so that I may pass similar ones to my own children.

Model Composition #2

Decision-Making and Problem-Solving[1]

[1] A leader is expected to get the job done. To do so, he or she must learn to plan, analyze situations, identify and solve problems (or potential problems), make decisions, and set realistic and attainable goals for the unit. These are the thinking or creative requirements of leadership and they set direction. These actions provide vision, purpose, and goal definition. They are your eyes to the future, and they are crucial to developing a disciplined, cohesive, and effective organization.

[2] Decision-making and problem-solving are basic ingredients of leadership. More than anything else, the ability to make sound, timely decisions separates a leader from a non-leader. It is the responsibility of leaders to make high quality decisions that are accepted and executed in a timely fashion.

[3] Leaders must be able to reason under the most critical conditions and decide quickly what action to take. If they delay or avoid making a decision, this indecisiveness may create hesitancy, loss of confidence, and confusion within the unit, and may cause the task to fail. Since leaders are frequently faced with unexpected circumstances, it is important to be flexible—leaders must be able to react promptly to each situation. Then, when circumstances dictate a change in plans, prompt reaction builds confidence in them.

[4] As a leader, you will make decisions involving not only yourself, but also the morale and welfare of others. Some decisions, such as when to take a break or where to hold a meeting, are simple decisions which have little effect on others. Other decisions are often more complex and may have a significant impact on many people. Therefore, having a decision making, problem-solving process can be a helpful tool. Such a process can help you to solve these different types of situations.

[5] Within business and the military today, leaders at all levels use some form of a decision-making, problem-solving process. There are at least several different approaches (or models) for decision-making and problem solving. We will present three such approaches: The first, and most common, is the seven-step problem-solving, decision-making process; the second is a simplified decision-making process; and the third is a more complex problem-solving model.

Seven-Step Problem-Solving, Decision-Making Process

[6] Having a logical thought process helps ensure that you will not neglect key factors that could influence the problem, and ultimately your decision. In fact, you should always apply a clear, logical thought process to *all* leadership situations that you encounter. The seven-step process is an excellent tool that can guide you in solving problems and making those sound and timely decisions. The seven steps are:

1. Identify (recognize/define) the problem.
2. Gather information (facts/assumptions).
3. Develop courses of action (solutions).
4. Analyze and compare courses of action (alternatives/solutions).

5. Make a decision; select the best course of action (solution).
6. Make a plan.
7. Implement the plan (assess the results).

Identify the Problem

[7] Being able to accurately identify the nature of a problem is a crucial undertaking. All leadership problems, whether they involve a work-related situation or a counseling session, are exploratory in nature—that is, leaders do not always identify the right cause of a problem or develop the best plan. In fact, two of the most common errors of leaders are identifying the wrong problem and identifying the wrong causes of a problem. Plus, the tendency for leaders to make mental errors increases as their levels of stress increase. We all make mistakes. If leaders are given false information, it may lead them to incorrect problem identification and to incorrect assumptions about the causes of a problem. Then, if leaders fail to determine the true source of a problem, they may develop an inadequate plan.

[8] Learn to identify the real problems. Consider all angles. Learn to seek only accurate information that leads to the real causes of a problem. To ensure that information is accurate, question its validity. In other words, leaders must take what accurate information they have, use their best judgment, and make educated assumptions about the causes of a problem. Then, they must consider the courses of action that will be most likely to succeed.

[9] Even though leaders may use the right problem-solving process, incorrect problem identification can lead to the wrong decision. It is a fallacy to think that using a correct formula or set of steps will lead you to the real problem and to a successful course of action. Your values, character, knowledge, and way of thinking have a direct and vital impact on the problems you identify as important. These inner qualities affect how you view, gather, and analyze information bearing on the identified problem.

Gather Information

[10] In this step, leaders must gather all available information that pertains to or can influence the situation (identified problem) from sources such as higher, lateral, and subordinate levels of command as well as from applicable outside agencies. Although some of the information may not bear on the problem at hand, it must be available for leaders to consider when developing and analyzing courses of action.

[11] The amount of available time in a leadership situation can be a limiting factor on how much time a leader spends performing the various steps of the problem-solving, decision making process. If time is extremely limited, this is the only step that leaders may omit so that they can quickly think through the remaining steps.

Develop Courses of Action

[12] With the problem identified and available information gathered, you are now ready to develop possible courses of action. Keep an open mind throughout this step and be prepared to anticipate change. "Sixty percent (of good problem-solving) is the ability to anticipate; 40 percent . . . is the ability to improvise, to reject a preconceived idea . . . , and to rule by action instead of acting by rules." *(S.L.A. Marshall)*

[13] Think of as many "what-ifs" as you can and prepare for them—do not be surprised. The laws of probability are strongly in favor of surprise. Develop courses of

actions to counteract events that might hinder accomplishment of your mission. Conducting "brainstorming" sessions is a good technique to use when there is difficulty in developing courses of action. Brainstorming is a creative technique that encourages several people to suggest as many solutions to a problem as possible. Generally, you want to have at least two or three possible courses of action—more if the situation dictates and time permits.

Analyze and Compare Courses of Action

[14] The next step is to determine which course of action will best solve the problem. Therefore, leaders should develop as many advantages and disadvantages for each course of action as possible. Then, they must objectively and logically analyze the advantages and disadvantages of each one against the advantages and disadvantages of the others.

[15] It is another fallacy to think that the course of action with the most advantages or the fewest disadvantages is the one that you should recommend or use. In most cases that may be true, but by weighing the importance of each advantage and disadvantage, there may be times when the "best" course of action has fewer advantages (all critical to mission accomplishment) and one or more disadvantages than another choice (but most are insignificant).

[16] Up to this point in the problem-solving, decision-making process, leaders should have involved subordinates to research the problem, gather information, and develop and analyze the various courses of action. *Subordinates are more likely to support a plan or decision if they took part in its development.* This technique will pay off in terms of increased interest, higher morale, and better efficiency by team members.

Make a Decision

[17] After you have carefully analyzed the possible courses of action using all available information, consider your intuitions and emotions. The decision-making process is not a purely objective, mathematical formula. The human mind does not work that way, especially under stress. Instead, the mind is both rational and intuitive, and since the decision-making process is a thought process, it is also both rational and intuitive. Your intuition is that aspect of your mind that tells you what "feels" right or wrong. Your intuition flows from your instincts and experience.

[18] However, never make the mistake of making decisions guided totally by emotions or intuitions and immediately doing what "feels" right. *This is a prescription for disaster.* Follow the problem-solving process as rationally and objectively as possible. Gather information; then develop, analyze, and compare courses of action. Consider your intuition or hunches, emotions, and values. Try to identify a "best" course of action that is logical and likely to succeed and that also "feels" right in terms of your intuition, values, and character. Finally, make your decision, make a plan, and take action.

Make a Plan

[19] Make a plan that includes who would do what, when, where, how, and why. Be as specific as time permits, but do not leave out vital information that could prevent mission accomplishment. Plus, ensure that you specify the what, when, where, how and why for all personnel or elements under your authority. Finally, include contingencies in your plan that address possible unexpected situations or actions. Develop these

contingencies based on the assumptions made when you identified the problem and gathered available information.

[20] As you did when developing the courses of action, be prepared to anticipate change. The ability to make appropriate changes in decisions and plans requires a certain flexibility of mind—a crucial trait of a good problem-solver, decision-maker, and planner.

Implement the Plan

[21] Once the decision and plan are made, it is time to act. In this final step, you must put the plan into action, then evaluate it to ensure that the desired results are being achieved. Evaluation is often a neglected step in the decision-making process.

[22] The key to evaluation is to seek feedback constantly on how your plan is doing. Get feedback from subordinates. Go to the point of the action and determine first hand if the plan is working or not. If not, determine why not and take immediate action to correct the plan. Mental flexibility is vital.

Sample Decision-Making Model

[23] Leaders often look for the simple decision, perhaps because it is easier to act on and explain. However, you must be extremely careful about making decisions too fast or too simplistically. Since you want to foster individual growth and/or improve the performance of your unit, do not automatically choose the first approach to solving a difficult situation. Leaders must evaluate each decision for its contribution toward the accomplishment of the task at hand and for future missions. If appropriate, a shared problem-solving, decision-making process with professionals, such as your instructors, will often help you to make wise decisions.

[24] The decision-making model described in this lesson is a quick and easy approach that leaders can use in many situations. First, briefly state the problem: For example, Connie has a drill practice on Friday night, but she forgot to cancel work for that night. Next, identify at least three options or courses of action. Concerning Connie's situation, she could:

- Speak to her drill leader about missing drill practice and working that night (*Option 1*).
- Find someone to cover for her at work while she participates in the drill practice (*Option 2*).
- Speak to her employer about showing up late for work after the drill practice is over (*Option 3*).

[25] Determine the positive and negative consequences for each of these options and whether you need more information upon which to make the best possible decision. The simplicity of this model allows anyone to use it almost anywhere and for any situation.

Sample Problem-Solving Model

[26] The problem-solving model shown below represents another approach that leaders can use to help them find solutions to problems and to make wise decisions. Within its three steps are numerous procedures that leaders can use as guides to solve a problem.

Step 1: Understanding the Problem

- Review the issue again.
- Write down what you know.
- Look for key phrases.
- Find the important information.
- Tell it in your own words.
- Tell what you are trying to find.

Step 2: Selecting Strategies

- Make a model—involve the senses.
- Make an organized list or table.
- Look for a pattern—find relationships.
- Guess (or conjecture) and test.
- Make an organized drawing or sketch.
- Work backwards—start with the consequence.
- Role-play—become an active player.
- Solve a simpler matter—try simulations.
- Use estimation.

Step 3: Looking Back: Checking the Answer

- Does the answer make sense?
- Is it reasonable?
- Can the issue be generalized?
- Is there a pattern?
- Are there other similar situations?

Source: Lesson 3: Decision-Making and Problem-Solving. The Air University. 19 June 2012. Web. 12 Aug. 2012.

Model Composition #3

I Drove Drunk And Killed Two Sisters

by Bethany Vaccaro

[1] After a day of partying, Brandy Graff got behind the wheel and slammed into an oncoming car. Since then, she's crusaded against the trend of young women driving drunk. But should she ever be forgiven?

[2] Brandy Graff can't remember the moment that changed her life. She does remember enjoying a gorgeous day at the beach, heading to a party at some college guys' house, drinking another beer, and waking up in a hospital room with a man in scrubs gripping her shoulders. She started yelling and fighting to get free when his voice cut through her confusion: "You've killed somebody!" Graff passed out again—her last, brief reprieve before the harsh new reality of the rest of her life.

[3] Wednesday, April 20, 2005, was forecast to be in the 80s—sunny and unseasonably warm for early spring in Rhode Island. A little after 9:00 A.M., 18-year-old Graff jumped into her stepfather's Mazda and went to Narragansett beach with a girlfriend and a 24-pack of Budweiser. "We drank in the car on the way to the beach and for the next several hours on the sand," Graff says. This was nothing out of the ordinary for her. "I loved to party. I'd go to house parties and play beer pong and card games, or go dancing at clubs, with my fake ID," she says. On the way home from the beach, she says, she and her friend decided to hit a college kegger before meeting up with Graff's boyfriend of six months. It was 3:30 P.M., and the two girls had finished most of the case of beer.

[4] A few towns away, Theodora "Dora" Mastracchio, 95, and her sister, Victoria "Vicky" Riccio, 86, had spent the afternoon dancing at the local seniors club. Afterward, Mastracchio's daughter, Karen Bucci, suggested they all go out for chowder and clam cakes, and the sisters were thrilled. They were always busy—knitting hats for the homeless, volunteering at a nursing home, spending time with their various grandchildren or great-grandchildren. They could often be seen cruising around town in a grandnephew's Mustang convertible, their white hair blowing in the wind. "They were always happy," Bucci, now 67, says. "Whatever anyone needed, they were there."

[5] After an early dinner, Mastracchio, Riccio and Bucci piled into Bucci's car for a scenic drive along the waterfront. Sometime before 6:30 P.M., Graff and her friend left their party. Graff can't recall if they discussed whether she should be getting behind the wheel. "I don't remember driving erratically," she admits. But Bucci remembers. "I saw a gold flash," she says, looking down as she replays the scene yet again in her mind. "All of a sudden—boom! It was like a slow-motion movie." Graff careened left on the two-lane road, slamming head-on into Bucci's car. Bucci hurt her ankle and broke her ribs, but Riccio died at the scene. Mastracchio succumbed to injuries three days later.

[6] The sisters were among the nearly 16,000 people killed that year in alcohol-related crashes. And although that figure has since declined, the number of women driving drunk has gone up: Federal Bureau of Investigation statistics show that since 2005, arrests of young women for driving under the influence jumped a staggering 36 percent. One reason for the spike is that groups like Mothers Against Drunk Driving

(MADD) have successfully pushed for better enforcement of laws, says José Alberto Uclés, a spokesman for the National Highway Traffic Safety Administration. But another major contributing factor is that women are drinking more, he says. (Under the same vigilant police efforts, arrests among young men were up only 4 percent.)

[7] The statistics, while startling, reflect the well-documented trend of women overindulging: According to one study, 37 percent of college women binge-drink. *Jersey Shore*'s Snooki and Angelina chug until they fall over, and multiple offender Lindsay Lohan is more punch line than cautionary tale, preening for the cameras wearing only a bikini and her sobriety-monitor ankle cuff. Women are working harder and partying harder, and often driving home afterward, sending a message that drinking and driving is not just tolerated; it's expected and even condoned. "It was so easy for Brandy—she got beer from adults," says Gabrielle Abbate of the Rhode Island chapter of MADD. "We need to start respecting the fact that alcohol is a drug and it causes harm."

[8] "I just couldn't wrap my mind around what had happened. Was I really responsible for ending a human life?"

"I Felt Like Prison Was Where I Belonged"

[9] The day after the accident, when Graff came to in the hospital, she was handcuffed to her bed, her worst injury a gash on the knee. (Her friend—whose name was never released because she was 16 at the time—also suffered minor wounds.) Graff was arraigned in her hospital room on multiple felonies, including reckless driving resulting in death. Authorities took her to the state correctional facility, where she was fingerprinted, photographed, and held for a few hours until her parents posted bail. "I just couldn't wrap my mind around what had happened," she says. "How could things go so terribly wrong? Was I really responsible for ending a human life? Could I kill someone and not even know it?"

[10] Graff spent the next two years out on bail, awaiting her sentencing through a plea bargain. She forced herself to go to community college classes and attended outpatient drug and alcohol treatment. "I didn't want to go out in public," she says. "I was so ashamed. I felt like prison was where I belonged." Watching the news coverage of her case, she saw for the first time the faces of the women she'd killed. "They were smiling; they were happy. They looked like people I could know, like my grandma," she says. Graff believed that she should have been the one killed. "There are times when I just wanted to die. When you do something like what I've done, you try to figure out how to fix it, how to make up for it. But there is no solution."

[11] In June 2007, a month before her twenty-first birthday, Graff was sentenced to 15 years, with at least 10 to serve at the Adult Correctional Institution in Cranston, Rhode Island. Superior Court judge Stephen Nugent said, "Hopefully, the word will go out: You drink, you drive, you hurt someone or kill someone, you will be seriously punished." Graff was led out of the courtroom by two police officers. She was now inmate #128457.

"I'm Brandy: Killer"

[12] Now Graff's typical morning starts with a cup of instant coffee in the cell she shares with another woman. She spends her days scrubbing toilets, lugging trash and mowing the lawn. The friends who used to be central in her life don't write or visit, but she does see her boyfriend and her stepdad. Her mom brings takeout three times a

week, which they eat with plastic forks under the watchful gaze of the guards. "Drive safe," Graff says to her mother before she walks into the night.

[13] A year into her sentence, Graff began speaking to groups of high schoolers about drinking and driving. Once a week during the school year, she'd tell her story, often breaking down in tears. But she says these talks have given her a reason for being alive. She wants to show the students that they could just as easily be in her shoes. "Never in a million years did I think I would be in jail. People like me don't go to jail. I wasn't a criminal," she tells them. "You don't want to be me. . . . I'm now Brandy: drunk driver. I'm now Brandy: killer." She's received letters from students who say that hearing her story helped them make better choices. But it can't undo the terrible one she made, she says. "I'll never be OK with what happened."

"Sorry Doesn't Even Scratch the Surface"

[14] While other members of the victims' families have not contacted Graff, Bucci and her daughter Melissa have visited her in prison—once when a student group came to hear Graff speak and once during regular visiting hours. "I have a broken heart, and that is never going to mend," Bucci says. "But I didn't want hatred on top of that." Bucci approached Graff before she was to speak and, seeing that she was nervous, hugged her and whispered in her ear, "What I want you to do for me is get up there and speak very strong so these kids understand that this cannot continue." Later, in a letter, she told Graff to be a good person, "and if it gets hard, you ask my mother and my aunt to help you and they will." Graff was stunned by her show of compassion. "I didn't understand why she was being so nice to me," she says. "You say sorry to someone, but it seems so stupid coming out of your mouth, because sorry doesn't even scratch the surface. I used to hope I could make it up to them; that if I kept talking to the kids and doing good things, I could make them feel better. But I've ruined their lives."

[15] Should Graff be forgiven? She was only 18 when she drove drunk, an age when many of us make foolish choices. But she didn't have a beer or two; she drank until she blacked out, and got behind the wheel several times that day. "She was old enough to reason," says Abbate of MADD. "And I'll bet she knew that what she was doing that day was wrong. So she goes through the justice system, and we hope that she will be rehabilitated." Some believe that making an example of someone like Graff will scare others straight. But Hugh Gusterson, Ph.D., a sociologist at George Mason University in Fairfax, Virginia, who has studied underage drinking, says that to come down hard on Graff is to ignore our collective culpability. "Brandy Graff was enabled by adults who provided the alcohol, and was incited by peers who considered it cool to drink to excess, then drive," he says. "She made her choices in a society that glorifies drinking." What we should be focusing on, he argues, is prevention: For every Graff, there are countless young women who slide behind the wheel after a few cosmos and barely make it home. Sending one or even a dozen Brandy Graffs to prison won't change that, Gusterson says. "The most important question is: What will stop this from happening? Why do young adults think drinking is the most exciting thing?"

[16] If Graff serves all 10 years, she will leave prison at age 31, although she'll likely get out sooner for good behavior. Last October she was eligible for her first chance at parole. She prepared a packet for the board, hoping that a woman who made a terrible mistake as a teenager might be given a second chance. But Bucci, for all of her forgiveness, did not support Graff's release. "Three years is not enough for killing two

people—my mom and my aunt were worth more than that," she told the parole board. Bucci still suffers from breathing problems and a limp, and often sees the crash flash in front of her; she remembers her aunt struggling to draw in her last breaths.

[17] The hearing didn't last very long. Parole was denied. Graff will be eligible again in two years.

Source: "I Drove Drunk And Killed Two Sisters" by Bethany Vaccaro, *Glamour* (Feb. 2011, pp. 127–129). Bethany Vaccaro/© Glamour/Conde Nast. Reprinted with permission.

Model Composition #4

Soft Skills: The Competitive Edge

[1] What do employers look for in new employees? According to the 2006 report *Are They Really Ready to Work? Employers' Perspectives on the Basic Knowledge and Applied Skills of New Entrants to the 21st Century U.S. Workforce,* it may not be what some young job seekers expect. This in-depth survey of 461 business leaders conducted by the Conference Board, Corporate Voices for Working Families, Partnership for 21st Century Skills, and Society for Human Resource Management reveals that while the three "R's" (reading, writing, and arithmetic) are still fundamental to every employee's ability to do the job, employers view "soft" skills as even more important to work readiness. The report also finds that younger workers frequently lack these skills, which include:

- Professionalism or work ethic
- Oral and written communication
- Teamwork and collaboration skills
- Critical thinking or problem-solving skills

[2] In 2007, the U.S. Department of Labor's Office of Disability Employment Policy (ODEP) discussed the importance of such skills with the *Circle of Champions,* a distinguished group of U.S. businesses that have received the *Secretary of Labor's New Freedom Initiative Award* for innovative and proactive efforts to recruit, hire, and promote people with disabilities. As part of this dialogue, the companies identified the following competencies as key to the success of young workers in the 21st Century workplace.

Networking

[3] Simply put, networking involves talking with friends, family members, and acquaintances about your employment goals, interests, and desires. It also involves reaching out beyond people you already know in order to expand the opportunities that may be available to you. When it comes to finding a job, networking is essential. According to Cornell University's Career Center, 80 percent of available jobs are not advertised. Therefore, if you are not connecting with other people, you are likely to miss out on many job opportunities.

[4] To start networking, make a list of everyone who may be able to help you job search. Next, talk to people on the list and tell them that you are looking for employment. Ask if they know of any openings and to introduce you if they do. But don't stop with the names on your list. Talk to cashiers, barbers, clergy, and anyone else you meet about their work and ask if they know of any jobs that match your interests. It is also essential to follow up with those with whom you have networked. Talking with a person once will only provide leads available at that point in time. But by establishing an ongoing relationship, you may learn of other opportunities as they arise.

[5] Once you find a job, it is important to continue to network effectively. Through ongoing networking you can develop relationships with colleagues and increase your ability to move up in the organization.

Enthusiasm

[6] Enthusiasm is also essential to success. When interviewing, you are likely to stand out in an employer's mind if you show excitement about the job. Prior to the interview, check out the company's Web site to learn about the business. Think of questions you might want answered, because asking questions is one way to show interest. Other strategies include arriving a few minutes early to the interview, dressing professionally, and staying engaged in the conversation. You should also bring a pad and pen so you can take notes during the interview; just make sure to ask if it is okay to take notes first. This shows the interviewer that you are actively engaged and paying close attention to what he or she is saying. It may also make it easier for you to think of additional questions to ask prior to accepting a job offer.

[7] Once employed, continue to demonstrate enthusiasm by taking initiative and seeking new and more challenging work. In some work settings, this may mean performing tasks needing to be done before being asked. In a restaurant, for instance, in between meal rushes, a server might show initiative by wiping off dirty menus or filling salt and pepper shakers. In other work settings, you can show initiative by volunteering to take on needed work or pitching a new project idea to your supervisor. If he or she likes the idea, offer to do more research and follow up with him or her. This provides you with some ownership of the project and shows your commitment to the company.

Professionalism

[8] Make sure your resume is "dressed to impress." Having an organized resume is essential to making a positive first impression. A good tip is to have a college professor or a career counselor read your resume and recommend edits before you submit it to a potential employer.

[9] Once you have been called for an interview, it is important to research the company and find out more about your potential job responsibilities. This will not only allow you to ask better questions during your interview, but also ensure you are well-informed should the company make you an offer.

[10] Business etiquette and work ethic go hand in hand for employers. Some tips when it comes to making a good impression once employed include:

- Dressing properly for the work setting
- Arriving on time and staying productive until you leave
- Turning cell phone ringers off while at work and returning phone calls and text messages while on breaks or after work hours
- Using computers, if you have access to them, only for work-related tasks
- Speaking in a respectful manner with supervisors, peers, and customers or clients

[11] Also remember that even when you are technically "off-duty" in the lunchroom or at a reception, you are representing the organization and are expected to act professionally. Don't contribute to office gossip or banter around too much with your co-workers. Although you are allowed to have fun and enjoy your job, you are still there to work.

Communication Skills

[12] Communicating ideas in the workplace is different than in an academic setting. In a classroom, the instructor usually leads group discussions or assigns written

homework, and students respond or ask questions when directed to do so. In the workplace, however, the format for interaction varies. Sometimes your supervisors may specifically ask you for your opinion or ask you to express that opinion in writing. More often than not, however, they assume that if they need to know something, you will bring it to their attention. The challenge of communicating in the workplace is learning how and when to share your ideas or concerns.

[13] If you need to tell your supervisor about something that is not going well, it is important to remember that both timing and your attitude are extremely important. For example, if you are a cashier at a carry-out restaurant and the long lines during the lunch rush "stress you out," causing you to give customers incorrect change, it is best to wait to talk to your supervisor about the problem during a slower period. At an appropriate time, you may want to ask if it would be possible to have someone assist you during busy periods. And if you are able to explain that this would not only allow you to make fewer mistakes, but also allow the business to provide better service by making the line move more quickly, he or she will be more likely to take your ideas seriously. Another proactive strategy would be to talk to your supervisor or another senior employee about how you could do your job more efficiently.

[14] Listening is also an important communication skill. Employers report that average entry-level candidates struggle with knowing how to listen carefully. They may not immediately process essential instructions or be able to understand how their tasks relate to the overall goals of the organization. One way to improve your listening comprehension skills is to ask questions. Other tactics include restating what you thought you heard to confirm you understood correctly, and taking notes.

Teamwork

[15] Successful businesses rely on team players. This skill is so important that an article in a *Society for Human Resource Management* magazine encourages employers to include teamwork as part of the performance appraisal process if collaboration is essential to the job. Understanding how to act as a member of a team may begin when you play sports or work on group projects in school. In the workplace, knowing how and when to lead and follow takes practice, as does knowing how to avoid unnecessary conflict. Working on a team also allows you to build closer relationships with your co-workers, which can make any job more fun and interesting. When working on a team, make sure that the workload is shared and that everyone is communicating. While some competition between team members is healthy and contributes to productivity, too much negative personal interaction can have the opposite effect.

Problem Solving and Critical Thinking

[16] Problem solving and critical thinking refers to the ability to use knowledge, facts, and data to effectively solve workplace problems. As a new employee, you may question why an organization follows certain steps to complete a task. It may seem to you that one of the steps could be eliminated saving time, effort, and money. But you may be hesitant to voice your opinion. Don't be; employers are usually appreciative when new employees are able to offer insight and fresh perspective into better and more efficient ways of doing things. It is important to remember, however, that as

someone new to the organization, you may not always have the full picture, and thus there may be factors you are unaware of that dictate that things be done a particular way. Another important thing to remember is that when you are tasked with solving a problem, you don't always need to answer immediately. The ability to develop a well thought out solution within a reasonable time frame, however, is a skill employers value greatly.

Source: Soft Skills: The Competitive Edge. United States Department of Labor. Web. 9 May 2012.

Model Composition #5

Television vs. Real-Life Criminal Investigations
by Jane Corbell

[1] Some of the most popular shows on television today are criminal investigation dramas such as *C.S.I.: Crime Scene Investigation, Cold Case,* and *Law & Order.* These shows typically begin with a homicide and follow police detectives as they work to figure out who the killer is. Like the agencies in these shows, real-life police departments combat crime and solve cases using crime scene investigators and special investigative units. However, the fictional TV dramas have led viewers to develop some misconceptions about these professionals and the procedures they use. The criminal investigations depicted in fictional television shows and actual crime scene investigative units differ in terms of manpower, resources, and time constraints.

[2] One significant difference between the TV crime dramas and real-life criminal investigations is manpower. Television crime shows have created a world in which a team of highly trained investigators show up at a crime scene and focus all of their efforts solely on that one case until it's solved. This simply is not reality. The vast majority of all law enforcement agencies in the United States are made up of very small departments, usually consisting of less than 50 employees. These small agencies have to assign staff to meet the most pressing needs of the community and usually cannot spare several officers for a specialized investigative unit. Although nearly every police agency has some type of investigation division, the assigned detective is often the only crime scene investigator for that case. Additionally, police detectives have to juggle a case load of several criminal investigations at one time. It is not uncommon for a single detective to have a dozen or more active investigations, so that person has to divide his or her attention among several cases, not just one.

[3] Another difference between television CSI and real-life crime scene investigation is resources. Although TV crime scene investigators arrive in top-shelf suits driving brand new SUVs with millions of dollars in technology stored in the back, real-life investigators usually have less to work with. The equipment seen on TV, such as laser range finders, alternate light sources (infra-red or ultraviolet lights), 3D digital mapping systems, and state-of-the-art crime scene labs, are all incredibly expensive. Police departments, especially the smaller ones, do not have the funding to provide these tools. In most cases, local authorities have to rely on a large, metropolitan department or a state-run agency for crime lab assistance. Most real-life detective work is still done the old fashioned way, by interviewing people face-to-face, reviewing the facts, asking the right people the right questions, and then putting the pieces together. The process is often not nearly as high-tech or glamorous as the TV shows make it appear.

[4] Probably the biggest difference between TV crime scene shows and reality is in the time factor. In TV land, evidence is always documented, collected, sent to the lab, analyzed and the results returned in a span of several hours. This just isn't true in the real world. In reality, evidence collected at a scene is sent to a lab, if one is available, within a day or two, depending on the nature and severity of the crime, and that's only if there's more than one detective available to work the scene. Once received at the lab, the evidence is handled based on its level of priority, with homicides, sexual

assaults, and child abuse cases taking precedence. Regardless of where the crime lab is located, its ability to process evidence in a timely fashion is limited to the number of available staff to perform the tests. Even crime lab folks get sick, take vacation, or attend training. So, real crime scene investigations tend to take a lot more time than television crime scene investigations do. Crime scene units, regardless of how big or how rich, cannot process a serious crime scene and see a case through to prosecution in the span of one hour (or even several days).

[5] Investigators know well the truth of the old adage, "Time is not your friend." The longer an investigation takes, the less likely it is to be solved. To be more effective in their jobs, they would love to have the manpower and the resources that are standard in the CSI-style television shows, but they don't. As a result, they are well acquainted with the difference between the facts and the fiction.

Model Composition #6

MEMORANDUM

TO: Mr. Charles Morgan, President

FROM: Jean McMullin, Lead Teller

DATE: November 16, 2013

SUBJECT: Tuition Reimbursement Program for Bank of Burke Employees

[1] For the last six years, I have been proud to tell people that I work as a teller at the Bank of Burke. In fact, I enjoy my job so much that I hope to be able to advance into positions of higher leadership here at the bank, and I recently decided to further my education and add to my qualifications. A few other Bank of Burke employees have also returned to school, so I would like to suggest that you consider adding another employee benefit to assist us in achieving our goals and, in turn, your goals for this institution. A tuition reimbursement program would be an excellent investment in one of Bank of Burke's greatest assets—its employees—and its benefits would far outweigh its costs.

[2] It's true that we already have a fine staff of employees who perform their duties very well. However, offering a tuition reimbursement program would encourage them to consider going back to school to take courses or to earn a college degree. Pursuing higher education would lead to improvements in our employees' knowledge, technical skills, soft skills, and professionalism. Courses in a college degree program typically strengthen students' oral and written communication skills, computer skills, and critical thinking skills, all of which would lead to improvements in our institution's productivity and customer service. Highly skilled and professional employees contribute to the bank's positive image and ensure our continued success in our community.

[3] Furthermore, a tuition refund program would allow us to attract excellent external candidates for job openings. When job hunters see that a company offers tuition reimbursement as an employee benefit, they conclude that the company not only cares about its employees but is also serious about rewarding them for their efforts to improve themselves and their job performance, and they want to be a part of that organization. Benefits like tuition reimbursement would draw a larger number of qualified candidates as well as candidates who are planning to continue to grow and develop their knowledge and skills. A high-caliber staff is able to maintain the smooth and efficient operation of our bank.

[4] I realize that assisting employees in furthering their education results in additional costs for the bank, but a tuition refund program would pay for itself. For example, assisting employees with their educational expenses could significantly reduce employee turnover. Staff members would more likely to stay with Bank of Burke and advance their careers here rather than seeking opportunities elsewhere, so the bank would save the costs associated with hiring and training new employees. In addition, retaining experienced, knowledgeable employees reduces the likelihood of costly mistakes. Plus, costs could be kept manageable. Bank of Burke's tuition refund program could include cost-sharing with employees. We could base tuition refunds on the grades each employee achieves. An A would be worth a 100 percent refund; a B, 85 percent; a C, 75 percent; and a D or below would earn no refund. Employees would be responsible

for purchasing their own books and materials. Implementing this kind of program would help build our employees' loyalty to this institution.

[5] Bank of Burke already compensates employees with fair wages and a benefits package, but adding a tuition refund program would place this institution a cut above the other banks in our community. We always strive to give our customers superior service and to remain a financially sound institution. Helping our employees further their education would directly contribute to our attainment of both of those goals.

Model Composition #7

Avoiding Plagiarism
by Dave Ellis

[1] Using another person's words, images, or other original creations without giving proper credit is called plagiarism. Plagiarism amounts to taking someone else's work and presenting it as your own—the equivalent of cheating on a test.

[2] Higher education consists of a community of scholars who trust one another to speak and write with integrity. Plagiarism undermines this trust. The consequences of plagiarism can range from a failing grade to expulsion from school.

[3] Plagiarism can be unintentional. Some students don't understand the research process. Sometimes they leave writing until the last minute and don't take the time to organize their sources of information. Also, some people are raised in cultures where identity is based on group membership rather than individual achievement. These students may find it hard to understanding how an individual can own creative work. Remember, however, that even accidental plagiarism can lead to a lowered grade and other penalties.

[4] To avoid plagiarism, ask an instructor where you can find your school's written policy on this issue. Read this document carefully, and ask questions about *anything* you don't understand.

[5] The basic guideline for preventing plagiarism is to cite a source for any fact or idea that is new to you. These include words and images created by another person. The overall goal is to clearly distinguish your own work from the work of others. A secondary goal is to give enough information about your sources so that they are easy to find. There are several ways to ensure that you meet both of these goals consistently.

Identify Direct Quotes

[6] If you use a direct quote from another writer or speaker, put that person's words in quotation marks. If you do research online, you might find yourself copying sentences or paragraphs from a Web page and pasting them directly into your notes. *This is the same as taking direct quotes from your source.* To avoid plagiarism, identify such passages in an obvious way. Besides enclosing them in quotation marks, you could format them in a different font or color to help you remember that these are quotes from other sources. Just remember to reverse the formatting before turning in your paper.

Paraphrase Carefully

[7] Instead of using a direct quote, you might choose to paraphrase an author's words. Paraphrasing means restating the original passage in your own words, usually making it shorter and simpler. Students who copy a passage word for word and then just rearrange or delete a few phases are running a serious risk of plagiarism. Consider this paragraph:

> Higher education also offers you the chance to learn how to learn. In fact, that's the subject of this book. Employers value the person who is a "quick study" when it comes to learning a new job. That makes your ability to learn a marketable skill.

Following is an improper paraphrase of that passage:

With higher education comes the change to learn how to learn. Employers value the person who is a "quick study" when it comes to learning a new job. Your ability to learn is a marketable skill.

A better paraphrase of the same passage would be this one:

The author notes that when we learn how to learn, we gain a skill that is valued by employers.

[8] Remember to cite a source for paraphrases, just as you do for direct quotes. When you use the same sequence of ideas as one of your sources—even if you have not paraphrased or directly quoted—cite that source.

Summarize Carefully

[9] For some of our notes, you may simply want to summarize your source in a few sentences or paragraphs. To do this effectively:

- Read your source several times for understanding.
- Put your source away; then write a summary in your own words.
- In your summary, include only the author's major points.
- Check your summary against your source for accuracy.

Identify Distinctive Terms and Phrases

[10] Some ideas are closely identified with their individual creators. Students who present such ideas without mentioning the individual are plagiarizing. This is true even if they do not copy words, sentence structure, or overall organization of ideas.

[11] For example, the phrase "seven habits of highly effective people" is closely linked to Stephen Covey, author of several books based on this idea. A student might write a paper titled "Habits of Effective People," using words, sentences, and a list of habits that differ completely from Covey's. However, the originality of this student's thinking could still be called into question. This student would be wise to directly mention Covey in the paper and acknowledge Covey's idea that effectiveness and habits are closely linked.

Note Details About Each Source

[12] Identify the source of any material that you quote, paraphrase, or summarize. For books, details about each source include the author, title, publisher, publication date, location of publisher, and page number. For articles from print sources, record the article title and the name of the magazine or journal as well. If you found the article in an academic or technical journal, also record the volume and number of the publication. A librarian can help identify these details.

[13] If your source is a Web page, record as many identifying details as you can find—author, title, sponsoring organization, URL, publication date, and revision date. In addition, list the date that you accessed the page.

Cite Your Sources as Endnotes
or Footnotes to Your Paper

[14] Ask your instructor for examples of the format to use.

Submit Only Your Own Work

[15] Turning in materials that have been written or revised by someone else puts your education at risk.

Allow Time to Digest Your Research

[16] If you view research as a task that you can squeeze into a few hours, then you may end up more confused than enlightened. Instead, allow for time to reread and reflect on the facts you gather. This creates conditions for genuine understanding and original thinking.

[17] In particular, take the time to do these things:

- Read over all your notes without feeling immediate pressure to write.
- Summarize major points of view on your topic, noting points of agreement and disagreement.
- Look for connections in your material—ideas, facts, and examples that occur in several sources.
- Note direct answers to your main and supporting research.
- Revise your thesis statement, based on discoveries from your research.
- Put all your notes away and write informally about what you want to say about your topic.
- Look for connections between your research and your life—ideas that you can verify based on personal experience.

Source: From Dave Ellis, *Becoming a Master Student*. 14th ed. Copyright © 2013 Cengage Learning.

Model Composition #8

Bias in the News Media

by Andrew R. Cline

[1] Is the news media biased toward liberals? Yes. Is the news media biased toward conservatives? Yes. These questions and answers are uninteresting because it is possible to find evidence—anecdotal and otherwise—to "prove" media bias of one stripe or another. Far more interesting and instructive is studying the inherent, or *structural*, biases of journalism as a professional practice—especially as mediated through television. I use the word "bias" here to challenge its current use by partisan critics. A more accepted, and perhaps more accurate, term would be "frame." These are some of the professional frames that structure what journalists can see and how they can present what they see.

Commercial bias: The news media are money-making businesses. As such, they must deliver a good product to their customers to make a profit. The customers of the news media are advertisers. The most important product the news media delivers to its customers are readers or viewers. Good is defined in numbers and quality of readers or viewers. The news media are biased toward conflict (re: bad news and narrative biases below) because conflict draws readers and viewers. Harmony is boring.

Temporal bias: The news media are biased toward the immediate. News is what's new and fresh. To be immediate and fresh, the news must be ever-changing even when there is little news to cover.

Visual bias: Television (and, increasingly, newspapers) is biased toward visual depictions of news. Television is nothing without pictures. Legitimate news that has no visual angle is likely to get little attention. Much of what is important in politics—policy—cannot be photographed.

Bad news bias: Good news is boring (and probably does not photograph well, either). This bias makes the world look like a more dangerous place than it really is. Plus, this bias makes politicians look far more crooked than they really are.

Narrative bias: The news media cover the news in terms of "stories" that must have a beginning, middle, and end—in other words, a plot with antagonists and protagonists. Much of what happens in our world, however, is ambiguous. The news media apply a narrative structure to ambiguous events suggesting that these events are easily understood and have clear cause-and-effect relationships. Good storytelling requires drama, and so this bias often leads journalists to add, or seek out, drama for the sake of drama. Controversy creates drama. Journalists often seek out the opinions of competing experts or officials in order to present conflict between two sides of an issue (sometimes referred to as the authority-disorder bias). Lastly, narrative bias leads many journalists to create, and then hang on to, master narratives—set story lines with set characters who act in set ways. Once a master narrative has been set, it is very difficult to get journalists to see that their narrative is simply one way, and not necessarily the correct or best way, of viewing people and events.

Status quo bias: The news media believe "the system works." During the "fiasco in Florida," recall that the news media were compelled to remind us that the Constitution was safe, the process was working, and all would be well. The mainstream news media never question the structure of the political system. The American way is the only way, politically and socially. In fact, the American way is news. The press spends vast amounts of time in unquestioning coverage of the process of political campaigns (but less so on the process of governance). This bias ensures that alternate points of view about how government might run and what government might do are effectively ignored.

Fairness bias: No, this is not an oxymoron. Ethical journalistic practice demands that reporters and editors be fair. In the news product this bias manifests as a contention between/among political actors (also re: narrative bias above). Whenever one faction or politician does something or says something newsworthy, the press is compelled by this bias to get a reaction from an opposing camp. This creates the illusion that the game of politics is always contentious and never cooperative. This bias can also create situations in which one faction appears to be attacked by the press. For example, politician A announces some positive accomplishment followed by the press seeking a negative comment from politician B. The point is not to disparage politician A but to be fair to politician B. When politician A is a conservative, this practice appears to be liberal bias.

Expediency bias: Journalism is a competitive, deadline-driven profession. Reporters compete among themselves for prime space or air time. News organizations compete for market share and reader/viewer attention. And the 24-hour news cycle—driven by the immediacy of television and the internet—creates a situation in which the job of competing never comes to a rest. Add financial pressures to this mix—the general desire of media groups for profit margins that exceed what's "normal" in many other industries—and you create a bias toward information that can be obtained quickly, easily, and inexpensively. Need an expert/official quote (status quo bias) to balance (fairness bias) a story (narrative bias)? Who can you get on the phone fast? Who is always ready with a quote and always willing to speak (i.e., say what you need them to say to balance the story)? Who sent a press release recently? Much of deadline decision making comes down to gathering information that is readily available from sources that are well known.

Glory bias: Journalists, especially television reporters, often assert themselves into the stories they cover. This happens most often in terms of proximity, i.e., to the locus of unfolding events or within the orbit of powerful political and civic actors. This bias helps journalists establish and maintain a cultural identity as knowledgeable insiders (although many journalists reject the notion that follows from this—that they are players in the game and not merely observers). The glory bias shows itself in particularly obnoxious ways in television journalism. News promos with stirring music and heroic pictures of individual reporters create the aura of omnipresence and omnipotence. I ascribe the use of the satellite phone to this bias. Note how often it's used in situations in which a normal video feed should be no problem to establish, e.g., a report from Tokyo I saw recently on CNN. The jerky pictures and fuzzy sound of the satellite phone create a romantic image of foreign adventure.

[2] The Accuracy in Media (AIM) organization claims the news media are biased toward liberal politics. The Fairness & Accuracy in Reporting (FAIR) organization claims the news media are biased toward conservative politics. Supporters of these views see one group as right and the other as wrong. But the reality is not that simple. Yes, AIM and FAIR each point out coverage that appears to bolster their various claims. At times, the media do seem to be biased one way or the other. What these groups don't say, however, is that their mistrust of the media is also a mistrust of the people. Those who complain most about media bias would see themselves as able to identify it and resist it. They get upset about it because they question whether the average American is able to do the same. If the average American can identify it and resist it, then there is little need to get upset about bias. The AIM and FAIR web sites are full of material to help hapless Americans avoid the cognitive ravages of the "evil" conservatives or the "slandering" liberals and their media lackeys. I believe the average American is quite capable of identifying problems with news coverage.

Critical Questions for Detecting Bias

1. What is the author's/speaker's socio-political position? With what social, political, or professional groups is the speaker identified?
2. Does the speaker have anything to gain personally from delivering the message?
3. Who is paying for the message? Where does the message appear? What is the bias of the medium? Who stands to gain?
4. What sources does the speaker use, and how credible are they? Does the speaker cite statistics? If so, how were the data gathered, who gathered the data, and are the data being presented fully?
5. How does the speaker present arguments? Is the message one-sided, or does it include alternative points of view? Does the speaker fairly present alternative arguments? Does the speaker ignore obviously conflicting arguments?
6. If the message includes alternative points of view, how are those views characterized? Does the speaker use positive words and images to describe his/her point of view and negative words and images to describe other points of view? Does the speaker ascribe positive motivations to his/her point of view and negative motivations to alternative points of view?

Source: Copyright © Andrew R. Cline. Reprinted with permission from the author. http://rhetorica.net/bias

Model Composition #9

Why Americans Think (Wrongly) That Illegal Immigrants Hurt the Economy

by Arian Campo-Flores

[1] At the heart of the debate over illegal immigration lies one key question: are immigrants good or bad for the economy? The American public overwhelmingly thinks they're bad. In a recent *New York Times*/CBS News poll, 74 percent of respondents said illegal immigrants weakened the economy, compared to only 17 percent who said they strengthened it. Yet the consensus among most economists is that immigration, both legal and illegal, provides a small net boost to the economy. Immigrants provide cheap labor, lower the prices of everything from produce to new homes, and leave consumers with a little more money in their pockets. They also replenish—and help fund benefits for—an aging American labor force that will retire in huge numbers over the next few decades. Also, an increase in the number of American workers is needed to prevent the U.S. from having too few working-age adults to pay for retiree benefits in a few decades, as many European nations currently do. So why is there such a discrepancy between the perception of immigrants' impact on the economy and the reality?

[2] There are a number of familiar theories. Some point to the ravages of the Great Recession, arguing that people are anxious and feel threatened by an influx of new workers (though anti-immigrant sentiment ran high at times prior to the crash of 2008). Others highlight the strain that undocumented immigrants place on public services, like schools, hospitals, and jails. Still others emphasize the role of race, arguing that foreigners provide a convenient repository for the nation's fears and insecurities. There's some truth to all of these explanations, but they aren't quite sufficient.

[3] To get a better understanding of what's going on, consider the way immigration's impact is felt. Though its overall effect may be positive, its costs and benefits are distributed unevenly. David Card, an economist at the University of California, Berkeley, notes that the ones who profit most directly from immigrants' low-cost labor are businesses and employers—meatpacking plants in Nebraska, for instance, or agribusinesses in California's Central Valley. Granted, these producers' savings probably translate into lower prices at the grocery store, but how many consumers make that mental connection at the checkout counter? As for the drawbacks of illegal immigration, these, too, are concentrated. Native low-skilled workers suffer most from the competition of foreign labor. According to a study by George Borjas, a Harvard economist, immigration reduced the wages of American high-school dropouts by 9 percent between 1980 and 2000. Not surprisingly, surveys show that those without a high-school diploma tend to oppose illegal immigration most fervently.

[4] There's another distortion in the way immigration's costs and benefits are parceled out. Many undocumented workers pay money to the federal government, in the form of Social Security contributions and income taxes, and take less in return, says Gordon Hanson, an economist at the University of California, San Diego. At the state and local level, however, it's a different story. There, illegal immigrants also make contributions, through property and sales taxes, but on balance, they use more in public services, such as schools, health benefits, and welfare assistance. As a result, says

Hanson, the federal government ends up with a net gain in its coffers, while "states get stuck with the bill."

[5] This breeds resentment among taxpayers. In a 2005 paper, Hanson analyzed how the size of the undocumented population and its use of public assistance affected attitudes toward immigration. He found that among low-skilled workers, opposition to immigration stemmed mainly from the competitive threat posed by the newcomers. Among high-skilled, better-educated employees, however, opposition was strongest in states with both high numbers of immigrants and relatively generous social services. What worried them most, in other words, was the fiscal burden of immigration. That conclusion was reinforced by another finding: that their opposition appeared to soften when that fiscal burden decreased, as occurred with welfare reform in the 1990s, which curbed immigrants' access to certain benefits.

[6] Beyond these economic rationales for anti-immigrant views, there's a demographic one as well. Illegal immigrants used to be clustered in a handful of big states, like California, Texas, and New York. But in the 1990s, they began dispersing en masse, chasing jobs in the remote reaches of the country. As a result, California's share of the undocumented population dropped from 42 percent in 1990 to 22 percent in 2008, according to the Pew Hispanic Center. A group of 28 fast-growing states, such as North Carolina and Georgia, more than doubled their share, from 14 percent in 1990 to 32 percent in 2008. Natives in those areas had barely any experience with undocumented immigrants, and they felt overwhelmed by the sudden change. The once distant debate over illegal immigration was now bubbling up in the heart of their communities.

[7] In a new book, *Brokered Boundaries*, Douglas Massey and Magaly Sánchez cite research showing that such rapid demographic change tends to trigger anti-immigrant sentiment when it gets entangled in inflammatory political rhetoric. They argue that in the past several decades, a "Latino threat narrative" has come to dominate political and media discourse. In the 1980s, President Ronald Reagan began framing immigration as an issue of "national security," they write. In the 1990s, the image of the immigrant-as-freeloader gained wide circulation. And in the 2000s, there was Lou Dobbs, railing against an "invasion of illegal aliens" that waged "war on the middle class." "The majority of Americans are more ambivalent than hostile [to undocumented immigration]," says Massey, a professor at Princeton. But "the hostile part can be mobilized from time to time," by what he calls "anti-immigrant entrepreneurs."

[8] The irony is that for all the overexcited debate, the net effect of immigration is minimal (about a one tenth of 1 percent gain in gross domestic product, according to Hanson). Even for those most acutely affected—say, low-skilled workers, or California residents—the impact isn't all that dramatic. "The shrill voices have tended to dominate our perceptions," says Daniel Tichenor, a political science professor at the University of Oregon. "But when all those factors are put together and the economists crunch the numbers, it ends up being a net positive, but a small one." Too bad most people don't realize it.

Model Composition #10

In Defense of Police Pursuits

by Marty A. McNeely

[1] Theodore Roosevelt, the 26th president of the United States, once said, "No man is above the law, nor do we ask any man's permission when we command him to obey it." To ensure citizens' compliance with the law, we invest authority and power in our police officers and assign them the duties of apprehending criminals, protecting the safety of the public, and, whenever possible, serving as a deterrent to crime. Because these officers take these duties seriously, they are willing to pursue a subject who is trying to flee from them, even though doing so often significantly endangers their own safety. Innocent bystanders, too, can sometimes be harmed when the police are forced to chase a fleeing suspect. However, most police departments still allow officers to pursue fleeing suspects under certain conditions. Police pursuits are a necessary and justifiable tool that officers must sometimes use to perform their duties.

[2] Police pursuits are justifiable because they lead, first of all, to the apprehension of offenders. Many examples show the need for law enforcement to pursue fleeing suspects to bring them to justice for their misdeeds. One such example is an incident that occurred in Rock Hill, South Carolina. On March 18, 2005, Rock Hill police officer Tim Greene responded to a reported bank robbery at the Bank of America and was met by an armed suspect emerging from the bank. The suspect fired several shots at Officer Greene before fleeing the scene in his SUV. Officer Greene pursued the suspect, who, more than once, stopped his vehicle to fire multiple shots from a semi-automatic long gun at police. As he tried to escape, the suspect continued to escalate the situation, endangering the public with his reckless driving and his indiscriminate gunfire. Unfortunately, the suspect was eventually killed in a gun battle with law enforcement, but Greene was fulfilling his duty in seeking to arrest a suspected thief.

[3] Pursuit of fleeing suspects is also necessary for police to fulfill their duty to maintain public safety. It's true that a suspect who is determined to get away from police will sometimes cause damage to property or injure innocent citizens. However, the public duty doctrine, a long-established legal precedent, holds that police do not owe a specific duty of protection to any one person, but instead have a general responsibility to society as a whole. If police allow a suspect to get away, they leave that individual free to continue to harm other people and their property. As the Greene pursuit demonstrates, police fulfill their ethical and moral obligation to ensure the general public's safety when they engage in a pursuit. Had the violent bank robber pursued by Officer Greene been allowed to escape, that robber may have gone on to injure or kill others. The United States Supreme Court has ruled that, in pursuit incidents, the police are deemed to be *reactive* and not proactive. In other words, the law views police in a pursuit situation as reacting to the need for immediate criminal apprehension, a need arising from a general duty owed to the public.

[4] Finally, police pursuits are necessary because they help police officers fulfill their duty to prevent crime. According to the deterrence theory of criminal behavior, individuals will often decide not to commit a crime because they know they risk detection, apprehension, and punishment. Deterrence theorists believe that the *certainty* of punishment is more important than the *severity* of the punishment. Under this model,

therefore, an individual will decide against engaging in criminal behavior more because of a perceived fear of pursuit and capture than a fear of the actual penalty for committing the criminal act. If police were not allowed to pursue suspects, an important obstacle to criminal behavior would be eliminated. Thus, more individuals might risk participating in a criminal activity because their chances of getting away with it would improve.

[5] If police are no longer permitted to pursue fleeing suspects, fewer criminals would be brought to justice. The threat to public safety would increase. And the crime rate would be likely to increase. Police officers are trained professionals who do everything they can to minimize the danger to the public as they perform their duties. We need to let them do their jobs and continue to pursue those who break our laws.

Model Composition #11

Make the Choice to Harness Time's Power
by Tom Rattle

[1] Time. It is the same for all of us. Time doesn't know, or care, if you use it wisely, or squander it foolishly. Once gone, it cannot be retrieved, changed, or reset.

[2] Time is also the main component of the most powerful financial tool at your disposal—the principle of compound interest. It has been called the eighth wonder of the world, and for good reason—with very little effort, astounding sums can be built over time from small initial amounts.

[3] The key to compounding is the cumulative effect of adding current investment earnings to existing capital, then having this new, larger amount generate investment earnings, which in turn are added to capital, which then generates a higher level of earnings, and so on. Do this for enough years, and even small amounts can grow to mighty sums. Here are a few examples:

- A newborn baby is given a gift—one share of stock in a company, purchased for $72.50. The company never pays dividends, but the share price appreciates at an average of 10 percent annually for a very long time. The baby grows too, and lives a very long life. On her 100th birthday, this single share of stock, which has compounded for many decades, is now worth $1 million.
- A young couple wisely decides to begin saving for retirement early. Beginning at age 25, both contribute $2,000 annually to an IRA. This continues for eight years—and then they stop. They never save another dime. But they started early, and that made all the difference. The investments made in their IRAs compounded at 10 percent annually, and by the time they reached 65, had grown to just over $1 million.
- You have probably heard the story about how the Indians of Manhattan sold their real estate to a group of immigrants in 1626 for $24 in beads and trinkets. The usual reaction to this story is that the Indians made a very bad deal. Actually, they made a very good deal; their mistake was in not converting their newfound wealth to cash and investing it. Their $24, compounded at 7 percent interest for 373 years, today would be worth about $2.1 trillion, or roughly 30 times today's value of that same real estate (including all the buildings).

[4] Although there are people who have amassed great fortunes because of their ability to compound capital at very high rates of return over long periods of time, it is very difficult to do (even for them!). The beauty of compounding is that high rates of return aren't necessary to achieve a satisfactory result. The process is simple, can be nearly effortless, is available to everyone, and always works if you follow a few simple rules:

- Focus on an investment approach that provides consistent returns. A significant loss in the later years of an investment plan can destroy a decade or more of steady growth.
- Don't touch the capital or its earnings. Reinvest everything. Resist the temptation to invade your ever-growing portfolio.

- Plant as many seeds as you can as early as you can. The more capital you start with, and the more years it is allowed to grow, the more you'll have in the end. The difference here can be dramatic. Had the couple in the second example begun saving five years earlier—still stopping after eight years— they would have accumulated 70 percent more money at retirement.
- Be patient. The race is long.

[5] Time. Compounding makes it work for you. But failure to follow the rules, or worse, failure to even get started, makes time your enemy. It can be a lever that moves the world with a small push, or an insurmountable barrier with no way around. Your choices will determine whether you leave a legacy of wisdom and wealth or an empty sack lined with regrets. Make the choice to harness time's power. The difference in your life day-to-day will be imperceptible; the difference in 30 years will be unbelievable.

Source: "Make the Choice to Harness Time's Power" by Tom Rattle. *The Enterprise* (Salt Lake City), July 5, 1999, p. 11. Reprinted with permission of The Enterprise—Utah's Business Journal, http://www.slenterprise.com

APPENDIX 2

Eleven Common Errors in English

In Chapter 3, you learned that the documents you write for most audiences—especially those in academic settings and the workplace—must adhere to Standard English. Unlike conversational English, Standard English demands that we follow a strict set of rules for grammar, punctuation, and spelling. The readers of your compositions will expect you to follow all of these rules.

In this Appendix, you will practice recognizing and correcting 11 common errors in English.

Error #1: Sentence Fragments

A **sentence** is a complete thought that includes both a subject and a verb. A **sentence fragment** lacks either a subject or a verb or does not express a complete thought. A fragment looks like a complete sentence because it begins with a capital letter an ends with a period, but it cannot stand by itself until the missing element or elements have been added. Although we commonly speak in sentence fragments, they are grammatically incorrect, so we cannot write them.

Fragments That Lack Subjects

One kind of sentence fragment lacks a subject, the noun or pronoun that performs the action or is being linked to more information. For example:

> Missing the point. [Who missed it?]
> Guarantees delivery in two days. [Who guarantees it?]
> Made her sad. [What made her sad?]

Fragments That Lack Verbs

Another kind of fragment lacks a verb. For example:

> Only one of my neighbors. [Did what?]
> Mr. Stanley, my favorite teacher. [Is what?]

The player who won the award. [This fragment has no verb. The clause *who won the award* functions as an adjective that identifies which player.]

The most common type of verbless fragment, though, is one that contains part of a verb, but not all of it. For example:

The cat licking its paw.
This two-story house designed for a large family.

In these cases, simply adding the missing part of the verb will correct the fragment:

The cat **is licking** its paw.
This two-story house **was designed** for a large family.

Fragments That Lack a Complete Thought

A third kind of fragment is one that expresses only part of a thought. Two types of these fragments are phrase fragments and dependent clause fragments. Neither can stand alone as a separate sentence.

Phrase Fragments. Phrases, which come in many types, are always *parts* of sentences because the whole group of words in the phrase acts as a specific part of speech in the sentence. When phrases stand alone, they become fragments. In the following examples, the information in parentheses gives one or more possible parts of speech for each phrase or group of phrases, depending on the context of the rest of the sentence.

On my way to work in the rain. [adverb]
Folding napkins. [noun or adjective]
Spinning out of control. [noun or adjective]
To get a good grade on the test. [noun or adverb]
A caring but firm woman. [noun]

Phrases must be combined with other elements to form complete sentences. Note how the previous phrases can be made into complete sentences:

On my way to work in the rain, I skidded into the back of a truck.
The servers always disliked folding napkins.
Spinning out of control, the model airplane crashed to the floor.
I hope to get a good grade on the test.
My son's teacher is a caring but firm woman.

Dependent-Clause Fragments. Dependent-clause fragments look deceptively like complete sentences because they are groups of words that may contain both a subject and/or a verb. However, they always begin with a certain kind of word—such as a relative pronoun or a subordinating conjunction—that causes the whole group to act as just one *part* of a complete sentence. Therefore, they cannot stand alone. Consider the following examples.

Who love to go fishing.

Who is a relative pronoun in a clause that could function as an adjective. Therefore, that clause is only part of a complete sentence, such as "Kids *who love to go fishing* will enjoy this camp." The clause acts an adjective modifying the word *kids*.

RELATIVE PRONOUNS THAT CREATE DEPENDENT ADJECTIVE CLAUSES

who	whom
which	that

If it's not raining.

The word *if* turns this whole group of words into an adverb. It should be part of a sentence such as "*If it's not raining*, she'll play golf." The clause becomes an adverb that modifies the verb *play*.

Because I can't be in two places at one time.

The word *because* turns this whole group of words into an adverb. It should be part of a sentence such as "You must give Megan a ride *because I can't be in two places at one time*." The clause becomes an adverb that modifies the verb *must give*.

SOME WORDS THAT CREATE DEPENDENT ADVERB CLAUSES

after	before	though	whenever
although	if	unless	where
as	since	until	wherever
because	so that	when	while

What I want.

This group of words can act as a noun. It should be part of a sentence such as "I can't decide *what I want*."

SOME WORDS THAT CREATE DEPENDENT NOUN CLAUSES

that	who	what
which	whatever	where
whichever	whoever	whose
when	why	how

Correcting Sentence Fragments

There are two ways to correct a sentence fragment:

1. Add the missing element.
2. Attach the fragment to the sentence before it or after it.

| **FRAGMENT:** | Maybe a mouse or a moth. [No verb] |
| **COMPLETE SENTENCE:** | Maybe a mouse or a moth chewed the quilt. [Adds the verb *chewed*] |

| **FRAGMENT:** | Got away with it. [No subject] |
| **COMPLETE SENTENCE:** | He got away with it. [Adds the subject *he*] |

FRAGMENT:	Singing in the tree outside the window. [Incomplete phrase fragment]
COMPLETE SENTENCE:	Singing in the tree outside the window, the bird kept me awake. [Attaches the phrase to the sentence that comes after it]
FRAGMENT:	Since I arrived home ill from Tennessee. [Incomplete dependent clause]
COMPLETE SENTENCE 1:	I arrived home ill from Tennessee. [Removes the word that creates the dependent clause]
COMPLETE SENTENCE 2:	I've had to stay home from school since I arrived home ill from Tennessee. [Attaches the dependent clause to a sentence that comes before it]

Grammar Exercise 1.1

On your own paper, rewrite each sentence fragment to add the missing element(s) and create a complete sentence.

1. In the afternoon.
2. If you suffer from insomnia.
3. Someone who likes dogs.
4. To write well.
5. Checking my e-mail.
6. Hopes to make the team.
7. When I finish my degree.
8. A person with a sense of humor.
9. Learning to speak Spanish.
10. Although the speed limit is only 45.

Grammar Exercise 1.2

The following passage contains ten sentence fragments. On your own paper, rewrite each one so that it is a complete sentence. If the best correction involves attaching the fragment to a sentence that comes before or after, include that sentence, too, as part of your rewritten sentence.

Effects of Sleep Deprivation

by Constance Staley

[1] Sleep restores us physically and emotionally. [2] It recharges our batteries. [3] College students who don't get enough sleep. [4] May be hurting their chances at college success. [5] Sleep deprivation causes a number of problems.

1. **Learning.** [6] During sleep, your brain creates sleep spindles. [7] Which are one to two-second bursts of brainwaves that help transfer information to long-term memory. [8] Sleeping less than six hours may

block the production of sleep spindles and result in less learning. [9] In tests comparing sleep-deprived students' learning with students who get eight hours of sleep. [10] Nonsleepers were less able to learn new information.

2. **Grade Point Average.** [11] In one study that compared college students who were short sleepers (six hours or less), average sleepers (seven to eight hours), and long sleepers (nine or more hours). [12] Average GPAs reported for the three groups were 2.74, 3.01, and 3.24, respectively.

3. **Relationship Strain.** [13] Who wants to interact with a cranky, sleep-deprived person? [14] Sleep deprivation may put your relationships at risk. [15] Because of increased irritability and decreased interpersonal sensitivity. [16] What's more, getting less sleep may start a chain reaction. [17] In one study of college students' sleep troubles, worrying about relationships was the most often cited reason for not getting enough sleep.

4. **Anxiety, Depression, and Illness.** [18] Sleep deprivation triggers all sorts of emotional, psychological, and physical risks. [19] Students who report getting less sleep appear to be less psychologically healthy. [20] And more prone to catching every bug that comes along. [21] Research indicates that sleep deprivation definitely puts a dent in your emotional intelligence and your ability to think constructively.

5. **Car Accidents.** [22] According to the National Highway Traffic Safety Administration. [23] Fatigue accounts for approximately 1,550 deaths, 71,000 injuries, and more than 100,000 police-reported automobile crashes on our highways each year. [24] Young drivers (ages 16–29) particularly at risk.

6. **Lowered Life Satisfaction.** [25] In the grand scheme of things, getting less sleep seems to throw off everything. [26] One study, for example, examined students' reported average length of sleep. [27] Also their scores on a well-known life satisfaction scale. [28] Getting less sleep was significantly related to being less satisfied with life in general.

Source: From Staley, Constance. *Focus on College Success.* 3rd ed. Copyright © 2013 Cengage Learning.

Error #2: Run-on Sentences and Comma Splices

A **sentence** is defined as a complete thought that contains a subject and a verb. A **run-on sentence** contains two complete sentences (independent clauses) that are not separated with adequate punctuation. Therefore, they "run together." For example:

> He bought tickets to the game I didn't want to go.
> Bob did the research Phil wrote the report.
> Mr. Patel's assistant is leaving he'll need to hire a replacement.
> You need to exercise it will improve your cardiovascular health.

The lack of appropriate punctuation in these example sentences makes them difficult to read. Usually, a reader has to stop and reread a run-on sentence to mentally correct where one thought ended and another began.

A **comma splice** contains two complete independent clauses separated only by a comma. For example:

> He bought tickets to the game, I didn't want to go.
> Bob did the research, Phil wrote the report.
> Mr. Patel's assistant is leaving, he'll need to hire a replacement.
> You need to exercise, it will improve your cardiovascular health.

Writers can correct run-on sentences and comma splices four different ways:

1. Create two separate sentences.
2. Insert a semicolon between the two sentences.
3. Add a coordinating conjunction.
4. Add a conjunctive adverb.
5. Add a subordinating conjunction to turn one of the sentences into a dependent clause.

Each method is explained next, with examples.

Create Two Separate Sentences

The easiest way to correct a run-on sentence or a comma splice is to divide it into two separate sentences, each of which ends in a period:

> He bought tickets to the game. I didn't want to go.
> Bob did the research. Phil wrote the report.
> Mr. Patel's assistant is leaving. He'll need to hire a replacement.
> You need to exercise. It will improve your cardiovascular health.

This separation will correct the mistake; however, it often results in short, monotonous sentences. It also causes a loss of direct connection between the two related ideas. The reader is then forced to figure out the relationship between them. Therefore, this method of correction—though simple—often results in less sophisticated writing that is more challenging to read. The next three correction methods better communicate how the two thoughts are related.

Insert a Semicolon

The second way to correct a run-on sentence or a comma splice involves inserting a semicolon between the two independent clauses:

> He bought tickets to the game; I didn't want to go.
> Bob did the research; Phil wrote the report.
> Mr. Patel's assistant is leaving; he'll need to hire a replacement.
> You need to exercise; it will improve your cardiovascular health.

The semicolon indicates to the reader that the two ideas are related. However, it still does not indicate *how*. The reader must figure out the relationship.

Add a Coordinating Conjunction

A more sophisticated way to correct a run-on sentence or a comma splice involves adding one of the seven coordinating conjunctions to indicate the relationship between the two sentences.

COORDINATING CONJUNCTIONS	
and	but
or	for
nor	so
yet	

In these examples, the coordinating conjunctions are highlighted in blue:

He bought tickets to the game, **but** I didn't want to go.
Bob did the research, **and** Phil wrote the report.
Mr. Patel's assistant is leaving, **so** he'll need to hire a replacement.
You need to exercise, **for** it will improve your cardiovascular health.

Note: When a coordinating conjunction links two independent clauses, it is always preceded by a comma.

Add a Conjunctive Adverb

Another sophisticated way to correct a run-on sentence or a comma splice is to add a conjunctive adverb between the two independent clauses.

COMMON CONJUNCTIVE ADVERBS	
therefore	finally
consequently	similarly
furthermore	also
then	likewise
meanwhile	moreover
for example	nevertheless

In these examples, the conjunctive adverbs are highlighted in blue:

He bought tickets to the game; **however**, I didn't want to go.
Bob did the research; **then**, Phil wrote the report.
Mr. Patel's assistant is leaving; **consequently**, he'll need to hire a replacement.
You need to exercise; **for example**, it will improve your cardiovascular health.

Note: When a conjunctive adverb links two independent clauses, it is always preceded by a semicolon and followed by a comma.

Add a Subordinating Conjunction

One final effective way to correct a run-on sentence or a comma splice is to turn one of the independent clauses into a dependent clause with the addition of a subordinating conjunction. Using this technique allows the writer to clearly state the relationship between the two ideas.

SOME COMMON SUBORDINATING CONJUNCTIONS			
after	before	though	whenever
although	if	unless	where
as	since	until	wherever
because	so that	when	while

In these examples, the subordinating conjunctions are highlighted in blue:

Although he bought tickets to the game, I didn't want to go.
Bob did the research **before** Phil wrote the report.
If Mr. Patel's assistant is leaving, he'll need to hire a replacement.
You need to exercise **because** it will improve your cardiovascular health.

Note: When the dependent clause comes first in the sentence, it should be followed by a comma.

Grammar Exercise 2.1

On your own paper, rewrite each of the following sentences twice to use two different methods of correcting run-on sentences and comma splices.

1. In the summer we go to the beach, in the winter we go to the mountains.
2. Yesterday I felt ill today I feel better.
3. Carl wants to lose weight, he is eating smaller portions.
4. The doors were all locked the thieves broke a window to enter.
5. You could buy a dress, you could make one yourself.
6. I am working three jobs, I am always tired.
7. This new software will save you money it will also save you time.
8. Angela overslept she still made it to class on time.

Grammar Exercise 2.2

The following passage contains nine run-on sentences and comma splices. On your own paper, rewrite each one to punctuate it correctly. Use a mixture of different methods to correct the errors.

The High Costs of Cheating

by Dave Ellis

[1] Cheating on tests can be a tempting strategy it offers the chance to get a good grade without having to study. [2] Remember, however, that cheating carries costs. [3] Here are some consequences to consider.

[4] **You risk failing the course or getting expelled from college.** [5] The consequences for cheating are serious, cheating can result in failing the assignment, failing the entire course, getting suspended, or getting expelled from college entirely. [6] Documentation of cheating may also prevent you from being accepted to other colleges.

[7] **You learn less.** [8] Although you might think that some courses offer little or no value, you can create value from any course. [9] If you look deeply enough, you can discover some idea or acquire some skill to prepare you for future courses or a career after graduation.

[10] **You lose time and money.** [11] Getting an education costs a lot of money it also calls for years of sustained effort. [12] Cheating sabotages your purchase. [13] You pay full tuition and invest your energy without getting full value for it, you shortchange yourself and possibly your future coworkers, customers, and clients. [14] Think about it you probably don't want a surgeon who cheated in medical school to operate on you.

[15] **Fear of getting caught promotes stress.** [16] When you're fully aware of your emotions about cheating, you might discover intense stress. [17] Even if you're not fully aware of your emotions, you're likely to feel some level of discomfort about getting caught.

[18] **Violating your values promotes stress.** [19] Even if you don't get caught cheating, you can feel stress about violating your own ethical standards. [20] Stress can compromise your physical health and overall quality of life.

[21] **Cheating on tests can make it easier to violate your integrity again.** [22] Human beings become comfortable with behaviors that they repeat cheating is no exception. [23] Think about the first time you drove a car. [24] You might have felt excited, even a little frightened. [25] Now driving is probably second nature, you don't give it much thought. [26] Repeated experience with driving creates familiarity, this lessens the intense feelings you had during your first time at the wheel.

[27] You can experience the same process with almost any behavior. [28] Cheating once will make it easier to cheat again. [29] You become comfortable with compromising your integrity in one area of life, you might find it easier to compromise in other areas.

Error #3: Noun Errors

Many noun errors occur when forming plurals or possessives.

Forming Plurals

The **plural** form of a noun indicates more than one. Most words are made plural by adding an –*s* to the end of the word. For example, add an –*s* to *flower* to make the plural *flowers*. Or add an *–s* to the word *cat* to make the plural *cats*. However, some words form the plural in other ways:

ADD *–ES*
witches
benches
taxes
tomatoes

CHANGE THE *–F OR –FE TO –VES*	
knife	knives
shelf	shelves
life	lives
calf	calves

CHANGE THE *–Y TO –IES*	
supply	supplies
sky	skies
cry	cries

USE THE SAME FORM FOR THE PLURAL
deer
sheep
fish

Some nouns are irregular and form the plural in other ways:

foot	feet
woman	women
child	children
mouse	mice
crisis	crises

Some nouns do not have plural forms:

happiness	paint
honesty	air
equipment	sunshine
homework	math
dust	fun
blood	

Some words and phrases indicate the use of a singular noun (one that refers to only one thing), and other words and phrases indicate the need for a plural noun.

SINGULAR	PLURAL
a song	**some** songs
one song	**two** songs
this song	**these** songs
that song	**many** songs
	one of the songs
	all songs

Forming Possessives

The possessive form of nouns, which indicates ownership, is formed by adding an apostrophe plus an -s to a singular noun:

Greg's glove
Shakespeare's plays
the house's roof
our money's worth
one year's experience

In plural possessive nouns, place the apostrophe *after* the -s unless the plural is irregular:

my parents' house
babies' bottles
the Joneses' car
men's cologne

Most apostrophe errors occur when writers mistakenly use apostrophes to form plurals.

INCORRECT	CORRECT
two hero's	two heroes
all Monday's	all Mondays
these course's	these courses

Grammar Exercise 3.1

A. On your own paper, write the plural form of each of the following words.

1. potato
2. fly
3. man
4. tooth
5. wolf
6. person
7. box
8. church
9. baby
10. reason

B. On your own paper, rewrite the possessive to add the apostrophe.

11. Mr. Chens garden
12. my brothers motorcycle
13. all of the actors scripts
14. the childrens coats
15. monkeys tails
16. storys ending
17. two years experience
18. a days pay

Grammar Exercise 3.2

The following passage contains ten sentences with noun errors (some of these sentences contain more than one error). On your own paper, rewrite every sentence that contains a noun error to correct that error.

Creating Flow

by Skip Downing

[1] Happiness has been called the goal of all goal, the true destination of all journeys. [2] After all, why do we pursue any goal or dream? [3] Isn't it for the positive inner experience our success will create?

[4] For centurys, explorers of human nature have pondered how we can consciously and naturally create happinesses. [5] Psychologist Mihaly Csikszentmihalyi has called highly enjoyable periods of time **flow states**. [6] Flow is characterized by a total absorption in what one is doing, by a loss of thoughts or concern's about oneself, and by a distorted sense of time (often passing very quickly). [7] His studys offer insights into how we can purposely create such positive inner experiences in college and beyond.

[8] Csikszentmihalyi believes that the key to creating flow lies in the interaction of two factor: the challenge a person perceives himself to be facing and the related skill's he perceives himself to possess. [9] Let's consider examples of three possible relationship of skill level and challenge. [10] First, when a persons perceived skill level is higher than a perceived challenge, the result is *boredoms*. [11] Think how bored you'd feel if you took an introductory course in a subjects in which you were already an expert.

[12] Second, when a person's perceived skill level is lower than that needed to meet a perceived challenge, the result is *anxiety*. [13] Think how anxious you'd feel if you took an advanced mathematics course before you could add and subtract.

[14] Third, when an individuals' perceived skill level is equal to or slightly below the challenge level, the result is often flow. [15] Recall one of those extraordinary moment when you lost yourself in the flow—maybe while conversing with a challenging thinker or playing a sport you love with a well-matched opponent. [16] In flow, participation in the activity is its own reward; the outcome doesn't matter.

Source: From Downing, Skip. *On Course*. 6th ed. Copyright © 2011 Cengage Learning.

Error #4: Pronoun Errors

Pronouns are words that substitute for and refer to another noun or pronoun. The three most common pronoun errors relate to pronoun case, pronoun agreement, and pronoun reference.

Pronoun-Case Errors

The **case** of a pronoun is the form it takes as determined by how it functions in the sentence. A pronoun that functions as a subject is in the **subjective case**. Here are examples of sentences with pronouns in the subjective case:

SUBJECTIVE PRONOUNS	
I	we
he	they
she	who
you	whoever

You and **she** have on the same dress.
Who knocked on the door?
He is taller than **I**.
We volunteers are meeting at noon.

A pronoun that functions as an object (an object of a preposition, a direct object, or an indirect object) is in the **objective case.**
Here are examples of sentences with pronouns in the objective case:

OBJECTIVE PRONOUNS	
me	us
him	you
her	them
it	whom, whomever

I sold **her** my textbook.
She tossed a peach to **him**.
From **whom** did you get that information?

A pronoun that indicates possession is in the **possessive case**.
Here are examples of possessive pronouns in sentences:

POSSESSIVE PRONOUNS	
my	our
mine	ours
your	yours
his	their
her	theirs
hers	its

Juanita is ready to give **her** speech.
Houa traded **his** peanut butter sandwich for **my** bag of jellybeans.

The pronouns most likely to be confused are those in the subjective and objective case. All of the following sentences contain pronoun-case errors:

Her and **me** left at the same time. [These are objective-case pronouns used as subjects.]
My grandfather gave the money to my brother and **I**. [This is a subjective-case pronoun used as an object.]
Us boys want to go swimming. [This is an objective-case pronoun used as a subject.]

To select the right pronoun, determine its function and then use the pronoun in the correct case. The incorrect pronouns in the sentences on page 255 are corrected below:

She and **I** left at the same time.
My grandfather gave the money to my brother and **me**.
We boys want to go swimming.

Pronoun-Agreement Errors

Like nouns, pronouns can be either singular or plural.

SINGULAR PRONOUNS			PLURAL PRONOUNS	
I	you	he	we	they
my	your	she	our	their
mine	yours	his	ours	theirs
myself	yourself	her	us	them
	it	him	ourselves	themselves
	its	hers	yourselves	
	itself	himself		
		herself		

A pronoun must agree in number with its **antecedent**, the word to which it refers. If that word is plural, you must use the matching plural pronoun form; if the word is singular, use the matching singular pronoun form. In the following examples, the antecedent is underlined, and the pronoun is highlighted in blue.

Each volunteer must bring **his** or **her** photo ID.
The children left **their** lunchboxes on the bus.
Try to understand your co-worker's perspective. **She** may be busy juggling many responsibilities.

When the word to which the pronoun refers is another pronoun, you must determine if the word is treated as singular or plural to select the correct pronoun.

SINGULAR		PLURAL	
each	no one	several	both
either	nobody	few	many
neither	anyone		
one	anybody		
everyone	someone		
everybody	somebody		

<u>Everyone</u> in the play forgot **her** lines at least once.
<u>Each</u> of the men checked **his** own safety equipment.
<u>Several</u> of the participants brought **their** lunch.
<u>Both</u> of the girls like to do the work **themselves**.

To avoid the inclusive but awkward *his or her* pronoun phrase, reword a sentence to use plural forms:

| **AWKWARD:** | A <u>person</u> should brush **his or her** teeth three times a day. |
| **BETTER:** | <u>People</u> should brush their teeth three times a day. |

| **AWKWARD:** | When <u>a school principal</u> discovers a weapon on **his or her** campus, **he or she** must act immediately. |
| **BETTER:** | When <u>school principals</u> discover weapons on their campuses, they must act immediately. |

Pronoun-Reference Errors

Another common pronoun problem is unclear reference. A pronoun must always refer to a clear antecedent. If a pronoun's antecedent is missing or unclear, confusion can result:

I took my son to get his teeth cleaned, and they said that he has two cavities.

Who is *they* in this sentence? Readers have to figure out for themselves that *they* refers to the people who work in the dentist's office. To correct this problem, rewrite the sentence to remove the unclear reference or to supply the missing antecedent:

I took my son to get his teeth cleaned, and **the dentist** said that he has two cavities.

Grammar Exercise 4.1

On your own paper, rewrite each of the following sentences to correct the pronoun error.

1. All of my co-workers were reading his or her e-mail.
2. Everyone in the class brings their own yoga mat.
3. To Jamal and I, this test was easy.
4. You run faster than her.
5. Each of the women selected their favorite shade of lipstick.
6. I went to the bookstore, but they said they were out of math textbooks.
7. Ken's mother told her and I to pick up a bag of ice.
8. A student should always bring their textbook to class.
9. Lisa feels nervous about giving speeches, but she hides it well.
10. After meeting a few lawyers, I realize it was not a good career choice for me.

The following passage contains eight sentences with pronoun errors [some of these sentences have more than one error]. On your own paper, rewrite every sentence that contains a pronoun error to correct that error.

Money and Values

by Dave Ellis

¹ People experience peace of mind when their behaviors align with their values. ² However, this is not always the case. ³ An individual who suspects that there's a conflict between their values and their behavior should look at the way they handle money.

⁴ For example, someone says that they value health. ⁵ After monitoring his expenses, he discovers that he spent $200 last month on fast food. ⁶ He's discovered a clear source of conflict. ⁷ He can resolve that conflict by redefining his values or changing his behavior. ⁸ People sometimes work to buy more things that he or she has no time to enjoy because they work too much. ⁹ This can be a vicious cycle.

¹⁰ Sometimes us Americans live values that are not our own. ¹¹ Values creep into our lives due to peer pressure or advertising that they bombard us with. ¹² Movies, TV, and magazines pump us full of images about the value of owning more stuff—bigger houses, bigger cars, better clothes. ¹³ All that stuff costs a lot of money. ¹⁴ The process of acquiring it can drive us into debt—and into jobs that pay well but deny our values.

¹⁵ Money provides plenty of opportunities for critical thinking. ¹⁶ For example, every college student should think about the wisdom of choosing to spend their money on the latest video game or digital gadget rather than a textbook or other resource needed for their education. ¹⁷ Games and gadgets can deliver many hours of entertainment before it breaks down. ¹⁸ Compare that to the value of doing well in a course, graduating with better grades, and acquiring skills for a career.

¹⁹ One way that you and me can align behaviors with beliefs is to ask one question when spending money: Is this expense consistent with my values? ²⁰ Over time, this question can lead to daily changes in behavior that make a big difference in peace of mind.

Source: From Ellis, Dave. *Becoming a Master Student*. 14th ed. Copyright © 2013 Cengage Learning.

Error #5: Relative-Pronoun Errors

Relative pronouns are words that create a type of dependent clause called a *relative clause*, which functions in a sentence as an adjective.

Relative pronouns cannot be used interchangeably, so writers need to learn to distinguish them from one another.

RELATIVE PRONOUNS	
that	which
who	whom

First of all, the relative pronouns *that* and *which* refer to things and animals. The relative pronouns *who* and *whom* refer to humans:

INCORRECT: A driver **that** observes the speed limit will not have to waste money on speeding tickets.

CORRECT: A driver **who** observes the speed limit will not have to waste money on speeding tickets.

Next, distinguish between *that* and *which*. *That* begins essential, or *restrictive*, relative clauses. These clauses are called restrictive because they are necessary for understanding which thing the writer is discussing. For example:

I will eat only at fast-food restaurants **that** offer healthy menu items.
Interviewers ask questions **that** help them assess candidates' qualifications.

Which begins nonessential, or *nonrestrictive*, relative clauses. These clauses interrupt the sentence with additional but unnecessary information. Therefore, they are set off from the rest of the sentence with commas, as in these examples:

Fruit and whole grains, **which** are both complex carbohydrates, are a staple of my diet.
A hummingbird, **which** weighs less than a penny, is the world's smallest bird.

Finally, learn the difference between *who* and *whom*. The relative pronoun *who* is the subjective case of the pronoun, whereas *whom* is the objective case (see pages 254–255 for an explanation of the subjective and objective pronoun cases). Note the difference in these two examples:

The player **who** earns the highest number of points wins the game.
My best friend from high school, **whom** I visit once or twice a year, lives in Maine.

Use commas before and after a clause that begins with *who* or *whom* if the information it provides is not essential to understanding the person being discussed. For example:

The person **who** is chosen for the job will begin work on the first day of August.
Professor Bonfield, **who** is retiring this year, was my favorite teacher.

Grammar Exercise 5.1

On your own paper, rewrite each of the following sentences to correct the relative-pronoun error.

1. I refuse to watch movies which are scary or gory.
2. Do people whom live in Florida get used to the high temperatures?
3. The woman which lives next door is an airline pilot.
4. The last person who we interviewed has valuable experience.
5. A vehicle which gets poor gas mileage will cost you more money to drive.
6. Students that prepare for class are usually more successful than students that don't.
7. Carol does not eat any foods which contain trans fats.
8. Rick is studying hapkido, that is a type of Korean martial art.

The following passage contains four sentences with five relative-pronoun errors. On your own paper, rewrite each of these sentences to correct the relative-pronoun error.

Can You Build a Better Brain?

by Constance Staley

¹ What's the secret to a healthy brain? ² When we think of fitness, most of us think from the neck down—strong abs, bulging pecs, and tight glutes. ³ But brain health tops them all. ⁴ According to new evidence, physical exercise helps our brains shrug off damage, reinforce old neural networks, and forge new ones.

⁵ Current research focuses on a protein called BDNF (for brain-derived neuro-tropic factor). ⁶ BDNF, that is sometimes referred to as "Miracle-Gro" for the brain, helps nerve cells in our brains grow and connect. ⁷ It's important for development in the womb, but it's also important in adult brains. ⁸ Simply put: it helps us learn. ⁹ According to researchers, rats which eat a high-calorie, fast-food diet and have a couch-potato lifestyle have less BDNF in their brains. ¹⁰ Omega-3 fatty acids found in fish normalize BDNF levels and counteract learning disabilities in rats who have brain injuries. ¹¹ Scientists are working to see if the same thing may be true for humans.

¹² "Exercise your brain. ¹³ Nourish it well. ¹⁴ And the earlier you start the better," scientists tell us. ¹⁵ New research indicates that education is a great way to nourish our brains. ¹⁶ People that are less educated have twice the risk of getting Alzheimer's disease in later life, and less educated people which have ho-hum, non-challenging jobs have three to four times the risk. ¹⁷ According to researchers, "College seems to pay off well into retirement." ¹⁸ It can help you build a better brain!

Source: From Staley, Constance. *Focus on College Success.* 3ʳᵈ ed. Copyright © 2013 Cengage Learning.

Error #6: Verb Errors

The most common verb errors include subject/verb-agreement errors, irregular-verb errors, and past-participle errors.

Subject/Verb-Agreement Errors

In the English language, subjects and verbs are either singular or plural. **Singular** means that the word refers to only one person or thing, and **plural** means that the word refers to more than one person or thing.

SUBJECTS		VERBS	
SINGULAR	PLURAL	SINGULAR	PLURAL
she	they	dance	dances
manager	managers	is	are
boy	boys	does	do

In a sentence, the subject and verb must agree (or match) in number. The writer must pair a singular subject with a singular form of the verb, and a plural subject with a plural verb. Agreement errors occur most frequently in sentences that contain compound subjects, collective nouns as subjects, pronouns as subjects, or an insertion between the subject and verb. These errors are explained in the next sections.

Compound Subjects

Two singular subjects joined by the word *and* form a compound subject. Compound subjects are plural, so they must be matched with a plural verb. For example:

> Her <u>brother and sister</u> **fight** all the time.
> The <u>Bahamas and Key West</u> **are** my favorite vacation destinations.

Note: Two singular subjects joined by the words *or* or *nor* are not treated as plural: Her brothers or her sister **picks** her up at school every day.

Collective Nouns

Collective nouns refer to a group of people or things. When functioning as subjects, they are singular if the verb refers to the whole group acting as a unit.

> The <u>public</u> **wants** details about celebrities' lives.
> Our <u>Social Committee</u> **arranges** fun events.
> <u>Sixty dollars</u> **is** the average ticket price.

Pronouns

Some pronouns are singular, and some are plural.

SINGULAR PRONOUNS		PLURAL PRONOUNS	
each	no one	several	both
either	nobody	few	many
neither	anyone		
one	anybody		
everyone	someone		
everybody	somebody		

> <u>Each</u> of us **needs** a canteen of water.
> <u>Everyone</u> in the audience **was** laughing.
> <u>Several</u> of the players **have** the flu.
> <u>Few</u> **realize** how difficult it is to ice skate.

Several pronouns (e.g., *some, all, most, any, none*) can be either singular or plural, depending on the words to which they refer. For example:

> <u>Some</u> of the play **was** dull.
> <u>Some</u> of the actors **were** nervous.
> <u>Most</u> of my family **has** red hair.
> <u>Most</u> of my cousins **have** freckles.

Insertions Between the Subject and the Verb

Often, a phrase that separates the subject and verb will result in a subject/verb-agreement error:

The planets in our solar system **varies** widely in size.

The subject of this sentence is *planets*, not *solar system*. The word *planets* is plural, so the verb should be in a plural form: *vary*.

To avoid subject/verb-agreement errors, disregard the phrase that separates the subject from the verb; then choose the appropriate verb. In the following examples, the phrases to disregard are enclosed in brackets:

Many citizens [in this state] **oppose** the governor's plan.
This system [of manually typing forms] **needs** to be automated.
Joe, [along with the other nurses,] **is** volunteering at the Blood Drive.

Irregular-Verb Errors

To form the past tense of verbs that are regular, we simply add *–d* or *–ed*. To form the past tense of verbs that are irregular, however, we must change one or more of the word's letters or change nothing at all. Here are some examples:

REGULAR VERBS		IRREGULAR VERBS	
PRESENT	PAST	PRESENT	PAST
hope	hoped	run	ran
walk	walked	take	took
believe	believed	sing	sang
laugh	laughed	leave	left
reach	reached	stand	stood
race	raced	feel	felt
		write	wrote
		go	went
		read	read

Past-Participle Errors

The **past-participle** form of the verb is used with helping verbs *has, have,* or *had.* If the verb is regular, the past participle needs to end in *–ed.* If the verb is irregular, its past participle will change form.

Past-Participle Form of Regular Verbs:

The team **has worked** on the problem for two weeks.
I **have searched** for a solution.
She **had considered** several options.

Past-Participle Form of Irregular Verbs:

We **have thought** about the various possibilities. [*Thought* is the past-participle form of the verb *to think.*]
The committee **has begun** the process.[*Begun* is the past-participle form of the verb *to begin.*]

I **have been** confused until now. [*Been* is the past-participle form of the verb *to be*.]

He **had hidden** his true feelings. [*Hidden* is the past-participle form of the verb *to hide*.]

Grammar Exercise 6.1

On your own paper, rewrite each of the following sentences to correct the verb errors.

1. The price of bananas have increased.
2. The players on our team is nervous about our first game.
3. Everybody recite the Pledge of Allegiance.
4. The front office staff collect the information for daily reports.
5. One of my co-workers leave at 4:00 p.m. every Tuesday.
6. My paper and my project is due in December.
7. Someone has ate all of the cake.
8. When Dan taked the test yesterday, he knowed all of the correct answers.
9. Last season, Carmen striked out every time she batted.
10. You have broke the school record.
11. Miguel and I have did the dishes.
12. She has stole my heart.

Grammar Exercise 6.2

The following passage contains 12 sentences with verb errors (two of these sentences contain more than one error). On your own paper, rewrite each of these sentences to correct the verb errors.

Keep Commitments

by Skip Downing

¹ The person we break commitments with the most are, ironically, ourselves. ² Keeping commitments often require overcoming enormous obstacles. ³ One of my students are a good example of this. ⁴ Rosalie had postpone her dream of becoming a nurse for eighteen years while raising her two children alone. ⁵ Shortly after she enrolled in college, her new husband asked her to drop out to take care of his two sons from a former marriage. ⁶ Rosalie agreed, postponing her dream once more. ⁷ Now back in college ten years later, she maked what she called a "sacred vow" to attend every class on time, to do her very best on all work, and to participate actively. ⁸ This time she was committed to getting her nursing degree. ⁹ Finally her time had came.

¹⁰ Then, one night she got a call from one of her sons who were now married and had a two-year-old baby girl. ¹¹ He had a serious problem: His wife was on drugs. ¹² Worse, that day she had buyed two hundred dollars worth of drugs on

credit, and the drug dealers were holding Rosalie's granddaughter until they got paid. [13] Rosalie spent the early evening gathering cash from every source she could, finally delivering the money to her son. [14] Then, all night she lay awake, waiting to hear if her grandchild would be return safely.

[15] At six in the morning, Rosalie got good news when her son brought the baby to her house. [16] He asked Rosalie to watch the child while he and his wife had a serious talk. [17] Hours passed, and still Rosalie cared for the baby. [18] Closer and closer crept the hour when her college classes would begin. [19] She started to get angrier and angrier as she realized that once again she was allowing others to pull her off course. [20] And then she remembered that she had a choice. [21] She could stay home and feel sorry for herself, or she could do something to get back on course.

[22] At about nine o'clock, Rosalie called her sister who lived on the other side of town. [23] She asked her sister to take a cab to Rosalie's house, promised to pay the cab fare, and even offered to pay her sister a bonus to watch the baby.

[24] "I didn't get to class on time," Rosalie said. "But I got there. And when I did, I just wanted to walk into the middle of the room and yell, "YEEAAH! I MADE IT!"

[25] If you could have saw her face when she told the class about her ordeal and her victory, you would have seen a woman who had just learn one of life's great lessons: When we break a commitment to ourselves, something inside of us die. [26] When we keeps a commitment to ourselves, something inside of us thrive. [27] That something is self-respect.

Source: From Downing, Skip. *On Course.* 6th ed. Copyright © 2013 Cengage Learning.

Error #7: Adjective and Adverb Errors

The most common adjective and adverb errors include adjectives incorrectly used as adverbs, past-participle adjective errors, and misplaced modifiers.

Adjectives Used as Adverbs

Adjectives are words that modify (describe or limit) nouns and pronouns. They tell *how many, what kind, or which one.* **Adverbs** are words that modify verbs, adjectives, and other adverbs by telling *when, where, how,* or *to what degree* an action occurred. Many adverbs end in *–ly,* but not all of them do.

ADJECTIVES	ADVERBS
sunny day	cried **loudly**
two gold stars	left **yesterday**
these tacos	**very** tall
more time	**skillfully** drove
unbelievable story	go **home**

Three pairs of adjectives and adverbs are easy to confuse and often misused in sentences. They cannot be used interchangeably:

ADJECTIVE	ADVERB
good	well
real	really
bad	badly

INCORRECT:	Sam pitched **good** at yesterday's game. [The word is modifying the verb *pitched*, so the adverb form is needed.]
CORRECT:	Sam pitched well at yesterday's game.
INCORRECT:	I am **real** sorry about this mistake. [The word is modifying the adjective *sorry*, so the adverb form is needed.]
CORRECT:	I am really sorry about this mistake.
INCORRECT:	She slept **bad** last night. [The word is modifying the verb *slept*, so the adverb form is needed.]
CORRECT:	She slept badly last night.

Past-Participle Adjective Errors

Past-participle forms of verbs are sometimes used as adjectives. See pages 262–263 for more about past participles.

broken window
sliced tomatoes
handwritten note
qualified applicant

If the verb is regular, the past participle needs to end in –*ed*. If the verb is irregular, its past participle will change form.

INCORRECT:	The freezer was filled with **froze** foods.
CORRECT:	The freezer was filled with frozen foods.
INCORRECT:	The **delay** flight to Phoenix finally departed at 3:00 p.m.
CORRECT:	The delayed flight to Phoenix finally departed at 3:00 p.m.
INCORRECT:	The **tire** children fell asleep in the car.
CORRECT:	The tired children fell asleep in the car.

Misplaced Modifiers

Modifiers are words, phrases, or clauses that explain or describe another word in the sentence. If a modifier doesn't come right before or right after the word it modifies, confusion can result. Misplaced modifiers are separated from what they explain or describe:

At only two years of age, my grandmother taught me to swim.

The highlighted phrase is the modifier that is supposed to describe *me* in this sentence. However, because it immediately precedes *my grandmother*, the sentence says that the grandmother was only two when she conducted these swimming lessons!

> She sent an e-mail to the president that made everyone mad.

This sentence makes it seem that the president—rather than the e-mail—angered everyone.

Note: If the writer *had* intended to say that the president made everyone mad, the correct relative pronoun would be *who* rather than *that*.

> Last year, I walked the same streets my father walked for the first time.

The highlighted phrase should modify the first *walked*. Its placement at the end of the sentence causes it to modify the second *walked*, which does not correctly state the writer's meaning.

Misplaced modifiers can also create ridiculous images in the reader's mind:

> Running down the street, my Poptart crumbled as I tried to catch the bus.

In this sentence, the Poptart is running down the street!

To correct a misplaced modifier, either move the modifier so that it's attached to the word it modifies, or reword the sentence completely to correct the error. Here are some examples:

MISPLACED:	I watch my children through the window playing in the sand.
CORRECTION 1:	Through the window, I watch my children playing in the sand.
CORRECTION 2:	As they play in the sand, I watch my children through the window.
MISPLACED:	The lottery winner was a teacher at the high school, who cried tears of joy.
CORRECTION 1:	The lottery winner, who cried tears of joy, was a teacher at the high school.
CORRECTION 2:	When the teacher at the high school won the lottery, she cried tears of joy.
MISPLACED:	In the bathtub, he discovered his son's collection of live frogs.
CORRECTION 1:	He discovered his son's collection of live frogs in the bathtub.
CORRECTION 2:	He looked into the bathtub and discovered his son's collection of live frogs.

Note: A **dangling modifier** is a related error to watch out for. When a modifier "dangles," the word it should modify has been left out of the sentence:

> While walking down the beach, her tension and stress melted away.

In this sentence, the tension and stress are walking down the beach because the sentence lacks the real subject: she. [*Correction:* While walking down the beach, she felt her tension and stress melt away.]

Grammar Exercise 7.1

On your own paper, rewrite each of the following sentences to correct the adjective and adverb errors.

1. My grandfather doesn't see good without his glasses.
2. Our teacher is a real good writer.
3. I bought a use car instead of a new one.
4. The explanation was complicate and difficult to understand.
5. I ordered the steak cover in grill onions.
6. The police found the stole car in Virginia.
7. Lying in the street, I spotted the newspaper.
8. Lee enjoys listening to music doing his homework.
9. Soaring overhead, my father pointed at the eagle.
10. We served cake to the guests on paper plates.

Grammar Exercise 7.2

The following passage contains five sentences with adjective and adverb errors (two of these sentences contain more than one error). On your own paper, rewrite each of these sentences to correct the errors.

Giving and Receiving

by Skip Downing

[1] A story is told of a man who prayed to know the difference between heaven and hell. [2] An angel came to take the man to see for himself. [3] In hell, overflowing with beautifully prepare meats, vegetables, drinks, and desserts, the man saw a huge banquet table. [4] Despite this bounty, the prisoners of hell had wither, sunk looks. [5] Then the man saw why. [6] The poor souls in hell could pick up all the food they wanted, but their elbows would not bend, so they could not place the food into their mouths. [7] Living amidst all that abundance, hell was filled with citizens who were starving.

[8] Then the angel whisked the man to heaven, where he saw another endless banquet table heap with a similar bounty of splendid food. [9] Amazingly, just as in hell, the citizens of heaven could not bend their elbows to feed themselves.

[10] "I don't understand," the man said. "Is heaven the same as hell?'

[11] The angel only pointed. [12] The residents of heaven were healthy, laughing, and real happy as they sat together at the banquet tables. [13] Then the man saw the difference.

[14] The citizens of heaven were feeding each other.

Source: From Downing, Skip. *On Course.* 6th ed. Copyright © 2011 Cengage Learning.

Error #8: Parallelism Errors

When you write a sentence that contains a series of words, phrases, or clauses, each item of that series should be **parallel**, or matching in form or structure. Parallelism errors occur when the writer mixes different parts of speech or forms of words. This type of error makes it more difficult for the reader to understand relationships between the sentence parts.

I enjoy **golfing**, **tennis**, and to hike.

This sentence mixes three different forms for the three activities in the series. We can correct this parallelism error by choosing one form for all three items:

CORRECTION 1:	I enjoy golf, tennis, and hiking.
CORRECTION 2:	I enjoy golfing, playing tennis, and hiking.
CORRECTION 3:	I like to play golf, to play tennis, and to hike.

Another example illustrates nonparallel phrases:

We searched for the missing file **in the drawers**, **on the desks**, and going through our briefcases.

The first two items in this series are prepositional phrases, but the last item breaks that pattern. It, too, should use the prepositional phrase structure:

We searched for the missing file *in the drawers, on the desks*, and *in our briefcases.*

One final example demonstrates nonparallel clauses:

She told us **that the memo is due** and **to finish the report**.

Both clauses in this sentence should begin with the same word to balance the two items in the series:

She told us **that the memo is due** and **that the report must be complete** by July.

Grammar Exercise 8.1

On your own paper, rewrite each of the following sentences to correct the parallelism errors.

1. We spent Saturday cleaning the house, doing the laundry, and prepared dinner.
2. The medical team worked with quickness, steadily, and efficiently.
3. My friend Jimmy is intelligent, funny, and has talent.
4. Sarah looked for her keys under her bed, in the fridge, and searched the car.
5. The teacher advised his students to take notes, to study daily, and that they should form study groups.
6. Most of us serve in many different roles our lives, including spouse, parent, co-worker, and friendships.

7. We have the money for a new toaster oven but not buying a new car.

8. Last night, my friends and I worked out at the gym, ate a light dinner, and the movie started at 9 o'clock.

The following passage contains ten sentences with parallelism errors. On your own paper, rewrite each of these sentences to correct the errors.

Benefits at the End of the Road

by Constance Staley

[1] There are plenty of benefits to graduating from a college or university. [2] According to a recent study, "The evidence is overwhelming that college is a better investment for most graduates than in the past . . ." even for people in jobs that don't require a degree, like secretaries, plumbers, and people who work as cash register operators. [3] "And, beyond money, education seems to make people happier and with good health." [4] Here's a quick look at some of them.

1. **Higher earning potential.** [5] On average, college graduates earn twice as much income as their peers with only a high school diploma.

2. **Lower unemployment rates.** [6] College graduates are more employable than their non-degreed peers. [7] This is especially helpful during cyclic downturns in the economy, when many people—even talented and committed employees—find themselves out of work.

3. **Wisdom.** [8] College students have the opportunity to gain understanding about a broad range of topics—politics, sociology, and subjects like history, to name a few. [9] A well-educated person knows Sigmund Freud's contribution to psychological theory, Charles Darwin's contribution to evolutionary theory, and the contribution to economic theory made by Adam Smith. [10] But beyond theories, facts, and dates, a well-educated person knows how to think critically, contribute to society, and management of his or her life.

4. **Insight.** [11] College students have the opportunity to understand themselves better as they participate in the academic, society, and co-curricular opportunities of higher education.

5. **True scholarship.** [12] College students have the opportunity to become lifelong learners. [13] True scholarship is not about making the grade. [14] It's about becoming the best student-learner you can be—inside or when you're out of the classroom. [15] The value of this benefit is beyond measure and serving you throughout your life.

6. **Lifelong friendships.** [16] Many college graduates report that some of their strongest lifelong relationships were formed during their time at college. [17] Choosing to attend college and the choice of a specific major puts you in touch with a network of people who share your specific interests.

Error #9: Comma Errors

Commas are probably the most misunderstood punctuation mark. Yet there are seven very clear rules that explain when they are necessary. To avoid comma errors in your own writing, memorize these rules. Then, when you are tempted to insert a comma, you can check yourself by thinking of the rule that requires a comma in that particular sentence.

Rule 1: Commas Separate Items in a Series

Items in a series can be words, phrases, or clauses, as in the following examples:

> Carol designs, builds, and sells wooden deck furniture.
> Please pick up milk, cheese, soda, and potato chips.
> We enjoyed relaxing on the beach, shopping at the mall, and eating out every night.
> The attorney interviewed him about where he went, what he did, and when he returned.

Rule 2: Commas Separate Two or More Adjectives Before a Noun

If you could insert the word *and* between two adjectives and the sentence would still make sense, separate those two adjectives with a comma:

> A smart, athletic senior won the scholarship.
> I bought the newest, smallest laptop computer.
> We ate at a crowded Chinese restaurant. [no comma]
> Take the first right turn after you exit the highway. [no comma]

Rule 3: Commas Separate Two Independent Clauses Joined by a Coordinating Conjunction

When two complete sentences (each with its own subject and verb) are linked together with a coordinating conjunction (*and, or, but, for, nor, so, yet*), a comma precedes the coordinating conjunction:

> The candidate reconsidered her decision to run for office, and she dropped out of the race.
> Air bags save lives, but they can injure very small children.
> You can pay the balance now, or you can wait until you receive your next bill.

Many comma errors occur when writers mistakenly put commas in sentences that do not contain two separate subject/verb relationships. The following sentences contain compound verbs, but they are not compound sentences. Therefore, commas are unnecessary.

> The candidate reconsidered her decision to run for office and dropped out of the race.
> Air bags save lives but can injure very small children.
> You can pay the balance now or wait until you receive your next bill.

Rule 4: Commas Separate Nonessential Clauses and Phrases That Interrupt the Rest of the Sentence

Commas need to come before and after extra information inserted into a sentence, as in the following examples:

> Bill, who has a lot of experience, is our first choice for the job.
> Monticello, which is in Virginia, was Thomas Jefferson's home.
> No one, not even the president, wants to work on Memorial Day.
> The marketing team, after working all night, finally readied all of the packages for mailing.
> Todd, her youngest son, bought her the necklace.

Look out for clauses and phrases that are *essential* to understanding the entire sentence—do not separate them with commas:

> The applicant who has the most experience will be our first choice for the job.
> Every person signing up for the soccer team must get a physical exam.

Rule 5: Commas Separate Introductory Elements of a Sentence

In the following examples, commas are used to separate the introductory elements:

> No, I didn't understand the diagram.
> By the end of the day, the staff was exhausted.
> Hoping for a big turnout, we plastered posters all over town.
> Because he has diabetes, he cannot eat the cake.
> For instance, you could walk a mile every day after work.
> Senator Perry, I do not support your proposal.

Rule 6: Commas Separate Information in Names, Titles, Dates, and Addresses

Note the commas in the following sentences that include dates and titles:

> The company opened for business on August 1, 2010, in Orlando, Florida.
> Alice Henson, Dean of Health Sciences, is retiring in December.

Rule 7: Commas Punctuate Direct Quotations

Note the following uses of commas to punctuate direct quotations:

> "By the end of this year," Mr. Roberts said, "we'll generate $100,000 in revenue."
> According to this week's *Wall Street Journal*, "Investors should quickly recover their losses."

▌ Grammar Exercise 9.1

On your own paper, rewrite each of the following sentences to correct the comma errors.

1. At the library, I checked out a cookbook a documentary on DVD and a bestselling novel.
2. After lying in a coma for a week the patient finally awoke.
3. Jorge will you play on our team?
4. On May 2 2014 I start my new job in Tulsa Oklahoma.
5. The instructor asked "Does anyone have any questions?"
6. Because Rashonda studied for weeks she passed the nursing exam on her first try.
7. The player intercepted the football but then he ran toward the wrong goal.
8. My father likes to tell long boring stories.

▌ Grammar Exercise 9.2

The following passage contains eleven sentences with comma errors. On your own paper, rewrite each of these sentences to correct the errors.

Instructors' Teaching Styles

by Carol Kanar

[1] Just as you have a learning style your instructors have teaching styles. [2] An instructor's teaching style determines to some extent the instructional methods he or she prefers to use. [3] Although educational researchers define a number of teaching styles we will consider only two basic types: independent and interactive. [4] Each of these styles represents an extreme of behavior. [5] However many instructors' styles fall somewhere between these extremes. [6] For example, an instructor may use mixed modes: a combination of teaching methods such as lecturing collaborative activities and group discussion.

[7] The instructor whose style is independent is usually formal and business-like with students, and places more importance on individual effort than on group effort. [8] This instructor expects students to assume responsibility for learning to work independently and to seek help when needed. [9] Lecturing is the preferred teaching method of this instructor who will often call on students rather than ask for volunteers. [10] Students often feel competitive in this instructor's class. [11] If you feel most comfortable in lecture courses and like working independently, then you may do your best work with an instructor, whose style is independent.

[12] On the other hand, the instructor whose style is interactive is usually informal with students and places more importance on group effort than on individual effort. [13] The interactive instructor guides students step by step through tasks and anticipates their needs. [14] Small group activities and large group discussions are this instructor's preferred teaching methods. [15] Rather than call on students he or she will

usually ask for volunteers. [16] Students often feel cooperative in this instructor's class. [17] If you feel more comfortable in classes where students do most of the talking, and if you would rather work with others than by yourself, then you may be able to do your best work with an instructor whose teaching style is interactive.

[18] If you do not like, or do not get along with one of your instructors, you may be reacting negatively to a teaching style that conflicts with your learning style. [19] However, don't let personal feelings keep you from being successful in the course. [20] Instead, you should focus on what you can do to meet the instructor's requirements and you should make an extra effort to adapt to his or her teaching style. [21] By making this effort, you may find that your relationship with your instructor will improve dramatically.

Source: From Kanar, Carol. *The Confident Student*. 7th ed. Copyright © 2011 Cengage Learning.

Error #10: Semicolon Errors

Semicolons have only two purposes: They separate independent clauses, or they separate items in a series when those items contain commas. You might think of the semicolon as a punctuation mark that communicates balance—what comes before and what comes after are always related and equal.

Semicolons Separate Two Independent Clauses

A semicolon divides the two equal parts of a compound sentence, as in the following examples:

> You wash the dishes; I'll sweep the floor.
> Retirement planning should begin early; people who start investing during their twenties often accumulate millions.
> I'd love to get a pet; however, I just don't have the time to properly care for one.
> The report was poorly written; furthermore, it included inaccurate data.

Before you use a semicolon, check to make sure that there is an independent clause (complete sentence that could stand alone) before it and another independent clause after it.

Note: Don't forget that in a compound sentence, two independent clauses joined by a coordinating conjunction (*and, or, but, for, nor, so, yet*) are separated by a comma. For example: The report was poorly written, and it included inaccurate data.

Semicolons Separate Items in a Series

If the items in a series contain commas, adding more commas to separate them would probably create confusion. Therefore, use semicolons when the list is more complex, as in these examples:

> My 10-day business trip will include stops in Seattle, Washington; Chicago, Illinois; and Charlotte, North Carolina.

This workshop targets a variety of people, such as business executives, including Human Resources managers; financial professionals, including stockbrokers and accountants; and attorneys.

Grammar Exercise 10.1

On your own paper, rewrite each of the following sentences to add the necessary semicolons.

1. The people in this photograph are Bruno, my grandfather Rose, my grandmother and George, my uncle.
2. My husband was raised on a farm I grew up in the city.
3. Much of the information posted on the Internet is inaccurate or unreliable therefore online researchers must carefully evaluate the worth of every website.
4. On our trip, we visited Savannah, Georgia Charleston, South Carolina and St. Augustine, Florida.
5. Always apply sunscreen a sunburn is both painful and dangerous.
6. Roger went out to get more boxes meanwhile, Anne began packing the contents of the drawers and cabinets.
7. Some things are easy to learn others are difficult and require more effort.
8. College students need to know how to use several types of computer software for example, coursework may require knowledge of Microsoft® Word®, PowerPoint®, and Excel®.

Grammar Exercise 10.2

The following passage contains eight sentences with semicolon errors. On your own paper, rewrite each of these sentences to correct the errors.

Be Proactive About Studying

by Carol Kanar

[1] Stephen R. Covey, author of *The Seven Habits of Highly Effective People*, says that people are either proactive or reactive in their responses to life's circumstances. [2] Proactive people take initiative; and accept responsibility for what happens to them. [3] Reactive people lack initiative instead of taking responsibility for what happens, they blame other people or outside events. [4] The first and most important of Covey's seven suggested habits is to be proactive. [5] Being proactive means being in control of how you feel, what you think, and what you do. [6] Being proactive means accepting responsibility for your own success or failure it also means choosing your actions, accepting the consequences, and modifying your behavior as needed to achieve success.

[7] When it comes to studying; are you reactive or proactive? [8] Language is a key. [9] The language of reactive people, according to Covey, relieves them of

responsibility. [10] For example, if you say, "I can't make a good grade in that class," what you are really saying is that you are not responsible. [11] Rather, someone or something is preventing you from making good grades in the class. [12] If you say, "I don't have time to study" instead of managing your time; you are allowing the factor of limited time to control you. [13] If you say, "I have to study," then you mean that you are not free to choose this action instead, someone or something is forcing you to do it.

[14] To be proactive about studying, you must first take control of your language. [15] The following is an example of how language can either limit or expand your horizons. [16] When you say, "I can't make a good grade in that class," you convince yourself that there is no reason to try. [17] As a result, you give up you stop studying. [18] The belief that you can't make a good grade becomes a self-fulfilling prophecy. [19] But if you become proactive and instead say, "I choose to make good grades in that class," then you realize that grades are the result of your own decisions and your own effort. [20] You can then accurately assess what your strengths and weaknesses are then, you can choose appropriate study systems or learning strategies that will get you the results you want.

Source: From Kanar, Carol. *The Confident Student.* 7th ed. Copyright © 2011 Cengage Learning.

Error #11: Usage and Word-Form Errors

Usage errors include words not in the correct form and commonly confused words.

Word-Form Errors

Many words in English can change form by changing their ending:

NOUN	VERB	ADJECTIVE	ADVERB
beauty	beautify	beautiful	beautifully
laughter	laugh	laughing	laughably
correction	correct	correct/corrected	correctly
analysis	analyze	analytical	analytically

Word endings that often indicate nouns include *–tion, –ion, –sion, –acy, –age, –ance, –ence, –hood, –ar, –or, –ism, –ist, –ment, –ty, –y,* and *–ness.*

> **EXAMPLES:** laziness, contentment, permanence, childhood, aviator, commercialism

Word endings that indicate verbs include *–ate, –ize, –ify,* and *–en.*

> **EXAMPLES:** modify, freshen, regulate, economize

Word endings that indicate adjectives include –al, –able, –ible, –ant, –ent, –ive, –ing, –en, –ed, –ic, –ical, –ish, –ful, –less, –like, –ly, –ous, and –y.

> **EXAMPLES:**   reliable, talkative, magical, harmless, ridiculous

Word endings that indicate adverbs include –ly and –ally.

> **EXAMPLES:**   logically, happily, angrily

Errors occur when the word is not in the correct form for its use in the sentence, as in the following examples:

> **INCORRECT:**   I decided to **sale** my house.
>
> **CORRECT:**   I decided to **sell** my house. [This word is a verb, so the verb form is needed.]

> **INCORRECT:**   My father is a very **success** businessman.
>
> **CORRECT:**   My father is a very **successful** businessman. [This word is an adjective, so the adjective form is needed.]

> **INCORRECT:**   Thinness does not **necessary** equate to healthiness.
>
> **CORRECT:**   Thinness does not **necessarily** equate to healthiness. [This word is an adverb, so the adverb form is needed.]

Commonly Confused Words

Here are pairs and groups of words that are often used incorrectly because they are not interchangeable:

its	a possessive pronoun used to indicate ownership
it's	contraction of *it is*
your	a possessive pronoun used to indicate ownership
you're	contraction of *you are*
there	in or at that place or that point
their	a possessive pronoun used to indicate ownership
they're	contraction of *they are*
then	a word that means "at that point" or "next"
than	a word used to show comparison

> **INCORRECT:**   **Your** going to love that movie.
>
> **CORRECT:**   **You're** going to love that movie.

> **INCORRECT:**   The Wilsons haul **there** recycling bins to the curb every other Tuesday.
>
> **CORRECT:**   The Wilsons haul **their** recycling bins to the curb every other Tuesday.

> **INCORRECT:**   The eagle spread **it's** wings.
>
> **CORRECT:**   The eagle spread **its** wings.

As you write, watch out for these and the many other words that sound alike but have different spellings and meanings.

Grammar Exercise 11.1

On your own paper, rewrite each of the following sentences to correct the usage errors.

1. Extremely low temperatures are creating danger conditions outside.
2. We are lucky to live in a country that provides free public school educate.
3. The informative he gave us may be incorrect.
4. She was fear of snakes and heights.
5. Our new neighbors' friendly and willing to help was a pleasant surprise.
6. I can now location and correction my usage errors.
7. In the United States, religious believes vary.
8. His dog obedient follows every one of his commands.

Grammar Exercise 11.2

The following passage contains fifteen sentences with usage errors. On your own paper, rewrite each of these sentences to correct the errors.

General Techniques for Note Taking

by Dave Ellis

[1] The format and structure of your notes are more important then how fast you write or how elegant your handwriting is. [2] The following techniques can improve the effectively of your notes.

Use Key Words. [3] An easy way to sort the extraneous material from the important points is to take notes using key words. [4] Key words or phrases contain the essence of communicate. [5] They include these:

- Concepts, technical terms, names, and numbers
- Linking words, including words that describe action, relationship, and degree (for example, *most, least,* and *faster*)

[6] Key words evoke images and associations with other words and ideas. [7] They trigger you're memory. [8] That characteristic makes them powerfully review tools. [9] One key word can initiate the recall of a whole cluster of ideas. [10] A few key words can form a chain from which you can reconstruction an entire lecture.

Copy Material from the Board or a PowerPoint® Presentation. [11] Record key formulas, diagrams, and problems that the teacher presentations on the board or in a PowerPoint presentation. [12] Copy dates, numbers, names, places, and other facts. [13] You can even use your own signal or code to flag important material.

Use a Three-Ring Binder. [14] Three-ring binders have several advantages over other kinds of notebooks. [15] First, pages can be removed and spread out when you review. [16] This way, you can get the whole picture of a lecture. [17] Second, the three-ringer-binder format allows you to insertion handouts right into your notes. [18] Third, you can insert your own out-of-class notes in the correct order.

Use an "I'm Lost" Signal. [19] No matter how attention and alert you are, you might get lost and confused in a lecture. [20] If its inappropriate to ask a question, record in your notes that you were lost. [21] Invent your own signal—for example, a circled question mark. [22] When you write down your code for "I'm lost," leave space for the explanation or clarify that you will get later. [23] The space will also be a signal that you missed something. [24] Later, you can speak to your instructor or ask your fellow students for there notes.

Label, Number, and Date All Notes. [25] Development the habit of labeling and dating your notes at the beginning of each class. [26] Number the page, too. [27] Sometimes the sequence of material in a lecture is important. [28] Write your name and phone number in each notebook in case you loose it.

Take Notes in Different Colors. [29] You can use colors as highly visible organizers. [30] For example, you can signal importance points with red. [31] Or use one color of ink for notes about the text and another color for lecture notes.

Source: From Ellis, Dave. *Becoming a Master Student.* 14th ed. Copyright © 2013 Cengage Learning.

Index